CHILD ABUSE
AND FAMILY LAW

Thea Brown is Professor of Social Work and Director of the Family Violence and Family Court Research Program at Monash University. She has served on Family Court committees and on the Commonwealth Family Law Pathways Advisory Group.

Dr Renata Alexander is Senior Lecturer in Law at Monash University and a member of the Victorian Bar. She was Deputy Reg istrar in the Family Court and is the author of *Domestic Violence in Australia*, 3rd edition.

THEA BROWN
RENATA ALEXANDER

CHILD ABUSE
AND FAMILY LAW

Understanding the issues facing
human service and legal professionals

Routledge
Taylor & Francis Group

LONDON AND NEW YORK

The authors wish to dedicate the book to their families.Thea Brown wishes to dedicate it to Rober t, her husband,andVictoria, her daughter. Renata Alexander wishes to dedicate it to her mother, her late father, and her sister Inka.They both wish to dedicate the book to those at its heart—the children entangled in the web of family law socio-legal services as a result of allegations of child abuse made in the context of parental separation and divorce.

First published 2007 by Allen & Unwin

Published 2020 by Routledge
2 Park Square, Milton Park, Abingdon, Oxon OX14 4RN
605 Third Avenue, New York, NY 10017

Routledge is an imprint of the Taylor & Francis Group, an informa business

National Library of Australia
Cataloguing-in-Publication entry:

Brown, Thea.
    Child abuse and family law : understanding the issues
    facing human service and legal professionals.

    Bibliography.
    Includes index.
    ISBN 978 1 86508 731 3.

    1. Child abuse - Law and legislation - Australia. 2.
    Family law - Australia. 3. Abused children -
    Services for - Australia. 4. Problem families - Services
    for - Australia. I. Alexander, Renata. II. Title.

Index by Nancy Sibtain
Set in 10.5/13 pt Bembo by Midland Typesetters, Australia

ISBN-13: 9781865087313 (pbk)

CONTENTS

Foreword by *The Honourable Alistair Nicholson*   ix
Acknowledgments   xiv

Introduction: A new problem   1
   Current knowledge   2
   The family law socio-legal service system   3
   Navigating the book   6
   Future directions   7

**1. A new understanding of child abuse in the context
of parental separation**   8
   The relationship between child abuse, parental separation and
     divorce   9
   The history of understanding of child abuse in the context
     of parental separation and divorce   10
   The distinctive nature of child abuse in this context 17
   The families   19
   Alleged and actual perpetrators   20
   Conclusion   23

2. Child abuse, family violence and family law legislation   24
   Background to the *Family Law Act* 1975 (Cth)   25

The *Family Law Reform Act* 1995   26
Changes in 2006 to the *Family Law Act* 1975   29
Case law under the *Family Law Act* 1975   32
Family violence between parents   33
Child abuse where children are direct or primary victims   40
Child sexual abuse   42
Australian research   46
Conclusion   48

3. Family law legislation and the protection of children   **50**
Best interests of the child   51
Myths   52
Let's blame Freud   53
Wishes of the child and separate representation of children   55
How the Family Court deals with child abuse cases   59
Protocols and legislation affecting state and territory agencies   59
The Magellan list   61
Children's Cases program   62
Conclusion   63

4. Child sexual abuse   **65**
Community attitudes to child sexual abuse   66
The discovery/rediscovery cycle in child sexual abuse   67
Reported incidence of child sexual abuse   68
Actual prevalence of child sexual abuse   70
Children's reporting of sexual abuse   71
Definition of sexual abuse   72
Evidence of abuse   73
Interviewing strategies   75
Delays and changes in telling of the abuse   76
Causes of child abuse   77
Marital partnership and partnership breakdown and
    divorce as risk factors   79
Perpetrators   80
Victims   81
Residence and contact arrangements for victims of child
    sexual abuse   82
The attitudes of socio-legal professionals to child sexual abuse   83
Conclusion   84

5. Other forms of child abuse   86
Community attitudes to other forms of child abuse   87
The puzzle of reported incidence   89
Patterns in reported incidence of other forms of child abuse   90
Patterns of abuse in the context of parental separation
    and divorce   91
Reported incidence of abduction   93
Reported attempted and actual homicide   93
Severity of abuse   94
Definition of physical abuse   94
Definition of neglect   96
Definition of emotional abuse   97
Forms of child abuse specific to parental separation and divorce   98
Causes of the other forms of child abuse   99
Parental separation and divorce as a cause   102
Perpetrators and victims   103
Effects of abuse   103
Arrangements for residence and contact   104
Attitudes of socio-legal professionals to the other forms of
    child abuse   105
Conclusion   106

6. Managing families and their problems   108
The impact of divorce on families and family members   109
Immediate impact on family members   109
The impact of the child abuse allegations   111
Impact of the allegations on the substantiated perpetrator
    of the child abuse   112
Working with substantiated perpetrators   113
Impact of the client and their violence on the professional   115
Impact of unsubstantiated allegations on the alleged
    perpetrators   116
Working with alleged perpetrators where the allegations
    are not substantiated   117
Impact on the partner making the allegations   118
Working with the parent making the allegations   119
Impact of the allegations and the process of investigation
    on the children   120

Working with children who are the alleged victims of
    family abuse   121
Other factors   121
Conclusion   127

7. Managing the family law service system   128
The family law socio-legal service system as a maze   128
The core of the system   129
The Commonwealth financial benefits agencies   131
Counselling agencies   132
Services for children   133
State child protection services   134
Lobby groups   135
Funding   137
Problems of a service system that has become a maze   138
No specialised services for child abuse allegations   139
New specialised services and pathways   141
    The Magellan program   141
    The Columbus program   143
    Other programs   144
Strategies for managing the maze   145
Conclusion   147

8. Case presentations: The professionals' contributions   148
The use of a common framework   148
Case presentation and discussion   150
The first family   150
The second family   162
Conclusion   175

Notes   177
References   180
Index   194

FOREWORD

This book is courageous, ground breaking and extremely comprehensive. The authors have extensive experience with the subject matter and have brought that experience to bear in a very effective way.

It is courageous first, because it swims against the current tide of an assumption that a relationship with both natural parents is invariably in the best interests of a child. This is not an assumption based upon established research, but rather an emotional assumption that has been assiduously fed by lobby groups to the point where the Federal Parliament has amended the *Family Law Act* in such a way as to give legislative force to it and, I believe, has therefore placed many of our children in much greater danger than was the case previously.

In the context of what might be described as 'normal' families, such an assumption may have some validity. However, many families who reach the point of litigation in the courts as to the disposition of their children are not normal in this sense. As the authors indicate, approximately 30 per cent of marriages break up because of domestic violence and they document the close link between domestic violence and child abuse. Further they make the point that approximately 90 per cent of abusers are male and approximately 73 per cent are fathers of the child/children in question, who is/are normally female. Many people in this category are litigants in the courts.

Unfortunately, the assumption is effectively applied to them by the legislation, with potentially disastrous results. It is true that the legislation provides that the protection of children from harm caused by abuse and family violence is an object of the Act and a primary consideration for a court in determining issues relating to children, but it is an inconsistent one with the Act's other emphasis on shared parenting. The expectations that the latter concept creates are such that courts are much more likely to make contact orders and particularly interim contact orders, even when faced with such allegations or finding them proved. As the authors say, child abuse is hard to detect or understand, the perpetrators usually deny it, the victims may either deny it or are too young to disclose it and the community also denies it.

The authors have therefore made the point that the new legislation endangers many vulnerable children by promoting the desirability of shared parenting as a concept for all families, by creating a climate where contact is the norm almost regardless of the behaviour of the parents and by forcing parents into mediation at the new family relationship centres.

As the authors comment, and about which they are rightly critical, the only exception to this last requirement is if a parent can first prove to a court that there are reasonable grounds to believe that abuse or family violence has occurred or may occur (see s 60I (7) *Family Law Act*). One needs only to ask how many parents, usually mothers, are prepared or financially or otherwise able to go to these lengths on the off chance that a court may relieve them of the necessity to attend a family relationship centre. Once there they are subjected to mediation in circumstances where there is general acceptance that such a procedure is inappropriate in cases of family violence and child abuse. This is inherently wrong.

Secondly, the authors are courageous in the way that they have roundly criticised the family law system, including the courts, and have suggested the need for a unified family court system in Australia combining child protection and traditional family law jurisdiction. Coupled with this they say that there should be a unified law as to child protection. This is a view that I have long advocated and it is the only way that real progress is likely to be achieved in reforming the family law and child protection system in this country.

They have also drawn attention to the extraordinary maze that operates in the area of family law and child protection, which seems to be exacerbated every time the legislature looks for another 'quick fix' to a difficult problem. Much of the recent legislation is yet another attempt at a 'quick fix' and is likely to be no more effective than its predecessors.

As to their criticism of the courts, I think it true to say that until the early 1990s, the Family Court paid insufficient regard to issues of violence and child abuse. I believe that this was a legacy of the view associated with the original rationale of the *Family Law Act* 1975 that the court was to pay no regard to the conduct of the parties. It was not a view that I shared, but it was one that took time to overcome.

The authors are also critical of the approach of the courts and particularly the Full Court of the Family Court to the issue of proof of child sexual abuse and again I think that this view has some justification. In this context they refer to the decision of the Full Court overturning my decision in one of the last cases that I adjudicated, *Re W* (*Sex abuse: standard of proof*), 2004. In that case I had accepted evidence of the mother and a sexual abuse counsellor as to separate and consistent disclosures of sex abuse by the child, coupled with similar disclosures made to a police officer in an interview that was recorded on video. I also accepted evidence of an expert psychiatrist that the admissions made in the video interview were likely to have been untainted and rejected the father's evidence that abuse had not occurred. I therefore made a positive finding that abuse had occurred.

As the authors point out the Full Court found that 'at its highest the evidence ought properly have left the Court with a lingering concern that something untoward might have happened'. This was a surprising finding since the argument before me had been conducted at the conclusion of the trial on the basis that counsel for the father conceded that I should find that there was an unacceptable risk that child abuse had occurred but urged that I should not make a positive finding that it had occurred.

The authors suggest that there may be elements of gender bias and double standards in this decision. While I do not share this view I think that the standard of proof nominated by the court was far too high. Courts need to be careful not to apply what appears to be almost a test of guilt beyond reasonable doubt before a finding of child sexual abuse can be made. This is not the law and runs contrary to the principles laid down by the High Court. It also has the effect of endangering vulnerable children, who should be the first concern of the court in such cases.

The authors rightly criticise delays in the courts as exacerbating problems in cases of child abuse and further endangering the children. It undoubtedly does so and is further exacerbated by governmental failure to properly fund the system or to appoint sufficient judicial officers.

They do however point to the successes of the Magellan and Columbus initiatives in the Family Court of Australia and Western Australia respectively. The Magellan project arose out of Professor Brown and her team's research, which I adopted, and it has proved to be a most useful initiative in the case management of all cases. It was one of the factors that led to the introduction of the Children's Cases program that I introduced as a pilot in Parramatta in 2004 and which is now incorporated into Division 12A of the *Family Law Act*, which came into force on 1 July 2006. Unlike many of the recent amendments it was a carefully researched and evaluated project which I believe, has great potential for the future conduct of all children's cases and perhaps others, at least in the family jurisdiction.

As I commented at the outset, the book is also ground breaking. It is ground breaking because it is undoubtedly the first attempt to bring together a comprehensive body of knowledge dealing with what I believe is a blight upon our society, namely child abuse in all its forms. It is surprising that this should be so, given the prevalence of child abuse and the knowledge of its existence over so many years. Admittedly community awareness of the prevalence of child abuse is a relatively recent phenomenon, but it has been the subject of many academic articles over the years where, as the authors say, various differing theories have been propounded. However, very few of these have been as child focused as this book is and almost none have addressed in a comprehensive way the problems encountered by professionals working in the field.

The book is comprehensive. It deals with all of the various forms of child abuse, including potential indicators and provides sound practical suggestions for dealing with problems on the ground. It points out the distinctive nature of child abuse in the context of parental separation and divorce and debunks many earlier myths. In particular the authors effectively demolish the myths propounded by some experts in relation to the so called 'parental alienation syndrome', which is usually coupled with another myth that most allegations of child abuse in a family law context are false and made with a view to preventing the other party from seeing the child. The evidence is that this is not so. In fact it is clear that many relationships break up as a direct result of child abuse and that the period following separation is in any event a danger period for children in all too many cases.

The book discusses the effect of allegations of child abuse on the victims, the person making the allegations and the person against whom they are made. It points to the fact that the children who are victims all too often lack proper support. In an interesting section the authors discuss the effect of child abuse cases on professionals and particularly on professionals who are dealing with and representing the alleged perpetrators and point to the danger that in such cases the professional may either identify too much with the client or become fearful of that person, with unfortunate consequences.

It also discusses in relation to child abuse, the problems posed by other cultures, including Indigenous cultures. I am not aware of any culture that sanctions child abuse, but different cultures have different attitudes to family law issues and the role of women and children and it is important that those working with people from other cultures make some attempt to understand such issues. As the authors point out, historically we have made little attempt to do so prior to certain Family Court initiatives in the 1990s. It is important that we continue to do so, despite current conservative mythology suggesting that the law should ignore cultural issues.

I have no doubt that this book will become an invaluable tool for family and children's court judges and magistrates, psychiatrists, psychologists, social workers, police and the many other professionals who work in this field. I commend it to them and also to legislators and those who advise them when it next becomes necessary to amend family and children's legislation.

Alastair Nicholson
Former Chief Justice of the
Family Court of Australia
Melbourne
14 July 2006

ACKNOWLEDGMENTS

Many generous professional and academic colleagues from the family law socio-legal service system have supported the writing of this book. Indeed, it was their requests for such a book that led to its birth.

The book is based on extensive research, much of which was carried out by the Family Violence and Family Court Research Program team, comprising one of the authors, Professor Thea Brown, and her Monash colleagues Lesley Hewitt and Dr Rosemary Sheehan, and their La Trobe colleague, Associate Professor Margarita Frederico. The research was under-taken in collaboration with many family law socio-legal services, the most important of which is the Family Court of Australia. The Honourable Justice Alastair Nicholson (former Chief Justice of the Family Court of Australia) authorised the first of the research projects and enthusiastically supported the recommendations of that research. That research led in turn to the further research around Project Magellan, a unique program inter-nationally led by the Honourable Linda Dessau both in its exploratory and in its ongoing phase. Justice Linda Dessau has played a vital ongoing role in the research. The initial research project was supported also by the Honourable John Faulks, who authorised the work at the Canberra Reg istry. In addition, many other judicial staff assisted and impressed by their interest and insights, in particular the Honourable Sally Brown, who was the first judge to work in the experimental Magellan program, and the Honourable Joe Kay. Subsequently, the new Chief Justice of the Family

Court, the Honourable Diana Bryant, has maintained a link with the research and both she and Justice Linda Dessau have kept the research team informed as to the court's work in this difficult area.

Many other services gave support, indicating a widespread shared concern for children involved in parental separation and divorce and allegations of child abuse. These organisations were the child protection services of all Australian states and territories, but especially the Department of Human Services Victoria, all the state legal aid commissions, but particularly Victoria Legal Aid (which was an active research collaborator), the Victorian Police Force, and the Commonwealth Attorney-General's Department, which supported the research strongly from the outset. More recently, other community-based non-government family relationship services have become involved.

Funding for the various research projects that underpin this book was provided by the Family Court of Australia, Monash University, the Australian Catholic University (Canberra), the Australian Institute of Criminology, the Australian Research Council and Victoria Legal Aid.

The authors wish to thank their academic colleagues from the faculties of Arts, Law and Medicine, Nursing and Health Sciences at Monash University in Melbourne. They wish also to thank the members of their families who have sustained them in their work, in this project and in all the other projects that culminated in this book.

INTRODUCTION: A NEW PROBLEM

Child abuse alleged and occurring in the context of parental separation and divorce has emerged as a growing and troubling problem in recent years. Consequently, building knowledge for the use of professionals who work with this problem has been an urgent task. However, it has not been an easy one because the distaste, the denial and the myths surrounding it have undermined the development of the professional knowledge required to deal with it.

This book aims to present the first comprehensive body of knowledge for professionals working with child abuse in the context of parental separation, divorce and family law proceedings. It is aimed at those professionals working in the world of the family law service system: legal practitioners—especially family law practitioners; the judiciary, judicial officers and administrators; social workers and psychologists—many of whom will be child protection workers; and medical practitioners—including general practitioners, paediatricians and psychiatrists. It is also for teachers and nurses, and for those who work in less defined roles in the specialised services, such as refuges and contact centres, as well as for staff who will work in the new Commonwealth-funded family relationship centres, the first fifteen of which opened across Australia on 1 July 2006.

The knowledge constructed for this book has been built from the cutting-edge research the authors have undertaken in the fields of child abuse and domestic violence, from the research of others, and from the authors' professional experiences in social work and family law. The knowledge presented has been developed for the Australian environment, but most of it is relevant to other countries—especially those that share with Australia the heritage of an English legal system: countries like New Zealand, Canada, the United States, Singapore, Malaysia, Sri Lanka and Hong Kong.

Reco gnition of the relationship between child abuse, parental separation and divorce has been slow. Although the problems of child abuse were noted in the earliest of the parental separation and divorce research, they were dismissed as being incidental to the real problem: that of the parental separation and the divorce (Wallerstein and Kelly, 1996). Subsequently, allegations of child abuse made at the time of separation and divorce were branded as false by the therapist Gardner who, in a flow of influential work, explained it as the malicious behaviour of manipulative divorcing parents, most particularly mothers (Gardner, 1986, 1987, 1989). Even those who have more recently explored the role of family violence in separation and divorce have tended to ignore child abuse, preferring to concentrate on one form of family violence: domestic violence (Johnston and Campbell, 1993). Furthermore, as many of the parents who brought the problem to professionals were mothers alleging that the child's father was the perpetrator of the abuse, the problems became suffused with the gender issues always prominent in parental separation and divorce, to the detriment of both the child victims and the development of a research-based body of professional knowledge.

CURRENT KNOWLEDGE

Despite these obstructions and distractions, knowledge has grown rapidly in the last decade. Child abuse and domestic violence—now seen as closely linked—are recognised as far more common causes of parental separation and divorce than had previously been realised (FLPAG, 2001). When one parent discovers the other parent is abusing their child, one obvious outcome is for the parent to decide to leave their partner either immediately or later. Sometimes, if the abuse has been notified to the child protection service, the service will require it. However, the mere fact of separation does not automatically overcome the abuse, and family law proceedings are a likely consequence as one parent seeks to protect their child from the other parent—and sometimes from other members of the family as well.

Furthermore, problems of child abuse relating to parental separation and divorce do not occur only at the point of separation: they can erupt many years later. We know that fresh events of child abuse—particularly child sexual abuse—occur more commonly among children of separated and divorced parents. Again, later allegations can bring families into the family law socio-legal system years after they thought they had left these services far behind.

Child abuse in this context has distinctive features, including types of abuse specific to separation and divorce, and particular perpetrators and victims. These distinctions necessitate the use of different professional strategies to assist the families concerned.

THE FAMILY LAW SOCIO-LEGAL SERVICE SYSTEM

Professionals working with problems of child abuse relating to parental separation and divorce confront major challenges. In addition to the slow development of knowledge on child abuse in this context, they have to manage a service system that is complex and confused—one that was not constructed to deal with this problem. Yet families with such problems have become half the caseload of disputes in the Family Court of Australia in children's matters (Brown et al., 1998), and one-third of the caseload of family law solicitors (Hunter et al., 2000).

The complexity of, and confusion surrounding, family law service provision are international. With little recognition of these problems, few services are designed to focus on them, and there are no clear pathways to the services that *are* there. In Australia, the confusion is worsened by the split in responsibilities for service delivery and service funding between the various levels of government, and between the government and non-government sectors—leading to a level of fragmentation that continues to worsen. Duplication of service provision when there are already too few services is also occurring, as governments seek to overcome old problems with new services that overlap existing ones that governments think will not reform.

Another challenge confronted by professionals in this area is the personal impact they face from working with child abuse victims, their families and the perpetrators. While some socio-legal professionals realise they are affected by vicarious trauma—suffered indirectly from learning of the trauma of the abuse—they may be unaware that there are identified reactions professionals have when working with child abuse that can affect their interventions. Such reactions have been shown to be unhelpful and even dangerous to the clients and the professionals alike. Thus deciding on and carrying out best professional action must be informed by an understanding of these issues.What might seem the most obvious response is not always the best one.

Many professionals find it difficult to recognise families who have these problems when they meet them. They reinterpret the families and their problems in the light of the myths that surround child abuse in the context of separation and divorce. The following families are based on the families encountered by the authors in their work and they are presented here to bring reality closer to the reader and to emphasise the need to understand these families within the framework proposed in this book. We stress that they are not actual families.

Jonathon was a young boy whose allegations, made directly by himself to many professionals over five years, were continually dismissed.

Jonathon was twelve when the police apprehended him after he stole cash and goods from a corner milk bar. He told the police he was living on the street for the weekend. He was supposed to be on a contact visit with his father, but instead he had run away from his father's home. He said his father sexually abused him and had done so for many years. Returning him to his father, the police found that the child had been the subject of family law proceedings for five years in a long-running contact dispute that involved child abuse allegations. This year he had begun running away to avoid the court-ordered contact visits. The police advised Jonathon to face up to life and to spend the alternate weekends with his father as the court had ordered.

One year later, after his father was charged with sexually abusing his five-year-old stepson, Jonathon's mother succeeded—after six years of proceedings—in gaining orders for no contact between the father and Jonathon.

Max and Sonia's father's suspicions about the care of his children seemed unreasonable to the professionals in his first encounters with them. They saw his fears as evidence of his anger at Jane, his wife, over her leaving him.

Max and Sonia, aged two and four, lived with their mother Jane after she left Grant. Grant had them for one day and night each week on an informal basis. The changeover arrangements, set up by Jane to protect herself after years of Grant's domestic violence, meant she would not let him enter her home. He collected and returned the children from the front garden. Over some weeks, he noticed the children were losing weight and were not clean or properly dressed. Questioning them did not reveal any information. He contacted the child protection service twice, but each time after discussion he did not proceed with a notification.

After a further month, Grant contacted the child protection service again, and on investigation they were surprised to learn that Jane was in gaol on remand following charges for drug offences and that Jane's sister, who lived next door to her, had been inadequately 'keeping an eye' on the children.

Banggla and Nadiri were two young Afghan refugees whose burns perplexed the local doctor.

Born in Australia and now aged five and three, Banggla and Nadiri were the sons of two Afghan refugees who had come to Australia via a refugee camp in Pakistan ten years before. The children had two older sisters who had been born in Afghanistan. After Nadiri was born, his mother developed diabetes and his father left his wife, taking the two sons but leaving the daughters. The father took the boys to visit their mother but he would not see his daughters. Neither parent took any action to formalise the separation. The mother took her two sons on three occasions to her local doctor with burns on their hands that she explained as an accident due to the overcrowding in her small kitchen on contact days. On the last visit, the daughter who interpreted for the mother said the burns were a punishment that the boys deserved. Confused and uncertain, the doctor referred the mother and the boys to the local hospital. The family did not attend the hospital. Three months later, after another episode of burns, the father took the mother to the hospital where it was decided the burns were a result of excessive discipline from the mother due to Afghan cultural norms for punishing children.

In fact, angry at the father's rejection of them, the sisters were inflicting the burns on contact visits, as a teacher at the older son's school was eventually informed.

In all these examples, professionals struggled to assist without the knowledge required to do so.

NAVIGATING THE BOOK

We begin in Chapter 1 by discussing the relationship between child abuse and parental separation and divorce. The chapter explains the relationship between them, and looks at how this link has developed. It considers the mythology, misunderstanding and misinformation about this complex relationship, and urges professionals to base their interventions in this area on tested and research-based information rather than on their subjective opinions. Chapter 2 examines the law framing problems of family violence after parental separation as set out initially in the *Family Law Act* of 1975 and subsequently amended as socio-legal understanding of family relationships and family violence has changed, culminating in the proposals for change enacted in the *Family Law Amendment (Shared Parental Responsibility) Act* 2006. The chapter considers case law under the *Family Law Act* in relation to abuse suffered directly and indirectly by children. Chapter 3 considers the protection offered to children and their parents by the legislation and its implementation where abuse has been alleged.

Child abuse is then discussed in considerable detail in Chapters 4 and 5. Chapter 4 discusses child sexual abuse, as this is a particularly common form of abuse in this context, despite being uncommon in others. It is a particularly troubling form of child abuse for professionals to address, for many reasons. Chapter 5 presents the other well-known types of child abuse—physical abuse, neglect and emotional abuse—as well as looking at the less well-known form, multi-type abuse, which is now more often acknowledged. This chapter also reviews some types of abuse not usually discussed as they tend to occur only in this context—like abduction, handover or changeover abuse and some new forms of neglect.

Chapter 6 marks the beginning of a new theme in the book: professional intervention. The chapter reviews the impact of abuse on victims and their families, and proposes ways of working with the affected victims and members of their families. Chapter 7 pursues this theme further by mapping the service system for the use of socio-legal professionals and their clients. It proposes ways through a service system so complicated that it has been likened to a maze (FLPAG, 2001).

Chapter 8 focuses on real case interventions. It presents two cases of child abuse, and considers the issues each case presents for intervention by the various professionals from the family law socio-legal services likely to be involved.

FUTURE DIRECTIONS

We wish to point out that this is the first book to tackle this area, and we hope more will follow. Professionals need more knowledge about the particular problems of child abuse in this context, and they need more knowledge about dealing with such abuse. It is vital to place a priority on finding out what supports and services the children need, including what they have to say about professional intervention with them and on their behalf. Often the voices and perspectives of children are lost during parental separation and divorce, as their parents and other adult family members speak more loudly and command more attention than the children can. Nevertheless, the children are the focus of the professionals' attention, and we need to approach their problems enlightened by their views about their experiences as well as by the views of their parents.

We believe we have approached this work objectively by stressing the importance of empirical research. Much of the discussion around parental separation and divorce is gender biased—indeed, the area is a gender war zone. As two women writers, we could well be accused of a gender bias. However, by focusing on the needs of the children and the development of professional knowledge to assist them, we hope any such bias has been avoided. To assist children, we have also presented ways of meeting the needs of the parents. We have not focused on the perpetrators here, although there is some consideration of their position.

1

A NEW UNDERSTANDING OF CHILD ABUSE
IN THE CONTEXT OF PARENTAL SEPARATION

Our understanding of child abuse in the context of parental separation and divorce has changed recently. In the past, allegations of child abuse—given as a reason for parental separation, and/or for restricted or no contact with a parent or other relative in family law proceedings after separation—were regarded as mostly false. They were seen as having been manufactured by a malicious parent who wished to exclude the other parent from the child's life for their own selfish reasons. However, we now have evidence that shows such allegations are no more likely to be false than allegations of child abuse raised in other contexts. Child abuse in this context is real, it is serious and it should not be dismissed. Moreover, there is a distinctive profile of abuse in this context which encompasses the nature of the abuse, the victims, their families and the abusers.

This chapter introduces the current knowledge about child abuse in this newly identified context of parental separation and divorce. It reviews past explanations for such abuse, because misunderstandings from the past persist today and continue to misinform and mislead professionals in their approaches to the problem. It also identifies the distinctive aspects of abuse in this context in terms of the types of abuse which occur, victims, families, and alleged and actual perpetrators.

Detailed consideration of each type of abuse is undertaken in Chapters 4 and 5.

THE RELATIONSHIP BETWEEN CHILD ABUSE, PARENTAL SEPARATION AND DIVORCE

The relationship between child abuse, parental separation and divorce is a complex one, and the picture of the relationship is not yet complete. We know that child abuse is a reason why some parents decide to separate, and for many of these couples child abuse and domestic violence have occurred at the same time (Hume, 1997; Brown et al., 1998, 2001). Indeed, some regard domestic violence as child abuse. When child abuse and domestic violence occur together, many parents state that domestic violence is the cause of the breakdown; however, some in this position regard the child abuse as the real reason for the separation. Separating couples seem to simplify family violence in their presentation of material for divorce. They tend to bring forward only one form of family violence as a cause of separation while simultaneously referring to the existence of other forms (Brown et al., 1998; Hume, 1998; Brown et al., 2001). Perhaps the family law legal system encourages this simplification.

But parental separation and divorce also appear to lead to subsequent child abuse. First, parental separation does not stop abuse from continuing after separation, as a parent who leaves a marriage in order to protect their child from continuing abuse within the family may imagine (Hester and Ratford, 1997). Second, abuse can occur for the first time after separation— and indeed does so slightly more frequently than it does before separation (Brown et al., 2001).

The reasons why such abuse should begin after separation are not clear. It is possible that the loss of one of the two original parents reduces overall parental vigilance over the child (Wilson, 2002a), and that the separation leaves the child in an emotional state that makes them vulnerable to abuse—especially by sexual predators (Wilson, 2002a). Possibly the stress of a separation, even a desire for revenge, overwhelms some parents, who then physically, emotionally or sexually abuse their children (Briggs, 2003).

Many of the consequences of parental separation and divorce—such as lower income levels, reduced physical and mental health, and housing problems—are also factors associated with child abuse (Hiller and Goddard, 1989; Cawson, et al., 2001). However, it is not yet known which factor, or combination of factors, is most implicated in causing child abuse in this context.

THE HISTORY OF UNDERSTANDING OF CHILD ABUSE IN THE CONTEXT OF PARENTAL SEPARATION AND DIVORCE

Since our current knowledge in this area is so recent, theories from the past need some detailed examination, as they are still a powerful influence on the way we think about and construct our actions when working with this problem. Professionals are still intervening on the basis of theories that we now know to be wrong, and that have no evidence to support them.

Looking back over the history of child abuse, we suggest that there have been three eras in our understanding of child abuse. These are the *era of concern without understanding*, followed by the *era of misunderstanding* and concluding with the current era, the *era of dawning understanding*.

Child abuse has been recognised as a social problem for many centuries. We can be said to have been concerned without having much under-standing during much of this time. Abuse was seen as a problem associated with ignorance and poverty until the revelations of US child abuse researcher Dr Henry Kempe, who used his research to expose child physical and sexual abuse internationally Kempe et al. (1962) showed that child abuse was more than a problem of ignorance and poverty, and that it occurred among parents who might have been expected to have known better and who went to great lengths to conceal it. Kempe's public campaigns increased community recognition of the issue as a family problem during the 1960s and 1970s. Subsequently, the incidence of child abuse notified to child protection authorities rose quickly and sharply in the major English-speaking countries—first in the United Kingdom, then in the United States and Canada, and more recently in Australia and New Zealand. The dramatic rises in reported incidence continued for three decades, plateauing (for the moment) at the end of the twentieth century in the United Kingdom and in the United States, but not yet in Australia (Berliner and Conte, 2003; AIHW, 2004: 5). These trends are discussed further in Chapter 4.

Paralleling the reported incidence of child abuse, the incidence of marital breakdown also increased—first in the United States, then in Australia and New Zealand, and then in the United Kingdom (Wallerstein and Kelly, 1996). Research on marital breakdown was instigated to explain the rise in marital breakdowns, but it was not underpinned by any knowl-edge of child abuse in families and any awareness of the sharp rise in reported child abuse that was paralleling the increase in the divorce rate.

Child abuse was not considered to be a part of marital breakdown, as either a cause or a consequence.

Nevertheless, the early researchers on marital breakdown (Wallerstein and Kelly, 1980) did discover some children who were abused by their parents among the 60 middle-class families they studied. However, they did not categorise this behaviour as child abuse, but rather as the problematic functioning of certain parents that resulted in risks to the safety of the children—a fine semantic subtlety that implied a huge difference in understanding. Their denial of the existence of child abuse was underscored by a similar approach to domestic violence. They saw it, they noted it, but they interpreted it as part of the end stage of a dying marriage rather than a cause of the death of the marriage or as a threat to a parent and to the children after the marriage had died. They did not see either child abuse or domestic violence as being related in any way to the partnership breakdown and subsequent divorce.

The combination of rising divorce rates and rising child abuse notification rates affected the professionals working in family law by the early 1980s. Increasing numbers of allegations of child abuse in the context of residence and contact disputes were presented to family and divorce courts, as well as to family law professionals, legal practitioners, social workers, psychologists, psychiatrists, paediatricians, the judiciary and other court staff. Soon family law professionals began to ask why there was such a marked increase in child abuse allegations in residence and contact disputes in family law proceedings (Thoeness and Pearson, 1988; Schudson, 1992; Toth, 1992). The answers presented at this time led to the era of misunderstanding.

The questions were tackled first in the writings of Gardner, a US psychiatrist with no background in either child abuse or the increase in its reported incidence. He put forward an explanation he called the 'parental alienation syndrome' (Gardner, 1986). The syndrome described a supposed family dynamic whereby mothers made false allegations against fathers about the sexual abuse of their children in order to prevent further contact between the fathers and their children, thus removing the fathers permanently from the children's lives. He suggested that the children were brainwashed by the mother into supporting the allegations, and argued that any allegations the children made should not be believed. His views struck a strong chord with many parents and professionals. Parental alienation syndrome was a plausible explanation: it covered all aspects of the problem; it left nothing unexplained; and it maintained an entrenched community view which lingers today—the desire to deny the existence of child sexual abuse within the family especially among economically secure families (AustraliansAgainst Child Abuse, 2002).

Gardner's views were attacked because of their perceived bias against women, their dismissalof children's complaints of abuse and their lack of grounding in or reference to any rigorous research (Faller, 1998; Dallam, 1999). Subsequently he revised his views and conceded the possibility that fathers were also likely to manufacture such allegationsand that child sexual abuse did in fact occur in some families. He produced a risk assessment tool, for professionals to use to determine the truth or otherwise of the allegations (Gardner, 1987).

Parental alienation syndrome (often known by its initials as PAS) and its originator became significant: PAS attracted considerable support, and Gardner wrote along these lines until his death in 2003. His views echoed a theme noted in the child protection literature whereby mothers are blamed for the allegations of abuse as well as for the abuse itself, even though the mother was not the perpetrator (Scourfield, 2002). Mothers were—and still are—seen as always responsible for the care and well-being of their children, while fathers are not (Humphreys, 1997). Thus fathers are ignored even when they are the perpetrators of the abuse (Fleming, 2002). Gardner's work supported another theme reported in child protection literature: that of reducing all parents—mothers and fathers—to stereotypes (Scourfield, 2002). Gardner stereotyped mothers as bad parents—as perpetrators of PAS—and fathers as innocent victims of their behaviour. His work reconstructed the reality of each parent's individual situation to their disadvantage (Brown, 2003).

Another outcome of his theory of PAS has been its metamorphosis into a broader notion of parental alienation, where one parent is believed to have alienated the child from the other not only in relation to child abuse allegations but also for a large number of possible reasons.This idea, again unsupported by research, persistsin family law as can be seen in the current policy the Family Court of Australia uses in assessingwhether or not to recommend the appointment of a separate representative for a child in a residence and contact dispute One of the stated priority criteria in deciding if a child requires representation is 'parental alienation'.Thus the false notion of parental alienation in the broad sense maintainsa belief in it in the specific sense and the specific sense maintainsbelief in the broad sense

Soon after Gardner's writings were published, the first substantial research about child abuse allegations made in the context of parental separation and family law proceedings appeared. The era of dawning understanding had begun. The study was commissioned by the US National Centre of Child Advocacy, which sponsored a large investigation of several hundred residence and contact disputes from twelve states in the United States in which allegations of child sexual abuse had been made. The study followed the cases from the time they first presented in a family or divorce court until the case was concluded (Thoeness and Pearson, 1988).

This work showed that Gardner was wrong. The study found that allegations raised in this context were no more likely to be false than in any other situation. False allegations represented some 12 per cent of the total of all allegations. More significantly the researchers found that the family and divorce courts did not deal well with the allegations, letting the cases drift, unresolved and with children remaining in danger, for long periods of time—if not indefinitely. The study concluded that the way the courts managed the cases was wrong, and it made a series of recommendations for the processing of the cases so the courts would provide better outcomes for children. The research pointed to what has since been identified as a major problem in child protection; coordinating the many services that are inevitably involved on behalf of children (Lyon and de Cruz, 1993; Hallett, 1995).

Following that landmark study, additional research revealed more of the reality of the relationship between child abuse and parental separation and divorce, providing much-needed detail about it. Three Australian studies (Hume, 1997; Brown et al., 1998, 2001) took a similar approach to the research in the United States and followed large numbers of cases where child abuse allegations had been raised in the context of residence and contact disputes in family law proceedings from the time the cases first presented to the court until they were concluded. However, in two of the three studies these cases included the entire spectrum of child abuse—that is, physical, sexual, emotional, neglect and anything else the court deemed to be child abuse—not only child sexual abuse (Brown et al., 1998, 2001).

The largest of the studies, reviewing the way the Family Court of Australia dealt with such cases, showed the court had become a forum for the resolution of all kinds of family violence, including child abuse. While the cases involving child abuse represented only some 5–7 per cent of the total number of cases presenting to the court in any one year (as was the situation in the United States), by the mid-point of potential court proceedings they had become half of the court's caseload in children's matters. As the cases progressed through the court's various steps and stages, they became an increasing proportion of the court's workload as they did not resolve like other cases—either of their own accord or through the use of the court's conciliation services. Thus the apparent epidemic noted in the United States was, to an extent, a result of the way the cases moved slowly and without resolution through the court processes.

Both studies showed that child abuse was real, that it was severe, that it most commonly involved multiple forms of abuse, that it was associated with domestic violence, and that it represented the more serious end of the child abuse continuum. Importantly, the child protection services were not already familiar with the families—they were a new group of cases. False allegations were low at 9 per cent—a similarly low proportion to that reported in other contexts. Moreover, when the state child protection services undertook investigations of the allegations, they encountered distinct difficulties with the families due to the nature of the families' problems and to the relationship between the child protection service and Family Court.

Once the child abuse allegations were made, the court faced many obstacles in coordinating a response from the child protection authorities, the police, legal aid authorities and other social services. Moreover, the court's traditional strategies did not seem effective when used in this context. Counselling, adjournments and other delays did not assist, and only made the distress of the children greater. Some strategies were effective, however. These were the use of the court's family welfare reports, quick and detailed reports from the state child protection services, and the use of separate legal representatives for the child. A special program was recommended to the court to assist in better managing these complex and difficult cases.

As the Australian studies were being completed, more large-scale research was undertaken in North America. A Canadian study, like two of the Australian studies, used a broad definition of child abuse and included all four customary forms (Bala and Schuman, 1999). However, this study followed only those residence and contact disputes that went to a full trial—a proportion shown in the Australian studies to be only some 30 per cent of all cases. They focused attention on the high proportion—again, some 30 per cent—of unsubstantiated allegations where the child protection authority could neither prove nor disprove the allegations. They believed these were possible false allegations that should be added to the number the child protection agency had already determined to be false.

The Canadian study did not link its cases of unsubstantiated allegations to the nature of investigations in the child protection services as the Australian studies had done. The latter had shown that the proportion of unsubstantiated allegations was the same in residence and contact disputes as it was in all child abuse notifications. The Australian studies saw the issue of unsubstantiated allegations as one that was associated with the policies and practices of the Family Court and of the child protection services— not one related to the truth and falsity of the allegations. In the Australian study, evaluating the new specialised Family Court program for residence and contact disputes where child abuse allegations were involved—known as Magellan—this position was shown to be correct. In that program, when the court's and the child protection authorities' policies and practices were changed, the proportion of unsubstantiated allegations was reduced by half.

Then a series of studies from the United States suggested another dimension to the relationship between parental separation and child abuse. The meta-research studies of Wilson (2002), using data from many child protection studies carried out by other teams, suggested that parental separation and divorce seemed to lead to the occurrence of child abuse. Moreover, it did not seem to matter what post-divorce parenting arrangements were put in place for children after the separation and divorce: the risk seemed to remain the same, and was highest for the sexual abuse of female children.

This research was not able to draw firm conclusions as to why abuse was a consequence of parental separation and divorce, but suggested the reduced parental vigilance was an obvious factor. Finkelhor's theory about the causes of child sexual abuse includes the vulnerability of the child such as would occur with the loss of the parental partnership, the absence of one of the child's guardians, and the distress of the child post-separation. It also supports the notion that the child offers an opportunity to potential predators. In addition, there are the negative social conditions that can be a consequence of separation and divorce, which impact on parents and their coping ability (Rodgers and Prior, 1998).

We know now that child abuse in this context has distinctive features, including the way the abuse presents, the types of abuse that the victim suffers, the types of victims, the types of families in which it happens, and the types of alleged and actual perpetrators.

The allegations of child abuse in the context of parental separation and divorce are generally presented within family law proceedings in the form of a residence and contact dispute where one parent suggests the other should not have either residence or contact or both because of past or present abuse of the child. With the allegation being raised in this way, there is an immediate suspicion about the accusing parent's motives. In other contexts where allegations are made, there is no parental dispute, and suspicions about a parent's motives for making the allegations do not automatically follow. When one or both parents report what they believe to be the abuse of their child by a minister or priest, for example, there is less suspicion expressed by the child protection authority that the allegation is being used by the parent or parents against the minister for their own ends. When a professional, a school teacher or medical practitioner reports that they suspect a parent is abusing their child, there is even less suspicion that the allegations are mischievously manufactured for the accuser's own ends.

As the research has shown, most of the children subject to abuse in the context of parental separation and divorce are very young—on average, aged between four and eight. Most are too young to carry forward the allegations on their own, leaving one parent to take action against the other. In some instances, one parent is taking action against the other because of the advice of the child protection service, which has seen the solution to the abuse as being the person they call 'the protective parent' ending the parental partnership (Fehlberg and Kelly, 2000). When the service urges the protective parent to take action through family law proceedings, rather than the service deciding to use its own power through the Children's Court, it propels one parent into attacking the other in the forum of the Family Court rather than planning cooperatively with the child protection service.

Child protection workers have described such parents as being very difficult to work with (Brown et al., 1998, 2001). They are described as angry, as wanting urgent action to protect the child from the other parent, and as not understanding the subtleties of either the child welfare or the family law system or the way both need coordinating for the protection of their child. For example, as one mother said:

> Why, if the police are investigating him [the children's father] for sexually abusing them and they say they expect a prosecution, do I have to go to the Family Court to reply to his application for contact? This is ridiculous! The police say he is going to gaol! Do I have to take them to see him in gaol?

Often, such parents are alone with the problem they have encountered and have no family support. Just as the allegations of abuse from one parent to another pit one parent against the other, they pit the extended family of each parent against the other. Each parent loses the support they may have had from one half of the extended family and sometimes from both halves as extended family members withdraw from the tension of such a bitter debate. Furthermore, as the abuse is likely to continue after separation, the parent who is making the allegation can become more and more frustrated as nothing they do seems to have any effect. The desperation of such parents has been documented (Briggs, 2003; Hay, 2003), and they can appear to be lacking reason, flexibility, patience and understanding—even to be beyond help.

THE DISTINCTIVE NATURE OF CHILD ABUSE IN THIS CONTEXT

The abuse inflicted on children in the context of parental separation is different from other forms of child abuse. It's a bit like being Alice in Wonderland: what has been learned about child abuse generally does not hold true in this context. Traditionally child abuse reported to the child protection authorities internationally is classified into one of four categories, with each category having been defined by the child welfare legislation in the particular jurisdiction. The four categories are neglect, physical abuse, sexual abuse and emotional or psychological abuse. Detailed definitions, description and discussion of each type of abuse are presented in Chapters 4 and 5. Chapter 4 focuses on child sexual abuse and Chapter 5 on the other types of abuse.

In other contexts, neglect and physical abuse are the most common forms of abuse, with psychological abuse being less common and sexual abuse the least common form. However, in the context of parental separation and divorce, neglect is rare, sexual abuse is very common, and multiple types of abuse suffered at the same time is the most common scenario. The reason for the absence of neglect is clear. Neglect is usually a problem of an entire family—of both parents, not just one. It does occur sometimes in this context, but it occurs in unusual ways. For example, in the case quoted in the Introduction, the father (Grant) noticed over weeks that when he collected the children for overnight contact they were dirty, poorly dressed and losing weight. Furthermore, the mother's changeover arrangements prohibited him from entering her house. After some weeks he discovered their mother was on remand in prison awaiting trial on drug charges and caring for the children through a care system led by her sister and assisted by babysitters. She did not want the children to go to the father despite her troubles, hence the deception and neglect.

The reason for the prevalence of sexual abuse in this context is similarly clear. When a parent discovers the other parent is sexually abusing their child, often the only way to protect that child or children is to exclude the parent from the family by way of a parental separation, especially if the parent denies substantiated abuse. Child protection workers may insist that the protective parent take this action as either a short- or long-term strategy for the child's protection. The betrayal of trust between the two parents is so great in these circumstances that it is almost inevitable that, when one parent discovers sexual abuse of a child by the other parent, it will lead to parental separation and to a subsequent residence and contact dispute.

The prevalence of multiple forms of abuse in this context—a type of abuse now termed multi-type abuse—is more difficult to explain. One explanation is that the artificial constructs set up for the use of four separate categories of abuse in notifications to child protection services mask the existence of multi-type abuse. Supporting this explanation are the findings of a recent English study of child abuse that took the description of abuse from the words of victims and noted multi-type abuse. They found it occurred infrequently, involving only 5 per cent of the children who were abused (Cawson, 2002), whereas it involves a much larger proportion—32–45 per cent—of children in the parental separation and divorce research. The higher incidence of multi-type abuse in this context is probably linked to the high incidence of domestic violence found among these families.

Some distinctive types of abuse arise from the particular situations of separated and divorced parents. These include changeover abuse, where the abuse happens at the time of the changeover from one parent to the other; contact abuse, where the abuse happens while the child is on a contact visit with only one parent; and abduction, where one parent removes the child to a new location without informing or seeking the agreement of the other parent and refuses to inform anyone of the child's whereabouts. These are dealt with further in Chapter 5.

As mentioned previously, the victims of abuse in this context are younger on average than other victims of abuse. As a result, many are unable to speak for themselves, and need their parents or other adults to speak for them. Furthermore, an even higher proportion than one might expect from the high incidence of sexual abuse are female children. Another feature is the high proportion—28 per cent—suffering from what mental health professionals term very disturbed emotional states, such as severe depression, high levels of anger and extreme anxiety.

THE FAMILIES

In most respects, the families in which abuse occurs in these circumstances are typical of their local communities in terms of family form, race, ethnicity and social class. The families represent current family forms. Most (58 per cent) are families where the parents have been legally married, some (37 per cent) are families where the partnership has been a de facto one, some (2 per cent) are families with non-cohabiting partnerships—a recent family form emerging in Australia as elsewhere (Hetherington and Kelly, 2002)—and some are grandparents (3 per cent) who are caring for their grandchildren. They are not drawn from a distinctly lower socio-economic group or disproportionately from any one ethnic or racial group. All classes and ethnic backgrounds are represented. Nevertheless, there are three main differences in these families.

The proportion of fathers who are unemployed is high. Male unemployment has been noted to be high following divorce, and to last for some years—this has been attributed to the personal toll partnership breakdown exacts (Jordan, 1996). At the same time, Gregory (1996) has suggested that male unemployment internationally is increasing, and that it particularly affects men with dependants. It may be that the experience of unemployment, which Gregory likens to falling off a cliff, is an underlying factor in the partnership breakdown that emerges clearly only after the partnership ends. Also, the high unemployment rate may be linked to the high incidence of criminal convictions among these men. Some of them are pursuing a career of crime.

At the same time, the proportion of unemployed women is higher than among all women with children. Since the protective social effects of employment are so often absent for both parents in this group, it may be that many have suffered a range of social problems as a result, including child abuse.

In addition, the families have a high incidence of domestic violence. Some 44 per cent of families had experienced confirmed domestic violence. In these families, there was other family violence as well, with children being violent to their parents at surprisingly young ages and with other family members also being violent to the parents. Domestic violence is increasingly reported as a cause of partnership breakdown, with two-thirds of couples in Australia attributing the separation to domestic violence and one-third to severe domestic violence (FLPAG, 2001), suggesting that domestic violence is widespread in the Australian community and that it is now a common reason for marital partnership collapse. Since the occurrence of domestic violence is linked to the occurrence of child abuse, the fact that this is a group high in domestic violence is not surprising. It is possible that the incidence of domestic violence is even higher than identified because of the effect that one form of abuse has in masking others—thus families report or emphasise one form when others also exist (Brown et al., 1998).

A high incidence of criminal offences, including crimes of violence, is also evident. Some 24 per cent of men had a history of criminal offences, with multiple offences including crimes of violence being the most common type. Women's incidence of criminal offences was higher than average at 10 per cent—though not as high as for men and with a narrower range of offences, such as social security fraud and drug offences, which are usually interrelated. Of those charged with criminal offences some 15 per cent of the men had been convicted of child abuse offences, but none of the women had. Furthermore, the more serious the child abuse, the higher the rate of past criminal offences for both men and women.

ALLEGED AND ACTUAL PERPETRATORS

In the context of parental separation and divorce, the alleged and actual perpetrators are almost always family members—either one or other and sometimes both parents, or a grandparent, or a sibling of one parent, or a sibling of the child who is the victim. Since allegations are mostly made by one parent against the other, with only 15 per cent of allegations made by professionals, the allegations take on the features of a gender battle, with mothers pitted against fathers and vice versa. The sense of a gender war is further heightened when there are allegations of sexual abuse—which, as already indicated, are more commonly made and more often substantiated in the context of parental separation and divorce than in the case of other such notifications to the child protection authorities. About double the number of these allegations are made by mothers than by fathers. A small proportion of other family members also make allegations, and occasionally a victim does so, but most children involved are too young to be able to do this. Allegations are most commonly made against fathers, then mothers, by both parents against each other, against step-parents, against a group of family members, against siblings and step-siblings, and against other relatives and family friends in that order.

The substantiated perpetrators are also generally family members, with fathers being the most commonly substantiated perpetrators; other relatives, such as grandparents, uncles, and step-parents are grouped together as the next most commonly substantiated group; and mothers are the least frequently substantiated person. Table 1.1 compares the incidence of perpetrators who were substantiated as abusers with that of those who were not.

Table 1.1: Frequency of alleged perpetrators compared with substantiated perpetrators of all types of abuse

Person	Frequency rate of perpetrators substantiated (%) (N=52)	Frequency rate of perpetrators not substantiated (%) (N=48)
Father	53	47
Mother	30	70
Both parents	42	58
Step-father	60	40
Step-mother	100	0
Grandfather/step-grandfather	100	0
Grandmother/step-grandmother	0	100
Sibling	50	50
Multiple family members	75	25

Source: Brown (2003).

Table 1.2 shows the frequency of those who are the perpetrators of abuse, placing the comparison of alleged and substantiated perpetrators in a broader context. The table shows that fathers are the most common perpetrators, followed by both parents and multiple family members, who

Table 1.2: Frequency of perpetrators of substantiated abuse on all types

Person	Frequency rate (%)
Father	53
Mother	11.5
Both parents	12.5
Step-father	4
Step-mother	2
Grandfather/step-grandfather	2
Grandmother/step-grandmother	1
Sibling or step-sibling	2
Multiple family members	9
Other relatives	2
Not known	1

include fathers, mothers, siblings, grandparents and cousins. When multiple family members were involved, there were usually three family members.

When the tables are reviewed, the subtleties and contradictions of the situation can be seen. The basis for some of the misleading beliefs about abuse in this context also becomes evident. For, while fathers are the most frequently substantiated perpetrators, at the same time they are almost as frequently *not* substantiated as perpetrators, whereas mothers are the least frequently accused and the least frequently substantiated. However, step-fathers, while less frequently accused, are more frequently substantiated than biological fathers. Grandparents and step-grandparents, while infrequently accused, are invariably substantiated. Of concern is the fact that, when multiple family members are accused, there is a high chance the abuse alleged against all of them will be substantiated.

The making of false allegations—a strong concern in this context— seems to be confined to the children's parents, with slightly more fathers (55 per cent) than mothers (45 per cent) making false allegations. When Gardner first wrote of his 'parental alienation syndrome', he saw mothers as being the sole source of these, although he later changed his mind. When false allegations are examined in depth, such allegations are often found to have come from parents with mental health problems or parents who have suffered abuse themselves rather than from mischievous or malicious parents (Brown et al., 2001).

CONCLUSION

Our knowledge of child abuse in the context of parental separation and divorce has been confused by many factors over the years. The areas of child abuse, parental separation and divorce and domestic violence have developed separately and proceeded without reference to each other, thereby producing clouds of confusion in our thinking that remain with us today. As knowledge grew in one area, it did not penetrate the others, so misunderstandings about child abuse in the context of parental separation and divorce and the relationship of each to domestic violence have continued.

Reliable research is shedding light on child abuse in this context, and it is showing that—while child abuse in this context shares some characteristics with child abuse in other contexts—it also has distinct characteristics of its own. As each type of abuse is scrutinised even further, it becomes clear that even more distinct characteristics emerge. These are outlined in Chapters 4 and 5.

2

CHILD ABUSE, FAMILY VIOLENCE AND FAMILY LAW LEGISLATION

In 1975, Australia enacted new Commonwealth family law legislation, the *Family Law Act*, seen at the time to represent a dramatic move forwards in achieving a more civilised and sympathetic approach to marital breakdown. The new approach was aimed at reducing the distress of the partnership breakdown and the acrimony of ensuing parental conflict. At the time, however, domestic violence and child abuse were not recognised as problems relating to family breakdown, and the legislation did not deal with them adequately.

This chapter presents the background to the legislation and the details of its provisions and implementation. It identifies the subsequent changes which have occurred to the legislation, including the substantial amendments which came into effect in 2006—the *Family Law Amendment (Shared Parental Responsibility) Act* 2006. It also shows how the Family Court of Australia, established as a new court, struggled unsuccessfully—and possibly unsympathetically—to accommodate to issues of child abuse and other family violence despite demands from separating parties for it to make residence and contact decisions that took such violence into account.

By reference to case law and legislation amendments, the chapter shows also how the Family Court began to take family violence—both child abuse and domestic violence—into greater consideration in decisions affecting parenting and children.

BACKGROUND TO THE *FAMILY LAW ACT* 1975 (CTH)

Sexual abuse is insidious. Its effects are far-reaching. Violence in the home can be equally insidious. Psychological or emotional abuse can have equally deleterious effects. Our society accepts a plurality of conduct and a plurality of attitude. It does its best to ensure the existence of certain minimal standards, and consistent with the maintenance of a relationship between parent and child, to ensure that parents do meet those minimum standards. (*K v B*, 1994)[1]

Australia has one of the highest divorce rates in the world. It is estimated that, of the 46 per cent or over of marriages and de facto[2] relationships in Australia that break down,[3] about 50 per cent of those separated couples actually approach lawyers, courts or alternative dispute resolution services for assistance with financial and/or children's matters. Of that population, comparatively few actually litigate and even fewer proceed right through to a final hearing. Overall, the Australian Bureau of Statistics (ABS) estimates that there are one million children in Australia living in separated families. Of these, only a minuscule number of cases involve post-separation parents contesting the residence and care of children. These parents do so under the *Family Law Act* 1975 (Cth).

The *Family Law Act* came into effect in January 1976. The Act revolutionised some aspects of family law in Australia. It abolished fault for the purposes of divorce by replacing fourteen grounds for divorce (thirteen of which were fault-based) with one ground of 'irretrievable breakdown', evidenced by twelve months' separation. It also reformed the law on children's matters, matrimonial property, child maintenance, spousal maintenance, injunctions and other relief, as well as establishing alternative dispute resolution and counselling services. Importantly, the Act established a new specialist federal court—the Family Court of Australia—to deal exclusively with matters under the *Family Law Act*. In addition, state courts of summary jurisdiction (e.g. the Magistrates' Court in Victoria) and the Federal Magistrates Court (a new federal court established in 2000) also have jurisdiction in respect of some family law matters.[4]

When the *Family Law Act* came into force, the principal provisions relating to children were in Part VII, headed 'Children'. Section 60D prescribed that 'the court shall regard the welfare of the child as the paramount consideration' in custody and access matters. Section 64(1) set out the factors to be considered in custody and access proceedings such as parental responsibilities, *status quo*, parental conduct and wishes of the child, but there was no mention of domestic violence or child abuse as a relevant factor. In the case of *Lythow and Lythow* (1976: 75,074), Watson J emphasised:

> the constant shifts in community mores and opinions and the increased psychological understanding by the courts of the dynamics of inter-relationships within the family. To that extent the cases should be read more as examples of how the courts seek to deal with varied sets of facts and relationships rather than as hard and fast precedents binding upon later decision-makers.

In 1991, section 60D was repealed but the paramountcy of the welfare of the child was incorporated into the new section 64(1). This section then contained a non-exhaustive non-prioritised list of eight factors to be considered in proceedings relating to guardianship custody, welfare or access. Again, there was no specific inclusion of domestic violence or child abuse as relevant factors, but—as shown later in this chapter—such factors were argued under section 64(1)(i) which allowed the court to take into account 'any other fact or circumstance'. Each case was to be determined on its particular facts, and the interpretation of and weight accorded to each factor was up to the individual presiding judge as influenced by his/her own beliefs and as upholders of 'general community standards and norms' (*Lythow and Lythow*, 1976, per Watson J at 75,075). As the case law reflects, sometimes findings of domestic violence or child abuse were deemed relevant to determining the outcome in a children's matter, more commonly, such findings were ignored.

THE *FAMILY LAW REFORM ACT* 1995

The next major amendments to the *Family Law Act* were introduced by the *Family Law Reform Act* 1995, which came into operation in June 1996. The 1995 Act inserted an entirely new Part VII relating to children. Although much of Part VII has since been re-worded or changed by the *Family Law Amendment (Shared Parental Responsibility) Act* 2006 which was passed in May 2006 and mostly came into effect in July 2006, parts of Part VII remain current law and the case law outlined in this chapter concerns both repealed and still existing provisions of the *Family Law Act*.

Until jurisprudence and case law are developed under the 2006 amendments, it is worthwhile setting out the 1995 amendments and former provisions in detail in order to understand case law and judicial attitudes in both historical and jurisprudential context.

The 1995 amendments were influenced by the *United Nations Convention on the Rights of the Child* (ratified by Australia on 17 December 1990) and were largely modelled on the UK *Children Act* 1989. The changes provided not just new terminology, but also shifts in ideology and precepts away from proprietary connotations of parenting towards the rights of children. 'Custody' was replaced by 'residence' and 'specific issues'; 'guardianship' was replaced by the expanded notion of 'parental responsibility'; and 'access' was replaced by 'contact'. New provisions were also introduced to encourage contact between children and parents post-separation, and to promote the use of primary dispute resolution and parenting plans to encourage parents to care for their children amicably and cooperatively.

In addition, the concept of the 'welfare of the child' was replaced by section 65E, which stated that 'a court must regard the best interests of the child as the paramount consideration' in making parenting orders as to residence, specific issues and contact. An expanded list of factors that a court must take into account in determining the best interests of a child appeared in section 68F(2).

This included the following:

(g) the need to protect the child from physical or psychological harm caused, or that may be caused, by:
   (i) being subjected or exposed to abuse, ill-treatment, violence or other behaviour; or
   (ii) being directly or indirectly exposed to abuse, ill-treatment, violence or other behaviour that is directed towards, or may affect, another person

. . .

(i) any family violence involving the child or a member of the child's family.

(j) any family violence order that applies to the child or a member of the child's family.

Once again, no guidelines were given as to the weight of the factors on this list, and it remained a matter for judicial discretion on the particular facts and merits of each individual case. However, in considering what parenting order to make, the court must have ensured that the order 'does not expose a person to an unacceptable risk of family violence' (section 68K(1)(b)), and this clearly included exposing a child to direct or indirect violence. The court must also apply certain principles enunciated in section 43 in the exercise of its jurisdiction under the Act, including '(ca) the need to ensure safety from family violence'.

Another positive amendment was the inclusion of a definition of 'family violence' for the first time in section 60D(1). 'Family violence' was defined as:

> conduct, whether actual or threatened, by a person towards, or towards the property of, a member of the person's family that causes that or any other member of the person's family to fear for, or to be apprehensive about, his or her personal well being or safety.

This broad definition was adopted and applied in some reported cases.

The 1995 amendments also introduced a new section 60B into the *Family Law Act* that sets out the object and principles underlying Part VII with regard to children. In particular, section 60B(2)(b) enunciated the principle that 'children have a right of contact, on a regular basis, with both their parents and with other people significant to their care, welfare and development'. This was in direct contrast to section 68K(1)(b), which stated that:

> in considering what order to make, the court must, to the extent that it is possible to do so consistently with the child's best interests being the paramount consideration, ensure that the order: does not expose a person to an unacceptable risk of family violence.

This has created an unresolved tension in the Family Court:

> This tension, the research tells us, has translated into a greater tendency for non-resident parents to expect contact, even when domestic violence is an issue, and for there to be pressure on resident parents to *agree* to contact, despite safety concerns. This is particularly the case at interim hearings which frequently become de facto final hearings because of the time that elapses until the matter can be fully considered at trial ... The research also documents a high breakdown rate of contact arrangements where violence is an issue. (Nicholson, 2001: 12)

CHANGES IN 2006 TO THE *FAMILY LAW ACT* 1975

Following various national and parliamentary inquiries and reports in 2003 and 2004, the federal government released the 120-page exposure draft of the Family Law Amendment (Shared Parental Responsibility) Bill 2005 in June 2005. The Act was passed in May 2006 and contains almost 190 pages with over 450 amendments to the principal Act and other Acts for related purposes.

In the area of children's orders, some of the changes are cosmetic and others appear significant, though time will tell as to the impact on litigants, legal practitioners, court and allied practices, and judicial decisions. Some of the amendments deal directly with child abuse and family violence.

First of all, it should be noted that the terminology and language of parenting orders have been changed in section 64B. 'Residence' has been replaced by 'the person or persons with whom a child is to live', and 'contact' has been replaced by 'the time a child is to spend with another person or other persons'. The list of different types of parenting orders has been expanded.

More importantly, section 60B has been expanded. It now contains four objects and five principles underlying the principal Act. It adds new object (1)(a) 'to ensure that children have the benefit of both their parents having a meaningful involvement in their lives, to the maximum extent consistent with the best interests of the child' and new object (1)(b) 'protecting children from physical or psychological harm from being subjected to, or exposed to, abuse, neglect, or family violence'. It also adds a new principle in section 60B(2)(b) that 'children have the right to spend time on a regular basis with, and communicate on a regular basis with, both their parents and other people significant to their care, welfare and development'.

Best interests of a child remains the paramount consideration in making a parenting order under new sections 60CA and 65DAA merely repeating and relocating former section 65E.

In addition, old section 68F(2) factors have been repealed and replaced by section 60CC which now divides how a court is to determine what is in a child's best interests into 'primary' and 'additional' considerations. Section 60CC(2) specifies that primary considerations are:

(a)   the benefit to the child of having a meaningful relationship with both of the child's parents; and

(b)   the need to protect the child from physical or psychological harm from being subjected to, or exposed to, abuse, neglect or family violence.

These two new primary considerationsmirror the first two new objects in section 60B. Section 60CC(3) then lists thirteen non-weighted and non-prioritised additional considerations which by and large replicate or re-word former section 68F(2).

How important are these changes? Clearly, it is not possible to predict the impact of such changes but they appear cosmetic rather than qualitative. New section 60B(1)(b) merely repeats and formally elevates former section 68F(2)(g) detailed above from a factor relevant in making parenting orders to an underlying object of courts exercising jurisdiction under the Act. Further, the new principle in section 60B(2)(b) only replaces the term 'contact' with the new phrase 'spending time and communicating with'. As for new section 60CC, it just reshuffles the previous factors listed in former section 68F(2) and *prima facie* accords greater weight to two factors labelled as 'primary'.

These changes do not remove the current conflict between competing principles discussed.The proposals in fact further advance and entrench the notion that children should have a meaningful relationship and spend time with each parent. This appears laudable, but the term meaningful is not defined and insufficient attention is drawn to issues of child abuse and family violence.

There is another more controversial amendment. New section 61DA provides that, when making a parenting order in relation to a child, 'the court must apply a presumption that it is in the best interests of the child for the child's parents to have equal shared parental responsibility for the child'. This of itself does not provide for a presumption about the amount of time spent with each of the parents, but new section 65DAA states that if a parenting order provides for equal shared parental responsibility then the court *must* consider making an order to provide for the child to spend equal time with each of the parents. If it is not in the best interests of the child and is not 'reasonably practicable' to make such an order, then the court must consider an order for the child to spend 'substantial and significant' time with each parent.

The presumption of equal shared parental responsibility is rebuttable. One exception (section 61DA(2)) is:

if there are reasonable grounds to believe that a parent of the child (or a person who lives with a parent of the child) has engaged in:

(a)   abuse of the child or another child who, at the time, was a member of the parent's family (or that other person's family); or

(b)   family violence.

In a similar vein, the word 'reasonably' has been inserted into the definition of family violence relocated from section 60D(1) to the definitions in section 4(1). A person must now 'reasonably' fear for or be apprehensive about his or her personal well-being or safety.

No definitions or guidelines are provided as to what 'reasonable grounds' or 'reasonably' may be. It is not clear whether reasonable grounds need to be substantiated by evidence and whether any such evidence will be tested at a preliminary hearing or needs to be corroborated. It is also not clear whether the belief that a person has engaged in child abuse or family violence is subjective or needs to be supported by a Notice of Child Abuse or Family Violence under the *Family Law Rules* or needs to also involve state welfare proceedings (in which case there are jurisdictional problems under section 69ZK of the *Family Law Act*) or a current protection order under local state family violence legislation. Also, 'abuse' of a child is only defined in section 4(1) as sexual assault of a child or involving a child in a sexual activity so other forms of child abuse, such as psychological or physical abuse, may not suffice for this presumption not to operate.

Again, this presumption virtually accords priority to parents, including abusive or violent parents, to spend equal or substantial time with, and be involved in decisions regarding the day-to-day welfare of a child over and above the rights of a child or the resident parent to be protected and safe from harm and abuse.

This vagueness of the term 'reasonable' is compounded by new section 117AB, which states that if the court is satisfied that a party to the proceedings made a false allegation or statement in the proceedings, 'the court must order that party to pay some, or all of the costs of another party, or other parties, to the proceedings'. This begs the question—what about false denials?

The rationale behind this new provision is flawed. The explanatory memorandum to the 2006 Act states that this new provision addresses 'concerns' that allegations of family violence and child abuse can be easily made and may be taken into account in family law proceedings. However, research tells us that the rate of false allegations of child abuse in the Family Court is the same as in cases notified to child protection services, namely 9 per cent (Brown et al., 1998: 89) which suggests that the 'concerns' were raised by small and vocal but disproportionately powerful groups of aggrieved litigants (mostly men) and listened to by the lawmakers (see Chapter 7).

This new provision is also dangerous for abused women and children, who are largely vulnerable, powerless and unable to access or afford legal representation or legal aid. This may have the undesirable and potentially life-threatening effect of driving family violence and child abuse underground and rendering victims more invisible, thereby re-victimising those we should be seeking to protect and assist.

Time will tell how the courts interpret the 2006 changes. In the meantime, we refer to existing case law and judicial thinking.

CASE LAW UNDER THE *FAMILY LAW ACT* 1975

Legislative changes to the *Family Law Act* 1975 up to the 2006 amendments have paralleled (or, some would argue, have been a consequence of) changes in judicial thinking as reflected in the case law. Family violence and child abuse were peripheral considerations in many reported cases until the mid-1990s. Since then, such issues have attained a higher profile on a par with community expectations and public awareness.

First, a few words about case law. It is important to remember that case law is subjective and selective, and not necessarily representative of the divorcing population nor of the process of decision-making. Only about 5 per cent of all applications seeking ancillary relief (such as children's matters and property settlement) actually proceed to final hearing for judicial determination (Family Court of Australia annual reports; Australia, Law Reform Commission *Review of the Federal Civil Justice System*, 1999). Of those, even fewer are reported (i.e. published in law reports) in either the Family Court of Australia or the Federal Magistrates Court. However, case law does provide a valuable window into judicial discretion and the processes of judicial reasoning and decision-making, as well as reflecting broader community attitudes and socio-political influences.

As stated earlier, fault and marital misconduct were abolished under the

Family Law Act for the purposes of divorce, but remain relevant in proceedings concerning children and financial settlements. Rather than pretending not to look at conduct at all in children's matters, or in property or maintenance proceedings, courts purport to adhere to what Wilczek terms 'the optimum distance', which is the distance between eliminating the necessity of investigating 'conduct' in family law proceedings from areas where such investigation or inquisition would prove to be senseless and a waste of time and expense, and retaining the relevance of 'conduct' in areas where commonsense and the community sense of natural justice decree that 'conduct' needs to be taken into account (Wilczek, 1987: 488–89).

In the next two sections, we examine case law pre-2006 amendments and whether 'optimum distance' has been applied in cases of family violence and child abuse. We consider these two sets of cases separately by applying a broad definition of child abuse as adopted by the *Family Law Act* itself. Questions of residence and contact concerning children arise in situations of violence or abuse between the parents (or other household members) where children are indirect or secondary victims. In other cases, children are the direct or primary victims of abuse or violence, and these cases are considered separately In all cases, the tension between the co-existing but competing principles of protecting children from exposure to family violence on the one hand, and promoting contact between a child and both parents on the other, is evident. It is predicted that under the 2006 amendments this tension will remain and, indeed, heighten.

FAMILY VIOLENCE BETWEEN PARENTS

In many cases, the Family Court has adopted different standards in relation to the fitness of the mother as a parent and the fitness of a father as a parent. This has certainly been the case where violence has been alleged by a wife against her husband. Such violence has traditionally not been taken into account because it has been deemed to be a separate matter unrelated to the welfare of the children and the suitability of the father as a potential custodial or contact parent. For example, in *Chandler and Chandler* (1981), Nygh J refused to hear allegations of the husband's violence upon the wife. To be even-handed, the trial judge similarly refused to hear allegations that the wife had run off with another man, as this would lead to using a double standard. There, the judge wrongly equated family violence (and its impact upon not only the wife but also the children) with a marital 'transgression' by the wife.

Many cases in the first twenty years of the operation of the *Family Law Act* could be categorised as supporting the theory that 'he may be a violent husband but he's a good father'. In applying the 'welfare' or 'best interests' of the child principle, it was not until the 1990s that the Family Court shifted its thinking and finally recognised that a violent home can be as indirectly detrimental and harmful to a child as the damage inflicted by direct abuse or violence. For almost two decades, the Family Court consistently rejected evidence of family violence, or else under-estimated the effects of violence upon mothers and children, thus privatising, marginalising and devaluing the experience of women.

In *Heidt and Heidt* (1976), the wife and others gave evidence of the husband's violence towards the wife. The case concerned competing custody applications with respect to three young children. Murray J granted custody to the wife and access to the husband, and refused to grant the wife an injunction for her personal protection. Her Honour noted that:

> there is no suggestion that Mr Heidt has ever treated his children with the violence with which he has treated his wife ... in assessing his potential as a custodial parent, I have largely disregarded his behaviour as a husband. (1976: 75,362)

In *Dean and Dean* (1977), which was a case involving the wife's application for sole use and exclusive occupancy of the former matrimonial home, there was evidence before the court that the husband had been physically abusive to his wife, and that the wife had had 'associations' with other men. Wood J stated that it was difficult to say who was at fault for the breakdown of the marriage as the wife had chosen to lead 'an independent social life' away from the family. His Honour refused to grant either party the sole use of the family home, and held that it was not intolerable (and therefore tolerable) that they continue to live together. His Honour also stated that it would accordingly help the situation if the wife were to moderate her conduct 'in pursuit of her own pleasures' and to behave like a 'good and conscientious mother' (1977: 76,098). This, in turn, would enable the husband to moderate his behaviour.

Similarly, in *Cartwright and Cartwright* (1977), the court found that the husband was violent to his wife, drank alcohol to excess and was generally irresponsible and immature. Even though his abusive conduct was deemed relevant and the wife was awarded custody, the wife was still criticised for working. The court held that 'it would be better if she did not have to work' (1977: 76,432), implying that it would be better if she would stay at home as the ideal full-time mother and homemaker.

The reported cases demonstrate that, for almost twenty years, the Family Court formally viewed family violence generally as an example of marital misconduct—if that—devoid of any gender considerations and removed from the welfare or best interests of children. Berns describes this as 'judicial insensitivity' or 'obtuseness':

> A significant feature of the frequently submerged discourse of the violent marriage is the degree to which the abuse and victimization of women by their partners has been characterized as an issue of 'marital fault', one which is concerned primarily, indeed often exclusively, with the relationship between the former husband and wife, rather than as a pattern of family relationships which inevitably has a profound impact upon the welfare of the children. Given the increasing evidence that violent relationships tend to reproduce themselves in succeeding generations, that they become socially normative, this judicial insensitivity, one might say obtuseness, is remarkable. (Berns, 1991: 240–41)

This early attitude dismissing the impact of family violence between parents (primarily with fathers as perpetrators) upon children as a form of child abuse persisted until the 1990s. It was not until 1994 that a string of reported cases sealed a significant shift in the Family Court's thinking and a formal recognition of the relevance of inter-spousal family violence in children's proceedings. The formal case law recognition was later enshrined in the 1995 amendments to the *Family Law Act* detailed previously.

In *Merryman and Merryman* (1994), Mullane J found that the violent husband was dangerous to the wife and children 'not just in the direct physical sense, but also as an inappropriate role model' (1994: 81,171). In *Jaeger and Jaeger* (1994), the Full Court overturned a trial judge who disallowed evidence of violence in the wife's household, perpetrated against her by her new de facto partner, by stating: 'I am not interested in whether the home [of the mother] is a peaceful haven ... or a bit rougher than that' (1994: 81,117). The Full Court ordered a re-hearing, holding that violence in the household is relevant to a custody application, even if not directed at the child. Again, in *Patsalou and Patsalou* (1995), the Full Court held that the denigration of one parent by the other, as well as physical violence, were relevant considerations in children's matters and could place doubt upon the suitability of the proposed custodial parent. Similarly, in *JG and BG* (1994), the trial judge confirmed that the court must consider all admissible evidence in determining children's issues, including the nature of any family violence and its direct and indirect effect upon any children.

These decisions are laudable for recognising the deleterious effects of family violence on children as secondary or indirect victims, and for challenging the historical separation and quarantining of inter-spousal family violence from child abuse. This significant shift in judicial thinking and attitude, together with a burgeoning body of social science literature, no doubt contributed to the substantial amendments to the *Family Law Act* which came into force in 1996. As already detailed, these were subsequently expanded in the 2006 amendments: the court *must* now consider the effects of family violence involving a child or a member of the child's family, and is required to ensure that parenting orders do not expose people (including children) to family violence. In doing so, a wide definition of family violence is to be applied.

Unfortunately, research and experience show that the legislatively raised profile of family violence issues in children's matters has 'only limited practical effect' (Dewar and Parker, 1999). The relevance of violence has been overshadowed by the legislation (and courts) promoting a child's right of contact with both parents (Rhoades et al., 1999; Kaye et al., 2003b), problems with waiting periods for interim and final hearings, legal aid issues (Dewar et al., 1999) and poor levels of awareness amongst legal practitioners and the broader community. Also, courts are not consistently recognising the link between family violence and the harm caused to children nor the fact that legal processes such as negotiations, court-sanctioned alternative dispute resolution and frequent court appearances can also perpetuate family violence and child abuse (Kaye et al., 2003b).

Most cases are determined at trial at first instance, and neither go on appeal to the Full Court nor get reported in official law reports. That means that we cannot state definitively that judges are not adhering to the traditional historical separation between family violence and child abuse. A few Australian cases do, however, recognise the impact of family violence on children and on parenting capacity, as did the English Court of Appeal in *Re L (A Child) (Contact: Domestic Violence), V, M and H* (2001):

> The family judges and justices need to have a heightened awareness of the existence of and consequences (some long-term) on children of

exposure to domestic violence between their parents or other partners. There has, perhaps, been a tendency in the past for courts not to tackle allegations of violence and to leave them in the background on the premise that they were matters affecting the adults and not relevant to issues regarding the children. The general principle that contact with the non-resident parent is in the interests of the child may sometimes have discouraged sufficient attention being paid to the adverse effects on children living in the household where violence has occurred. It may not necessarily be widely appreciated that violence to a partner involves a significant failure in parenting—failure to protect the child's carer and failure to protect the child emotionally. (2000: 272–73, per Butler-Sloss P)

For example, in *Blanch and Blanch* (1999), the Full Court ordered a re-hearing of a residence matter concerning three young children where the wife had given detailed evidence of a sustained course of severe domestic violence at the hands of her husband. The Full Court held that domestic violence is an important factor in parenting cases under section 68F(2) factors, and the trial judge had given insufficient weight to the domestic violence and to the relevance of such violence to the overall welfare of the children. The Full Court stated that the trial judge must turn his or her mind to risks to children flowing from domestic violence other than just the risk of direct future violence. These risks include the potential damage to children's emotional development from exposure to a violent role model; the risk of insecurity, fear, unhappiness, anxiety and hyper-vigilance from witnessing abusive behaviour of a parent; the risk of serious long-term emotional problems such as poor self-esteem and lack of self-confidence; and the risk of using violence themselves in dealing with other people, destroying intimate relationships and coming into conflict with other people, the police and the law.

In *A and A* (1998), the wife was violently assaulted in the home in what appeared to be an attempt to kill her. She suffered serious injuries, including a sexual assault. The wife believed that her attacker was the husband, and there were a number of objective facts which supported that belief. The wife also gave evidence of a number of assaults upon her by the husband during the course of the marriage. The husband sought unsupervised contact with the three young children. The wife was opposed to any contact. The trial judge held that it was not the role of the Family Court to 'investigate criminal activity', but still concluded in the wife's favour that she had reasonable grounds for believing that the husband was the perpetrator. His Honour ordered regular supervised and then unsupervised contact after some time. On appeal, the Full Court found that there would be an unacceptable risk to the children if unsupervised contact took place. The Full Court ordered that the husband only have supervised contact each weekend for a day and did not envisage the likelihood of any change in the predictable future.

Similarly, in *M and M* (2000), the trial judge found that the father's abusive and aggressive behaviour posed a multi-faceted danger to the children, with a risk of injury and fear and a risk that the children would learn from the abusive behaviour and ultimately treat it as acceptable. The court recognised the far-reaching effects of inter-spousal violence upon children and family dynamics.

Again, in *T and S* (2001), the Full Court held that a trial judge had not sufficiently considered how children are affected by the consequences of violence upon the victimised parent's caregiving capacity. The trial judge did not accept the evidence of a self-represented mother as to domestic violence by the former partner. The judge found that she was erratic, impulsive and inconsistent, contradictory and prone to exaggerate the allegations of violence. His Honour largely discounted all her evidence in this regard. The Full Court did not criticise how the judge had conducted the trial, but allowed an appeal and ordered a re-hearing. The court held amongst other things that the case highlights a serious problem where women have suffered serious family violence and have to present their case unrepresented and unaided by legal aid.

Again, in *D and D* (2005), the trial judge found that the father of two girls, then aged fourteen and twelve years, refused to accept responsibility for his past violence perpetrated on the wife, some of which was witnessed and experienced by the children. The father was in deep denial about his behaviour and its ill effects and harmful impact upon the children. Carmody J concluded that their best interests dictated that the father have no communication or contact at all, save for contact initiated by the children. This order also accorded with the children's wishes, the opinion of expert witnesses and the recommendation of the children's separate representative.

By contrast, in two unreported decisions of *Bartholomew v Kelly* (2000) and *Grant and Grant* (2001), the Full Court noted the seriousness of the husband's physical and sexual violence towards the wife in each case, but nonetheless refused to interfere with the trial judge's discretionary findings as to the relevance of such family violence in parenting orders. In the first case, the husband was granted shared residence of two young girls. In the second case, the husband was granted sole residence of a teenage boy, over-turning a long *status quo* in favour of the wife. In both cases, the appellate court upheld the original decisions.

These are but a few cases, mostly on appeal, where the discounting of personal accounts or the lack of legal representation was scrutinised and led to a new hearing. Given the small number of appeals heard each year, the time and costs involved in an appeal, cuts in legal aid, the individual approaches and levels of 'consciousness' of different judges, the growing number of self-represented litigants, and the traditional private and 'behind closed doors' nature of family violence, the question remains as to the number of decisions made without scrutiny or accountability to a higher court. That question casts a long and disturbing shadow on the administration of justice and the protection of family members in family law proceedings involving inter-spousal family violence.

A relatively recent reported decision shines some light into this shadow. In *T and N* (2004), the trial judge refused to make consent orders for un-supervised contact by two young children with their father. The father had been physically violent to the mother (and allegedly to the older child), leading the mother to relocate to an undisclosed address with the children. Both parties were legally represented and proposed unsupervised contact with the consent of the child representative. The trial judge would only approve alternative consent orders limited to supervised contact. Her judgment is an isolated example of raised judicial consciousness and informed decision-making:

It also hardly needs to be said that violent and abusive conduct by one parent against the other is highly detrimental to the well-being of children, whether they are witness to it or not. If they do witness it, anyone can see that such conduct can only be a traumatic experience for them. There is an abundance of research from social scientists about the highly detrimental effect upon young children of exposure to violence and the serious consequences such experiences have for their personality formation. They are terrified and simultaneously come to accept it as an expected part of life; they may learn that violence is acceptable behaviour and an integral part of intimate relationships; or that violence and fear can be used to exert control over family members; they may suffer significant emotional trauma from fear, anxiety, confusion, anger, helplessness and disruption in their lives; they may have higher levels of aggression than children who do not have that exposure; and they may suffer from higher anxiety, more behaviour problems and lower self-esteem than children not exposed to violence. Clinical profiles for children who witness domestic violence include post-traumatic play, diminished ability to regulate affect in the forms of hyper-arousal, numbness, emotional constriction, a low frustration threshold, multiple nightmares and other sleep disturbances, aggressive behaviours, intense and multiple fears, regression in developmental achievements, and disturbances in peer relations ... One could go on to the impact upon their ability to form attachments, and so on. (2004: 264–65, Moore J)

CHILD ABUSE WHERE CHILDREN ARE DIRECT OR PRIMARY VICTIMS

As stated above, the *Family Law Act* 1975 contains a broad definition of family violence in section 4(1) (formerly in section 60D(1)), and at times courts exercising jurisdiction under the Act have adopted and applied that definition and perspective by acknowledging the impact upon children of family violence within a household or between parents.

In respect of cases involving allegations of abuse or violence directly perpetrated on children under eighteen years, the Act and courts appear to be more proactive and interventionist. Some decisions reflect a cautious and protective approach; however, other decisions accord greater priority to ensuring contact (or even residence) between children and parents, notwithstanding serious and sometimes substantiated allegations, suggesting that decision-makers disbelieve or minimise the effect of child abuse on parent–child dynamics and relationships.

This seems to confuse the clear distinction drawn in the legislation since the major 1995 amendments between responsibilities, duties and obligations of parents on the one hand, and the rights of children on the other. Parents do not have 'rights' *per se*, but in some cases of child abuse the courts are replacing the legislatively enshrined right of children to have contact or spend time with both parents with the non-existent 'right' of an abusive parent to see a child without restrictions. This clearly flies in the face of the principles of paramountcy of the best interests of the child (new section 60CA replicating former section 65E)[5] as well as the rights of children to achieve their full potential (section 60B(1)) and not to be exposed to family violence (new section 60CG replicating former section 68K and see also section 68R). [6]

There has been a definition of child abuse in the *Family Law Act* since 1991. Section 60D(1) states:

abuse, in relation to a child means:

(a)   an assault, including a sexual assault, of the child which is an offence under a law, written or unwritten, in force in the State or Territory in which the act constituting the assault occurs; or

(b)   a person involving the child in a sexual activity with that person or another person in which the child is used, directly or indirectly, as a sexual object by the first-mentioned person or the other person, and where there is unequal power in the relationship between the child and the first-mentioned person.

This would appear to be a very restrictive definition, as it focuses on sexual assault that is illegal or a sexual activity that involves power imbalance It goes without saying that any form of child abuse involves power differences, and thus focusing on sexual impropriety ignores the many other forms of child abuse. The 2006 amendments did not change this definition. The legislators continue to take a very narrow view of child abuse at a federal level in contrast to state child welfare legislation. For example, section 63 of the *Children and Young Persons Act* 1989 (Vic.), which is replicated in most other states and territories regarding the protection of children and young persons (up to the age of seventeen or eighteen years), contains six grounds or contexts when a child is deemed to be in need of protection. Four of these grounds constitute child abuse: physical injury, sexual abuse, emotional or psychological harm, and environmental neglect. [7] This is a very broad definition, which encompasses all aspects of a child's emotional, physical and developmental well-being (see Chapters 4 and 5 for a discussion of different forms of child abuse).

Unfortunately, the *Family Law Act* does not legislatively mirror this all-encompassing understanding; however, case law certainly recognises the diversity of children's needs and the different commissions and omissions which may constitute child abuse. For example, there are reported cases where, even though allegations of abuse have not been raised, the child cannot separate from the distress or fear or anger or conflict felt by their resident (custodial) parent towards the absent parent. Here the court has had to recognise that such apprehension or anxiety experienced by the child may constitute a form of abuse requiring sensitivity and a long-term view (*Cooper v Cooper*, 1977; *Litchfield and Litchfield*, 1987). In other cases, the apprehension in the resident parent of spousal violence and/or child abuse by the other parent (most commonly the father), and the impact of that fear or anxiety on parenting capacity are relevant factors. In some decisions, the court has refused all contact. In other cases, the court has allowed supervised or limited contact (see *Russell and Close*, 1992; *Sedgley and Sedgley*, 1995; *Irvine and Irvine*, 1995; *Re Andrew*, 1996).

CHILD SEXUAL ABUSE

Unfortunately the magnetising force of the simple *allegation* of a heinous event such as child sexual abuse, which legitimately invokes consideration of the *possibility* of that event, draws the clinician—and perhaps even Judges and jurors as well ... away from what ought always to be the starting point of her or his evaluation enquiries, which is that the event did not (or very highly probably did not) occur. Because the null hypothesis (and, correlatively the absence of an event) cannot be proved, in their testimonies concerning *possibilities* of alleged events, clinicians strongly resist exonerating the targets of their evaluation. Because it is always *possible* that a given individual—even one randomly drawn from the general or a specific population—has sexually molested a child, an inconvertible *proof* that the individual has *not* molested a child is impossible. (Horner et al., 1992)

In the area of child abuse, child sexual abuse strikes the deepest chord in the community. It involves a power imbalance, the abuse of trust, exploitation, fear and assault, and it causes often irreparable physical and psychological harm. Child sexual abuse, the most common form of abuse presented to the Family Court, is clearly a gendered phenomenon: in the domestic context, the majority of perpetrators are adult male relatives and the majority of victims are girls. (A full discussion of sexual abuse is presented in Chapter 4.)

The most common allegations of child abuse in the Family Court or Federal Magistrates Court revolve around fathers, and to a lesser extent step-fathers and other male relatives, sexually abusing young children of both sexes. There is a growing repository of case law around child sexual abuse informed by a substantial base of social and psychological science research and literature paralleled by an equally substantial body of myths and unsourced 'common knowledge'.

Case law

For over a decade, the Family Court formulated an 'imposing array' of tests (High Court in *M and M*, 1988: 77,081) to determine whether or not to grant access to a parent accused of sexually abusing their child. These tests included an assessment as to whether the risk to the child was 'real or substantial','grave', 'likely or probable' or 'possible', or simply whether there was any risk at all. These attempts at constructing a definitive consistent approach reflected the Family Court's endeavours 'to achieve a balance between the risk of detriment to the child from sexual abuse and the possibility of benefit to the child from parental access' (*M and M*, 1988: 77,081).

As shown below, this remains a fine balance to this day, given the interplay between the provisions of the Act, judicial attitudes, community expectations, and research and myths about this sensitive area.

In *B and B* (1988) and *M and M* (1988), the Full Court of the High Court of Australia unanimously determined and formulated the test to be applied in considering whether or not to grant custody or access (now called 'living with' and 'spending time with') under the *Family Law Act* in cases involving allegations of child sexual abuse. Both cases were heard together, as they revolved around the same substantive issue. In *B and B*, the husband had an order for access every alternate weekend to his two children, then aged six and four. The wife sought a suspension of access on the ground that the husband had interfered with the older child during overnight access. Both sides relied on expert evidence. The Full Court of the Family Court (with Nicholson CJ dissenting) dismissed the husband's appeal and upheld the suspension of access. Similarly, in *M and M*, the husband had access to his then five-year-old daughter suspended after allegations of sexual abuse were aired by the wife and were supported by expert evidence. On appeal, the same Full Court by majority upheld the suspension of access and dismissed the husband's appeal.

In both matters, the High Court unanimously dismissed the husbands' appeals, finding that in both cases the trial judge had concluded that there existed an unacceptable risk that the child would be exposed to sexual abuse if the husband were awarded access. The authoritative test enunciated by the High Court is a three-pronged test—namely, to determine whether there is a risk of sexual abuse occurring if custody or access is granted, to assess the magnitude of that risk, and then to assess whether awarding custody or access would expose the child to an unacceptable risk of sexual abuse. In addition, the High Court states that, in considering an allegation of sexual abuse, the court should not make a positive finding that the allegation is true unless the court is so satisfied on the civil standard of proof on the balance of probabilities with due regard to the factors in the earlier High Court decision of *Briginshaw v Briginshaw* (1938).[8] Those factors include the seriousness of the allegation made and the gravity of consequences flowing from a particular finding.

Subsequent cases have reinforced that the standard of proof to make a positive finding of sexual abuse, as opposed to a finding of unacceptable risk, must be towards the highest, more rigorous and strictest end of the civil spectrum[9] (*K v B*, 1994; *N and S and the Separate Representative*, 1996; *WK and SR*, 1997; *Re W (Sex abuse: standard of proof)*, 2004).

The term 'unacceptable risk' is not defined in either the *Family Law Act* or the case law. The test has been applied to parenting orders such as where a child lives (residence), specific issues and who a child spends time with (contact) and, in respect of contact, whether contact should be supervised or not or be subject to certain conditions or restrictions. The test has also been broadened to apply to other forms of child abuse, not just child sexual abuse. For example, in *B and B* (1993), the Full Court of the Family Court recognised the broader impact of sexual abuse such that all access was denied:

> In our opinion, a trial Judge who has made a finding that an unacceptable risk of sexual abuse exists, or that sexual abuse did occur, should look to the level of trauma in the widest sense, that has been occasioned to the child or children or may be occasioned in the future, to determine whether supervised access is appropriate. If there is an unacceptable risk of the child or children being exposed to physical, emotional or psychological harm by reason of contact with the abusing parent, then an order for supervised access is not appropriate because of the Court's obligation to protect children from such harm. (1993: 79,780)

Notwithstanding this decision, generally speaking the Family Court (and Federal Magistrates Court) prefers to grant conditional or supervised or limited contact rather than no contact at all, even in cases where child abuse has actually been determined to have taken place. This is borne out in case law and in available research.

In the Family Court case of *Re W (Sex abuse: standard of proof)* (2004), the trial judge (who was then the Chief Justice) found that a father had sexually abused his daughter when she was four years old and accordingly made orders that the father have no contact with his two children, now aged six (daughter) and ten (son). On appeal, the Full Court overturned the trial judge's findings and orders, claiming the reasons for positive findings of abuse were unsound. The Full Court also questioned the trial judge's reliance upon expert evidence supporting the mother's allegations and child's disclosures, and disapproved of the trial judge's rejection of the father's denials:

> The termination of a worthwhile relationship between the parent and child ought in most cases to be the course of last resort. The Court should not shy away from reaching such a result in an appropriate case but at all times judges should be conscious that the adversarial or inquisitorial systems often reach results that are artificial. The truth does not always come out. (2004: 79,217)

The Full Court found that 'at its highest the evidence ought properly have left the Court with a lingering concern that something untoward might have happened' (2004: 79,226), and remitted the case back to a single judge to determine whether the father should be allowed supervised contact to his children.

Contact is viewed as an almost inalienable right of the child, and it appears that the court will bend over backwards—even in the face of genuine allegations or positive findings of child abuse—to ensure that some contact takes place. For example, in *S and S* (2001), the Federal Magistrate was not satisfied on the *Briginshaw* test that the five-year-old girl had been sexually abused by her father (as alleged by the mother following disclosures), but was left with 'very grave concerns' that such abuse had occurred. Nevertheless, even though finding the mother to be a credible witness and the disclosures to be genuine, His Honour rejected the mother's application for no contact and granted the father supervised, though limited, contact. This attitude certainly seems to be bordering the notion that some risk of child abuse may be viewed as 'acceptable', as arguably suggested in *Re W (Sex abuse: standard of proof)* (2004):

The truth does not always come out. A false negative finding accompanied by appropriate safeguards as to the future relationship between parent and child such as adequate supervision to guard against possible abuse, may be far less disastrous for the child than an erroneous positive finding that leads to the cessation of the parent–child relationship ...

The risk that the court will find heinous behaviour where none has occurred needs to be borne in mind at all times. The harm and injustice that flows to both parent and child from an erroneous positive is almost too horrible to contemplate. (2004: 79,217–18)

There may be an element of gender bias and double standards in these strongly worded statements when contrasted with the Full Court's earlier decision of *Re David* (1997). In that case, the Full Court upheld the orders made by the trial judge whereby the six-year-old child was to live with the father and have no contact with the mother (with whom he had lived for the past three years) because the mother had deliberately undermined the father's relationship with the child by making false allegations of child sexual abuse. In the previous cases, the father perpetrating the alleged or substantiated abuse was 'rewarded' with contact, albeit supervised or limited contact. In this case, the mother making false accusations was 'punished' by an order reversing a long *status quo* and granting no contact at all.

AUSTRALIAN RESEARCH

Studies measuring the impact of the *Family Law Reform Act* 1995's changes to the *Family Law Act* described earlier in this chapter confirm case law and anecdotal experience that 'no contact' orders are rare, especially at interim hearings, even in cases where there have been positive findings of family violence or child abuse, including child sexual abuse.

In respect of family violence, the 1995 reforms created:

something of a tension between the underlying principles set out in section 60B(2) (particularly the 'right to contact' principle), and the requirement in section 68K that the Court ensure that a parenting order does not expose a person to 'an unacceptable risk of family violence'. It appears that the *Reform Act*'s 'right to contact' principle has been given greater emphasis by most practitioners and judges than the domestic violence aspect of the reforms ... The research suggests that an interim order refusing contact has become more difficult to obtain since the *Reform Act* came into being, despite allegations of domestic violence, and this is attributable, at least in part, to the 'right to contact' principle. (Rhoades et al., 1999: xi; see also Dewar and Parker, 1999; and Kaye et al., 2003b)

Similarly, in respect of child abuse, time and resources and formal procedural requirements mean that allegations are not tested at an interim level, and 'decisions at interim hearings were generally likely to preserve contact if possible, and thus to work in favour of the non-resident parent' (Dewar and Parker, 1999). This is important because, given the high settlement rate, problems with legal aid, expense and delay in litigation and the role of alternative dispute resolution, most cases do not proceed beyond an interim stage, and interim orders more often than not become final orders:

> Yet the reality is that many matters reach a conclusion following such hearings, conclusions that may not have been arrived at a full trial. There must be a real possibility that arrangements are being sanctioned at the interim stage that would not withstand closer scrutiny. (Dewar and Parker, 1999: 78)

In those cases which proceed to final determination, the waiting period in some registries of the Family Court or Federal Magistrates Court can be up to eighteen months.This is disturbing,and means that the welfare of some children may be further jeopardised,and that these children and their caregivers may continue to be victimised and harmed until the allegations are fully explored.

The available research referred to in Chapter 1 highlights how little actual knowledge exists about child abuse in family courts generally, and in the Family Court of Australia in particular. In terms of child abuse, the 1998 study by Brown et al. shattered commonly held views and myths (see Chapter 1). Most significantly child abuse allegations made in the Family Court were found to be no more frequently false than in other circumstances; the abuse alleged in Family Court cases was of a more serious nature than that dealt with by state child protection services; and the child abuse alleged did not exist in isolation from other forms of abuse.

This last finding is important, as it highlights the need to recognise and forge links in research, service provision, legislation and judicial attitudes between family violence and child abuse. These findings and subsequent evaluation of the pilot project Magellan (see Brown et al., 2001 and Chapter 1) led to the establishment of the permanent Magellan list—a list of cases lodged in the Family Court, which manages and determines children's matters involving allegations of serious physical or sexual child abuse. This list is described in the next chapter and in Chapter 7.

CONCLUSION

The authors' view that no contact may be less harmful and more beneficial long term to a child's development than some form of contact with an abusive parent has not been popular with the courts since the 1995 amendments to the *Family Law Act* came into operation in June 1996. It will predictably be even less popular once the 2006 changes to parental responsibility detailed above are evaluated and case law starts evolving.

The newly amended legislation creates a conflict between a child having a right of contact with both parents following separation versus the right of a child not to be exposed to family violence or child abuse. However, the growing number of contact/spending time with orders (virtually at all costs), and the increasing injection of funds into nationwide contact centres (where supervised contact can take place) (see Chapter 7), together with a proliferation of men's lobby groups (see Chapter 7) and popular literature on the significance of fathering and fatherhood have all rendered the conflict one-sided. Judging by case law and the rationale behind the 2006 amendments, the side that favours exposure to and spending time with (contact) or even living with (residence) a husband/father, notwithstanding allegations or findings of spousal and/or child abuse, is gaining prominence.

This is reflected in some of the 2006 reforms to the *Family Law Act*. It is also reinforced by the allocation of $400 million in the federal budget in 2005 to the establishment of 65 new family relationship centres across Australia over the next three years and the establishment of a family dispute resolution telephone advice line.

Another change pursuant to the *Family Law Amendment (Parental Responsibility) Act* 2006 is a requirement that from 1 July 2007 parents must attend a centre and must be assessed for family dispute resolution services like counselling or mediation before filing court proceedings (section 60I). There are limited exceptions to this mandatory requirement of participating in such services—for example, cases where there has been family violence or child abuse, or where there is a risk of such violence—but only a court can grant such an exemption. A court must be satisfied on 'reasonable grounds' to believe that violence or abuse has occurred or may occur (section 60I(9)). No guidelines or tests are prescribed. As stated above, a court has the power to make cost orders against a parent or party who has falsely alleged violence or child abuse to avoid compulsory family dispute resolution (section 117AB).

These amendments present numerous problems for parties, children and legal practitioners. Parties may be under emotional and/or financial pressure not to disclose violence or abuse to avoid further delays and costs; judges have no criteria to follow in determining 'reasonable grounds'; family dispute resolution is now mandatory—thereby negating the benefits of voluntary and consensual alternative dispute resolution; and the new centres may overlook or dilute the effects and impact of family violence or child abuse, because of inadequate screening processes or given their vested interests to achieve settlements and maintain financial viability. In addition, this may expose victims, including children, to further risk and danger and serve to privatise family violence away from public consciousness and public resources.

The effects on community awareness, court processes, judicial attitudes, decision-making within and outside formal litigation, alternative dispute resolution practice and on the community at large, by the 2006 amendments, all remain uncharted territory. Ongoing research, evaluation and education are necessary to see whether the experience post-1995 amendments, particularly for children, is repeated or improved.

3

FAMILY LAW LEGISLATION AND THE PROTECTION OF CHILDREN

The ultimate and paramount issue to be decided in proceedings for custody of, or access to, a child is whether the making of the order sought is in the interests of the welfare of the child. The fact that the proceedings involve an allegation that the child has been sexually abused by the parent who seeks custody or access does not alter the paramount and ultimate issue which the court has to determine, though the court's finding on the disputed allegation of sexual abuse will naturally have an important, perhaps a decisive, impact on the resolution of that issue.

But it is a mistake to think that the Family Court is under the same duty to resolve in a definitive way the disputed allegation of sexual abuse as a court exercising criminal jurisdiction would be if it were trying the party for a criminal offence ... [the] court is not enforcing a parental right of custody or right to access. The court is concerned to make such an order for custody or access which will in the opinion of the court best promote and protect the interests of the child. (*M and M*, 1988: 77,080)

Family law legislation, despite not originally being designed to offer children protection from abuse, has effectively been asked to take on that role through its decision-making powers to make orders determining the residence and contact arrangements for children after marital breakdown. This chapter considers the somewhat disappointing impact of the legislation on the protection of children involved in family court disputes since the original family law legislation was enacted.

This chapter also considers the evolution of the concept of the 'best interests of the child'—which has long been used to determine parenting arrangements post-separation and divorce—and examines the degree of protection this has provided for children. It traces changes in this concept and shows when and how children's interests and wishes are taken into account by the court. It covers the amendments pursuant to the *Family Law Amendment* (*Shared Parental Responsibility*) *Act* 2006 that came into effect on 1 July 2006. It also covers the problem of the relationship between the federal Family Court and various state Children's Courts, now governed by protocols to overcome past poor coordination, and concludes with two new Family Court programs that offer more protection for children than has been the case previously.

BEST INTERESTS OF THE CHILD

The principle that children's issues should be decided according to 'the welfare of the child' was adopted by English and Australian courts well before it was formally enshrined in legislation. In Australia, this idea was first articulated at the federal level in the *Matrimonial Causes Act* 1959 (Cth), and then reiterated when the *Family Law Act* was passed in 1975. Since 1995, this has been reworded to become 'the best interests of the child'. Under the 2006 amendments, new section 60CA repeats former section 65E and states that the best interests of the child must be regarded as the paramount consideration in making parenting orders. Case law since the earlier 1995 amendments suggests that the court must treat the child's interests as prevailing and determinative, though not as the sole consideration, with other factors or considerations and other people's interests also regarded as relevant (*B and B: Family Law Reform Act 1995,* 1997; *AMS v AIF; AIF v AMS,* 1999).

As stated in Chapter 2, new section 60CC mandates the court to consider two primary and twelve additional considerations, including family violence and child abuse. It is anticipated that as was the case under the former section 68F(2) judicial discretion will determine the weight of each of these factors and, as the case law reflects, statutory guidelines are of little value (*House of Representatives, Standing Committee* 2003: 6). 'In the end, the choice (between competing parties) inevitably falls to the intuition, hunch and prejudice of the deciding judge' (Uviller, 1978: 125), or simply 'the judge's sense of right' comes to the fore (Chisholm, 2002: 114). That clearly applies to the issue of child abuse. In the end, it falls on the judge to determine whether a parenting order may place the child at any risk, and whether such a parenting order is in the best interests of the child.

The best interests of the child standard is fundamental to the treatment of child abuse in the Family Court and Federal Magistrates Court, but it continues to attract criticism from all sides. There is broad agreement that the standard is a 'vague platitude rather than a legal or scientific standard' (Charlow, 1987: 267) and is too subjective and sociologically based, enabling broad judicial discretion:

> It invites each parent to engage in a full-scale attack on the other parent's worth as a parent and as a human being, a process that leaves scars of humiliation and rage on both combatants ... An imprecise standard also means that judges are given wide latitude in deciding the best interests of a child in any particular case. This leaves courts vulnerable to accusations that gender bias and subjective value judgements influence their custody dispositions. (Warshak, 1996: 398)

Such broad judicial discretion inevitably involves consideration of gender stereotypes, myths versus facts and reliance on experts and behavioural sciences.

MYTHS

Coexisting with community (and judicial) disgust regarding child abuse, and consequently attraction to severe punitive and retributive measures against perpetrators, lies an attitude of disbelief about and trivialisation of child abuse.

Disbelief emanates from various sources. Obviously a dogged desire not to believe because of the gravity and inappropriateness of an allegation of child abuse is one source. Another reason is a failure to understand family dynamics—particularly for someone not exposed to such behaviour in their own family and experience. Third, from a court's point of view, there needs to be a strict adherence to rules of law and evidence. It is often difficult—if not impossible—to substantiate child abuse, especially sexual abuse, through corroboration of physical evidence or of witnesses. Often the children in question are very young, so their statements may be unreliable or capable of different interpretations. Even in civil courts, where the standard of proof is lower, many child abuse allegations are not investigated, even though they may be relevant to parenting orders.

Most commonly, myths are the source of disbelief or trivialisation of allegations of child abuse. Many of these myths have been dispelled through indisputable research, yet they have a strangleholdon much of the community—including the legal profession and judiciary. Gender stereotypes have a role here, and many of the commonly held views focus on and blame mothers. For example, mothers make up allegations to obtain advantages in family law proceedings; mothers coach their children to make up stories; a mother would know if abuse was taking place and so is to blame for allowing the abuse to continue; the mother is at fault if her partner sexually abuses a child because she has a poor or unsatisfactory sexual relationship with her partner. Other misconceptions are that children make up stories; children are more likely to be sexually abused by strangers ('stranger danger') or that sexual abuse is consensual and an appropriate manifestation of bonding and affection between a parent-figure and a child. Research shows that false allegations are rare, and these other commonly held views lack any foundation. (These issues, presented in Chapter 1 as central to consideration of child abuse in this context, are discussed further in Chapters 4 and 5.)

LET'S BLAME FREUD

It would be easy to attribute disbelief about or trivialisation of sexual abuse of children to myths and misconceptions, or to gender bias against women and their perceived 'failures' as mothers. It would also be easy to blame psychoanalysis and Freudians for many of the myths since Sigmund Freud abandoned his seduction theory and in its stead developed his theories of infantile sexuality and the Oedipus complex back in the 1920s (Malcolm, 1997). According to Freud, young children (especially boys) experience sexuality by having a subconscious sexual desire for the parents of the opposite sex and a wish to exclude or remove the parents of the same sex. This Oedipus complex represents the pivotal experience of childhood.

However, it is important to remember that, 'although Freud came to believe that many or most of childhood seductions by family members reported by his adult patients had never taken place and were merely "wishful fantasies"', even Freud recognised that seductions and rapes (and physical abuse) of children did sometimes take place (Freud, 1925, cited in Malcolm, 1997: 16–17, 77).

Although lawyers, judges and magistrates cannot identifiably be categorised as Freudian, neo-Freudian, post-Freudian or anti-Freudian—and certainly do not overtly subscribe to such theories or counter-theories—vestiges of Freudian analysis continue to inform the legal profession and judiciary through the various behavioural science professions, and through personal experiences and what judicial officers and legal practitioners alike call 'common knowledge'.

The social and behavioural science professions filtered into family law in the 1970s, impacting on the meaning of 'best interests' and, within that, the understanding of child abuse as a factor. Social and behavioural sciences, psychiatry and psychology, and therapeutic models of alternative dispute resolution such as mediation all play a part in determining 'the best interests of the child'.

Most notably, the adoption of the best interests standard was heavily influenced by Goldstein et al. (1979a, 1979b, 1986) and their much-publicised psychoanalytic theory of child development. These authors emphasise the need for children to maintain a relationship with a 'psychological' parent who meets their daily emotional and physical needs. They view the psychological and emotional relationship between a parent and child as more important than biological ties, and they express a preference in custody disputes in favour of the parent who was the primary caregiver during marriage or cohabitation—traditionally (and still) the mother. The authors then make their most controversial claim that it is the custodial parent, and not the courts, who should determine and control what contact—if any—the children should have with the other parent.

These views, along with a growing body of research and literature on the effects of separation on children, continue to inform the courts and legal profession, and sit side by side with the legislation and case law—often in direct contradiction. Certainly there are varying short-term and long-term effects of separation (as explored in Chapter 6). The effect of separation and divorce on children may be positive, negative or neutral, and is subject to many variables, many of which also exist in intact families. Research is limited in its usefulness due to methodological problems, ignoring external factors and the absence of consistent, objective measures (Kelly, 1991; Rodgers and Prior, 1998). Nevertheless, the influence and impact of data produced and claims proffered by social and behavioural scientists should not be under-estimated.

Goldstein et al. (1979b and 1986), for example, intimate that it is more harmful to expose a child to parental conflict and possible child abuse than to sever the child's contact with the non-custodial parent. In some cases (detailed in Chapter 2), the Family Court has conformed to that view. In other cases, however, the much-publicised views of American pioneering divorce researcher Judith Wallerstein predominate, reinforcing the desirability and centrality of a child having a continuing relationship with both parents during the post-separation years (Wallerstein and Blakeslee, 1989; Wallerstein and Kelly, 1996; Wallerstein et al., 2000). In these cases, the court has emphasised that contact between a parent and child is sacred, and to be protected and promoted virtually at all costs to avoid psychological scarring and to promote the overall welfare of the child.

The position in Australian family law is that there are no legal or statutory presumptions, and the best interests standard is applied on a case-by-case basis. However, determining best interests including protection from child abuse is a subjective, variable, imprecise, value-laden judgement. There is no provision in the *Family Law Act* that allows the court to rely upon research from the sociological and psychological sciences, and judges and federal magistrates vary enormously in their reliance upon, or even taking judicial notice of, research material and publications referred to by parties or their advocates during proceedings or within their own private knowledge and understanding (Mullane, 1998). There is also enormous variability and imprecision as to the findings and recommendations of experts and the reliance by judges upon such expertise in determining children's cases (Horner et al., 1992). There is no professional framework set out to guide lawyers and judges in determining such potentially life-changing matters.

WISHES OF THE CHILD AND SEPARATE REPRESENTATION OF CHILDREN

One of the factors listed in new section 60CC which the court must consider to determine what is in the best interests of a child is:

(3)   (a) any views expressed by the child and any factors (such as the child's maturity or level of understanding) that the court thinks are relevant to the weight it should give to the child's views.

This replicates former section 68F(2)(a) except that the word 'views' has replaced the former reference to 'wishes'. The wishes or views of a child have always been a factor to be considered by the court since the *Family Law Act* came into operation in January 1976. This was well before Australia ratified the *United Nations Convention on the Rights of the Child* (UNCR OC) in December 1990[1] and, within that Convention, Article 12 which reads:

1. States Parties shall assure to the child who is capable of forming his or her own views the right to express those views freely in all matters affecting the child, the views of the child being given due weight in accordance with the age and maturity of the child.

2. For this purpose, the child shall in particular be provided the opportunity to be heard in any judicial or administrative proceedings affecting the child, either directly, or through a representative or an appropriate body, in a manner consistent with the procedural rules of national law.

Prior to the 1983 amendments, the court was bound to follow the wishes of a child aged fourteen years or over. Now there is no age prescribed, and the court can inform itself of a child's wishes or views in various ways, although it is clear in section 60CE (formerly section 68H) that neither the court nor any person can require a child to express his or her views in relation to any matter.

The court may inform itself of wishes expressed by a child through a family or welfare report prepared by a family and child counsellor under section 62G (section 60CD(2)(a)), through the appointment of a separate legal representative for the child under section 68L (section 60CD(2)(b)) or by any other means the court thinks appropriate (section 60CD(2)(c)), such as through an expert report by a psychologist or psychiatrist or even by a judge interviewing a child confidentially in chambers (Rule 15.02, *Family Law Rules*). This last way is done rarely and has been frowned upon.

Parents and other parties to children's proceedings can give evidence of children's wishes. New section 69ZV replicates and expands former section 100A. It provides that evidence of a representation made by a child that is relevant to the welfare of the child may be admissible, notwithstanding the rule against hearsay, and subsection (5) defines 'representation' to include an express or implied representation, whether oral or in writing, and a representation inferred from conduct. In rare cases, where a child is of mature teenage years though still under eighteen years, leave may be granted by a court for that child to give sworn oral or affidavit evidence in person (section 100B).

The weight accorded to a child's wishes or views, if expressed, depends upon the child's age, maturity, intelligence and level of understanding:

> In the ultimate … whilst the wishes of children are important and should be given real and not token weight the court is still required to determine the matter in the child's best interests and that may in some circumstances involve the rejection of the wishes of the child …
>
> As a matter of practical day-to-day experience, the problem in this area usually relates to the ascertainment of the wishes of the child and their interpretation and assessment in the face of conflicting evidence. Against that background the court will attach varying degrees of weight to a child's stated wishes depending upon, amongst other factors, the strength and duration of their wishes, their basis, and the maturity of the child including the degree of appreciation by the child of the factors involved in the issue before the court and their longer term implications. (H and W, 1995: 81,947–48, per Fogarty and Kay JJ; approved in R and R: Children's Wishes, 2000)

The appointment of an independent children's lawyer (formerly called a 'child representative') is the most common method through which a court can be informed of a child's views or wishes and be addressed on the issue of the child's best interests. New schedule 5 of the 2006 amendments expands section 68L and incorporates much of the case law into legislation. New sections 68L and 68LA and case law on the role of the child representative make it clear that the separate representative is a party to the adversarial proceedings with the powers of a litigant, such as the right to commission expert reports, call witnesses, cross-examine, subpoena, make submissions, seek costs and lodge an appeal. The independent children's lawyer also has the right to seek whatever orders are deemed appropriate in a particular case. Unlike child representatives in state welfare proceedings, a *Family Law Act* independent children's lawyer is not bound by a child's instructions. The role is not only to convey the child's views and wishes and instructions to a court, but also to make submissions, provide evidence and present a view to help the presiding judicial officer reach a determination in children's matters (section 68LA outlines the role of an independent children's lawyer).

Historically, a child representative was usually only appointed in cases involving allegations of child abuse. The Full Court in *Re K* (1994), however, set out thirteen circumstances in which a child ought to be represented, and that list is used by the Family Court and Federal Magistrates Court in a *pro forma* one-or-more tick-a-box format when appointing an independent child representative. Allegations of physical, sexual or psychological abuse of a child are one of those circumstances. Others include an 'apparently intractable conflict' between the parents; where the child is allegedly alienated from one or both parents; where significant illness or personality disorder is involved; where there are cultural or religious differences affecting the child; proposed relocation or splitting of siblings; where none of the parties is legally represented; and where 'the child is of mature years and is expressing strong views, which if given effect to will involve the changing of a long-standing custodial arrangement or a complete denial of contact with one parent'. Overall, when there are significant issues affecting the welfare of a child, the court will appoint an independent children's lawyer under section 68L to facilitate independent and theoretically objective representation of the child's wishes or views (where expressed) and best interests.

Separate child representation is certainly in accord with UNCR OC and the philosophy of the *Family Law Act*, but there are problems. First, there is the issue of training and accreditation. Legal aid bodies in each state and territory keep a list of solicitors approved to act as child representatives, but with only limited requirements as to years of practice and ongoing professional education. Second, child representation is generally funded by legal aid bodies out of their family law budgets and so can cause a strain on already precious legal aid funds.[2] Third, there are various practices and models amongst lawyers acting as separate representatives (e.g. whether or not to interview a child), and such personalised approaches and biases may not necessarily protect and promote a child's best interests.

Fourth, there remains debate as to whether children themselves should be able to appear in proceedings, to be called as witnesses by their own separate representatives and able to test the evidence of other participants in the case. Finally, although there is a procedure in the Act and guidelines for the appointment and role of an independent children's lawyer, there is no process to monitor the separate representative in a particular case, no guidelines as to accountability (other than financial) and no procedure stipulated for the removal of such a child representative.[3]

HOW THE FAMILY COURT DEALS WITH CHILD ABUSE CASES

Pre-court and trial processes in state and territory courts in child protection cases are regularly reviewed in various reports and inquiries, and often attract rigorous media attention—usually negative in nature. Child abuse in state and territory courts is a serious business, justifiably attracting constant scrutiny—though some would argue little action in terms of change in policy and procedure or allocation of realistic funds and resources. Child abuse in federal courts, however, rarely scores a mention,[4] highlighting the inappropriateness and unworkability of parallel state and federal schemes and systems in each state and territory, different courts and legislation, and an array of seemingly uncoordinated court-allied and community support networks dealing with children and their futures.

Pending the establishment of one court (and one system) with exclusive jurisdiction over civil matters related to the welfare and best interests of children, the federal system has taken some steps towards grappling with child abuse cases.

PROTOCOLS AND LEGISLATION AFFECTING STATE AND TERRITORY AGENCIES

All states and territories have developed a protocol between prescribed child protection agencies and the Family Court (and Federal Magistrates Court) in cases involving allegations of child abuse.[5] In addition, the *Family Law Act*, including 2006 amendments (new section 69ZW) prescribes relevant procedures facilitating these protocols. Together, these provide a channel of communication and exchange of information between agencies so that the federal court is fully informed and aware of investigations and outcomes conducted by the state or territory department or agency which has state responsibility for child protection. In practice, this means that any proceedings involving children in the Family Court or Federal Magistrates Court will be suspended whilst the department makes its investigations. The department is alerted either by the court itself—through court personnel, including counsellors and registrars (see section 10D (confidentiality in family counselling), section 60D (definition) and section 67ZA) and judges (section 91B), following a set procedure—or by the independent children's lawyer, or by any party with an interest in the particular proceedings alleging abuse or risk of abuse filing a Notice of Child Abuse or Family Violence in a prescribed form (section 67Z, Rule 2.04, *Family Law Rules* 2004 and expanded prescribed form 4).

Whether the department investigates and advises the Family Court that no action will be taken or whether the department intervenes and acts as a party to the proceedings under section 91B, the court can then continue to hear and determine the proceedings. It can authorise the department file to be produced (section 69ZW), so that evidence relating to child abuse or family violence can be provided to the court. This file can then be accessed (with certain parts such as names of notifiers generally excluded) by the independent children's lawyer, parties and/or their lawyers and any counsellor or other expert preparing a report. If the department advises the Family Court that proceedings will be initiated in the Family Division of the Children's Court, then the jurisdiction of the federal court is ousted under section 69ZK of the *Family Law Act*. That section prescribes that:

> a court having jurisdiction under this Act must not make an order under this Act (other than an order under Division 7) in relation to a child who is under the care (however described) of a person under a child welfare law unless:
>
> (a)   the order is expressed to come into effect when the child ceases to be under that care; or
>
> (b)   the order is made in proceedings relating to the child in respect of the institution or continuation of which the written consent of a child welfare officer or the relevant State or Territory has been obtained.

Courts exercising jurisdiction under the *Family Law Act* cannot affect the operation of a child welfare law in relation to a child (section 69ZK(2)), and most commonly the state or territory court exercises exclusive jurisdiction as to the welfare of the child and related issues such as residence or placement, contact and supervision by the welfare authority.

Alternatively, the child welfare authority can approve the federal court continuing to hear and determine a children's matter, and can choose to intervene in those proceedings where it is alleged that a child has been abused or is at risk of being abused; the authority thus becomes a party to those proceedings (section 92A *Family Law Act*), with all the rights, duties and liabilities this entails.

THE MAGELLAN LIST

One of the main problems in litigation under the *Family Law Act* is the delay in having matters determined. As stated in Chapter 2, only 5 per cent of cases proceed through to final hearing and judicial determination. That can involve a waiting period of twelve to eighteen months in most registries of the Family Court and Federal Magistrates Court. However, many cases require interim hearings, and delays in those lists also mean lengthy waiting periods of several months. In cases involving allegations of child abuse, this is clearly undesirable as such matters need speedy and sensitive determination. There are more cases involving child sexual abuse in the Family Court than in state courts dealing with child protection. Cases involving child abuse allegations comprise 50 per cent of the Family Court's workload in contested children's matters, despite the low incidence of such cases, and consume court and community resources. Research dispels the common belief that parties to family law disputes raise spurious or false allegations of abuse for tactical reasons. In fact, a low number (less than 10 per cent) of allegations of child abuse are false (see Chapter 1; Brown et al., 1998, 2001).

Studies in Australia in the late 1990s showed that:

> the court had difficulties in dealing with the cases, largely due to the problematic nature of the interface between the child protection system and the family law system. Once again, parents rather than children were the focus of the legal process even though the care of the children was the central issue. Outcomes for the children were poor; they included long delays, many hearings, frequent changes of residency and many children experiencing high levels of distress. (Brown et al., 2001: 5)

Children were suffering and remained exposed to child abuse, and were then re-victimised through systems abuse by the adversarial court system and its inherent problems.

This has partly been addressed in the Family Court through the establishment of the Magellan program.[6] Specific case management processes have been introduced to more efficiently and effectively manage the most resource-intensive children's cases involving serious allegations of direct physical and/or sexual child abuse. Cases involving domestic violence between parents but not directed at children are not included. A panel of senior court staff, including designated judges, manages such matters. Once a matter is placed on the Magellan list, that case is fast-tracked and usually finalised within six months if judges are available for hearings.[7]

This has proved to be an effective and time-reducing program and is now operating to some extent in all states. Western Australia has introduced a similar case management strategy called the Columbus program. Chapter 7 further details the history of the Magellan and Columbus programs and evaluations confirming their effectiveness.

CHILDREN'S CASES PROGRAM

This program originally operated as a pilot project in the Parramatta and Sydney registries of the Family Court from March 2004 where the Magellan program did not operate and in the Melbourne Reg istry from October 2005 where Magellan did. It is compulsory for all registries from 1 July 2006 (Practice Direction No. 3 of 2005 for all registries except Victoria and Practice Direction No. 2 for Victoria where the Children's Cases program incorporates a Child Responsive Dispute Resolution Model).

The program applies to all new children's cases promoting the principle in Rule 5.03(1) of the *Family Law Rules* 2004 that, subject to exceptions, 'before filing, a party must make a reasonable and genuine attempt to settle the issue to which the application relates'. It only applies to Family Court and not to Federal Magistrates Court matters. Magellan list cases, Hague Convention applications (abductions into or out of Australia) and applications for contempt or contravention are excluded.

Entry into the Children's Cases Program was optional at the start and has been mandatory since 1 July 2006. Each party completes a 'client questionnaire' which then forms part of the evidence before the judge. New Division 12A of the *Family Law Act* (introduced 1 July 2006) prescribes the principles for conducting child-related proceedings including Children's Cases program cases. Strict rules of evidence do not apply, and the process is far less adversarial. The matter is handled by the same judge at all times, and the hearing commences from the first intake or appearance when the judge speaks to the clients directly—a process akin to an inquisitorial process. Lawyers assist in defining the issues, but clients can be unrepresented. The judge may use any dispute resolution tools, including mediation, a formal hearing, ordering a family report or the appointment of an independent children's lawyer. Children are heard through an expert or a family report, and the judge may interview the child.

Evaluation of the program in Sydney and Parramatta over a twelve-month period shows completion of children's matters within three months. Over a third (38 per cent) involve evidence or allegations of domestic violence or child abuse: 40 per cent of matters settled fully or in part; and 18 per cent of matters involved allegations or evidence of family violence or child abuse and still required determination by a judge.

The program involves an inquisitorial process, but with fewer court resources; it is more child inclusive, cheaper and faster, and more flexible. It is too soon to tell whether cases involving family violence or child abuse are better suited to this model or to the formal adversarial litigation process and judicial determination. Outcomes for victims, especially children, need to be critically evaluated and analysed.

CONCLUSION

In its bipartisan report *Every Picture Tells a Story*, published in December 2003 the House of Representatives Standing Committee on Family and Community Affairs reported the results of a random sample of Family Court children's cases judicially determined over six months in the court's three largest registries—Sydney, Melbourne and Brisbane The sample provided by the court itself provided an indication of the high or moderate importance of the then existing section 68F(2) criteria used in parenting orders to determine the best interests of a child. In 38.5 per cent of cases, the protection of a child from harm (former section 68F(2)(g)) was considered to be of high or moderate importance in judicially deter-mined cases. Time will tell if the 2006 amendments to the *Family Law Act* provisions and procedures will alter this focus of the courts.

Clearly, the definition of the best interests of a child is always evolving and changing. However, protection of a child from abuse of whatever form is a constant. We have coexisting state and federal systems informed and controlled by different governments, bureaucracies, social policies, legisla-tive requirements, and court structures and jurisdictions. Children being abused or at risk of abuse are falling into the gaps of these schemes which have only minimal conduits for exchange of information and operate under diverse laws and methods for protecting children. Notwithstanding recent changes, the federal system, via the *Family Law Act*, is dysfunctional and ill-equipped to deal with child protection and family violence cases offering *ad hoc* token and Band-aid type strategies without clear discipline direction or coordination.

One solution recommended by the Family Law Council in 2002 was to adopt a 'one court principle' (Family Law Council, 2002: 86–92) so that, in child protection matters, a decision is taken as early as possible whether a matter should proceed under the *Family Law Act* or under child welfare law. Only one court should deal with the matter. This would avoid duplication of resources, reduce court processes and legal costs, and limit the exposure of vulnerable children and families to unnecessary investigations and assessments.

The recommendation, however, falls short of the idea of one dedicated specialist court exercising child welfare and *Family Law Act* jurisdiction, and determining child protection matters alongside making parenting orders. Without such a unified approach and national protection system, child exploitation and child abuse will continue to occur largely unchecked.

4

CHILD SEXUAL ABUSE

Intra-familial child sexual abuse—that is, when the perpetrator of the abuse is a parent, step-parent, uncle, aunt, grandparent, step-grandparent, sibling or step-sibling of the victim—presents more frequently within the context of parental separation and divorce than in other contexts.

Any child sexual abuse is an emotional subject to deal with, even for professionals. It inspires individual and community revulsion as well as denial of the problem (see Chapter 3). The feelings aroused in professionals are rarely admitted, making it even harder for them to manage families when this problem occurs. The presentation of child sexual abuse within the highly charged emotions of parental separation and divorce compounds the difficulties. The atmosphere of suspicion surrounding any allegations of abuse in this context of parental separation, divorce and family law proceedings is intensified if the allegations are about sexual abuse. It is therefore vital for professionals within the family law service system to gain a full understanding of child sexual abuse as a basis for its management—especially since the behaviour of victims and their families can seem irrational when in fact it is understandable and common in such circumstances.

This chapter will present our current understanding of intra-familial child sexual abuse in the context of parental separation, divorce and family law proceedings. It will examine what it is and how it occurs, and look at its links—to the extent that they exist—with other forms of abuse. We will present the special problems attached to this form of abuse for professionals in the family law services: problems of detection including the place of the grooming of victims and the victims' desire for secrecy and denial; and problems of devising strategies to ensure the safety of children in these circumstances.

COMMUNITY ATTITUDES TO CHILD SEXUAL ABUSE

It is important to understand that the few brief glimpses history allows us of children in the past suggests we have always held an ambivalent attitude towards child sexual abuse. Sometimes sexual abuse has been tolerated and sometimes it has not; at times, certain types of child sexual abuse have been acceptable whereas others have not (Gillham, 1994; Corby, 2000). Nevertheless, the sexual abuse of children by adults has been regarded as morally wrong and as a crime in the United Kingdom and in Europe for many hundreds of years. In England, from which Australia derives its broad socio-legal system, the rape of female children was known to be outlawed before the Norman conquest (Myers et al., 2002).

Protection for children from sexual abuse by family members began somewhat later. Incest—meaning sexual relations between a child and a family member within specific categories of kinship, such as parents and grandparents, aunts and uncles—was forbidden in England through canon law from the Middle Ages, and was prosecuted through the ecclesiastical courts. It was not introduced into English criminal law until 1857 although it had been introduced in Scottish criminal law much earlier, in 1567 (La Fontaine, 1990). Unfortunately, we know little of the prosecutions that resulted in these earlier times, so we do not know the extent of the community's vigilance or of its punishment of offenders.

A new strand of protection for children from sexual abuse within the family emerged towards the end of the nineteenth century in the child rescue movement, comprising the many local child rescue societies that were established in various cities of the United States, England, Europe, Australia and New Zealand (Brown, 1982). These societies sought to protect children from all forms of abuse within the family, and case workers visiting the families clearly regarded the sexual abuse of children as reprehensible (Brown, 1982; Myers et al., 2002). However, the families were poor and the abuse, when detected, was interpreted as a function of the threatening social conditions suffered by the working classes of that era.

The child rescue services of the nineteenth century are extremely significant because they formed the basis of today's child protection services internationally They became the basis of both the non-government services and those provided directly by government. In Australia, this strand of protection culminated in child welfare legislation and the establishment of a range of services provided by each state prior to Federation in 1901. Today, state child welfare legislation, with its associated state government services and children's courts, together with the government-subsidised non-government child protection services, provides the most significant protection for children against sexual abuse within the family.

Being state- and territory-based, the pattern of provision varies. In each state, the governmental and non-governmental child protection services are controlled by different legislation, introduced at different times and expressing different policies and approaches. If there is any national characteristic shared by the Australian child protection services, it is the state-to-state differences that are exacerbated by the fragmentation of services between the non-government and government sectors.

THE DISCOVERY/REDISCOVERY CYCLE IN CHILD SEXUAL ABUSE

Despite the growth of the child protection services internationally during the twentieth century, child sexual abuse received little attention during most of this period. Physical abuse and neglect among poor families commanded the attention of the growing services (Brown, 1982). Some contend that recognition of child sexual abuse during the twentieth century was prevented by a strong community denial, stemming from an unspoken conspiracy that included professionals who possessed case-based evidence to the contrary (Cox et al., 2000). This argument proposes that the denial of child sexual abuse by professionals began with Freud and continues to the present day (Schultz, 1982).

However, the denial of child sexual abuse was challenged by an outpouring of professional literature on child sexual abuse around 1975, which came to be known as the year of the 'continental divide of child sexual abuse' (Myers et al., 2002). The literature flowed from the feminist movement of the early 1960s and continued in successive waves. The feminists' focus on the experiences of individual women, coupled with their challenges to the patriarchal nature of the social system, drew attention to child sexual abuse at a very personal level (Kelly, 2000). Their writings challenged the denial of child sexual abuse in episodes of discovery and rediscovery that have continued to the present day. Many feminists believe that community denial of child sexual abuse is so strong it will never disappear, and the discovery/avoidance/rediscovery cycle will continue indefinitely (Kelly, 2000).

The feminists also drew on the medical research and campaigns of Dr Henry Kempe (Kempe et al., 1962). His campaigns, supported by medical practitioners internationally like the Birrell brothers in Victoria, focused the attention of a wide range of professionals on child abuse of all kinds, including child sexual abuse. So professional expertise combined with the outrage of the feminists led to further writing from medical, legal, social work and psychology professionals—some of whom espoused feminist beliefs. They presented a new view of child sexual abuse, seeing it as a problem also of mainstream families, not just of those who were marginalised (La Fontaine, 1990).

REPORTED INCIDENCE OF CHILD SEXUAL ABUSE

Following the year of the continental divide, the incidence of child sexual abuse reported to the child protection services internationally rose rapidly, driven to an extent by the recognition for the problem won by professionals among their colleagues internationally The professionals defined the problem, formulated its causes and advocated ways of dealing with it. Now professionals knew of the problem, they reported its occurrence.

The first country to experience this rise was the United States, where reported incidence of child sexual abuse rose very quickly from 1975, sometimes doubling from one year to another (Finkelhor, 1986). At the beginning of the twenty-first century, this growth rate slowed, and some believe it has peaked and is now in decline (Finklehor and Jones, 2001; Conte and Berliner, 2002). A similar trend occurred in the United Kingdom, with a sharp rise beginning around 1983 followed by a slight decline (La Fontaine, 1990; Gillham, 1994).

The same rise in reported incidence took place in Australia, but since national reported incidence figures have been presented only from 1991— when the Commonwealth body, the Australian Institute of Health and Social Welfare, began collecting and presenting national data—the rise is for a shorter period of time. The introduction of mandatory reporting of child abuse by professional groups was introduced in most states during this period, and may have inflated reported incidence. It may also account for the fact that Australia has not yet experienced any decline (AIHW, 2004: 5). However, while the reported incidence of notifications has not peaked, the incidence of substantiated notifications has, as from 2004. The continuing rise in notifications can be explained by changes in policies on notification criteria that have allowed a greater number of less serious cases to be included whereas once they were not.

Whether or not changes in policy have led to continual rises in notifications, it is clear that each state and territory reports remarkably different rates of sexual abuse. The variation is so great that it cannot be correct. For example, Victoria, Queensland and the Australian Capital Territory report rates that are one-third the rate of child sexual abuse that Western Australia and New South Wales—the two highest reporting states—report to the AIHW (AIHW, 2002). Such problems make it clear that Australia still has insufficient knowledge about the real prevalence of child sexual abuse.

We know little about the trends in the reported incidence of child sexual abuse in the context of parental separation and divorce. We do know that the first clues to a rise in reported incidence emerged in the United States in the 1980s and 1990s when family law professionals drew attention to the increased incidence of allegations of child sexual abuse in residence and contact disputes (Gardner, 1986; Schudson, 1992; Toth, 1992). Those reporting the increase in allegations did not understand why this had occurred, and did not consider that it was probably a product of the increasing divorce rate, the growing professional recognition of child sexual abuse and the relationship between the two. We know that parents and professionals are now more likely to recognise intra-familial child sexual abuse when it occurs, and that mothers—more frequently the innocent parent—are more prepared to leave their partner in these circumstances. Today, discovery of intra-familial child sexual abuse more often leads to parental separation, divorce and family law proceedings.

Information from the United States, combined with that from Australia, suggests that the rise in reported incidence of child sexual abuse in this context has continued since the 1980s, but at a slower pace in more recent times. The rise in incidence may continue in this context but not in others if the rise in incidence of domestic violence as a cause of marital breakdown continues, because of the link between domestic violence and child sexual abuse. Furthermore, if Wilson (2002) is correct in her view that children are at a heightened risk of child sexual abuse post-divorce, the rise in incidence is likely to continue.

We do know that intra-familial child sexual abuse remains atypically high in the context of residence and contact disputes in family law proceedings, compared with the variety of contexts reflected in notifications to all child protection authorities. In the first study of abuse allegations in residence and contact disputes in Australia (Brown et al., 1998), some 37 per cent of the cases involved alleged sexual abuse: some 12 per cent involved sexual abuse alone, while 25 per cent involved sexual abuse plus other forms of abuse— most commonly physical abuse (Brown et al., 1998). Only 26 per cent of these cases had been reported to the state child protection authorities. In the second study, where the cases were selected by the court to enter a special program because of allegations of serious physical and/or sexual abuse, the proportion of cases with sexual abuse allegations was higher again. Some 51 per cent of cases involved sexual abuse allegations alone, with 31 per cent involving sexual abuse alone and 29 per cent involving sexual plus other forms of abuse—again, mostly physical abuse. Only 36 per cent of these cases had been reported to the state child protection service (Brown et al., 2001). By way of contrast, the incidence of substantiated child sexual abuse reported to the child protection authorities in the same period was 15 per cent in Victoria and 12 per cent in Queensland (AIHW, 2004).

ACTUAL PREVALENCE OF CHILD SEXUAL ABUSE

The actual prevalence of child sexual abuse has been shown to be greater than the incidence of abuse that is reported, although the prevalence rates vary considerably from study to study. Almost twenty years ago, Finkelhor et al. (1986) attempted to pinpoint the actual prevalence by reviewing all studies of large populations that sought to determine actual prevalence.

Finkelhor's review showed marked differences in research design from one study to another that had resulted in different reports of actual prevalence. The design differences included definitional differences (whether contact or non-contact sexual experiences or both were included), differences in collecting data (whether sensitive, expert, face-to-face inter-viewing was used, whether multiple screening questions were used and whether the population studies were representative of the community), and differences in the gender of the respondents (whether women or men or both were studied). The most scrupulous of the studies he covered—unfortunately carried out only with women—showed 54 per cent had experienced some sexual abuse before the age of eighteen with some 16 per cent having experienced incest (Russell, 1984). A later study covering both men and women (but with poorer interviewing techniques than used in the Russell study) showed 27 per cent of women and 16 per cent of men had experienced sexual abuse as children (Finkelhor et al., 1990). The most recent large study, a UK study of males and females, found that 19 per cent of all adults had experienced sexual abuse as children, with a further 5 per cent being involved in what was termed borderline sexual activities; some 4 per cent were abused by family members, and females were by far the most frequent victim of the abuse (Cawson et al., 2001).

CHILDREN'S REPORTING OF SEXUAL ABUSE

A cause of the difference between actual prevalence and reported incidence lies in the fact that children do not tell adults of the abuse when it happens. Even if they do tell eventually, they may later deny what they have said. Some children do not ever concede it has happened, although the evidence to support it excludes all other possibilities. Both parents and professionals find the children's denial—either consistently or episodically—very hard to understand.

The proportion of children who tell anyone about their sexual abuse at all is small. Primarily due to fear, few say anything to anyone immediately and most say nothing in the longer term (Cawson et al., 2001; Lyon, 2002). When children are abused sexually, the abuse is usually carried out in secret, and the perpetrator binds the child to maintaining the silence (Corwin, 2002). The child's commitment to maintaining the silence can be very strong. Lyon used a number of existing studies to show that some 25 per cent to 57 per cent of children with a diagnosis of a sexually transmitted disease (strong evidence for the existence of sexual abuse, according to medical experts such as Oates, 1996) denied their abuse when questioned by multi-disciplinary medical teams (Lyon, 2002). Some children who concede the abuse then go on to 'forget' it, either intermittently or for very long periods of time (Cox et al., 2001). This group is small in number, and these children are not those described as having retrieved 'recovered memories' through the intervention of a therapist.

DEFINITION OF SEXUAL ABUSE

Child sexual abuse is often defined very loosely—for example, even professionals use the term 'child abuse' interchangeably with the term 'child sexual abuse' and vice versa. However, there are precise definitions of child sexual abuse established both in legislation and by the services administering the legislation. It is important to know what is defined as child sexual abuse and what is not. The differences arise from different views about the age at which childhood ends, whether non-contact sexual experience should be included, and what the age difference between a child and the perpetrator should be to constitute abuse. Furthermore, community denial about child sexual abuse encourages the exclusion from any definition of all except the most obvious and undeniable sexual abuse.

An example of one definition is the one used by the child protection staff in the Western Australia Department of Community Services. It is typical of many of the definitions currently used by child protection services. It defines sexual abuse as occurring when:

An adult or someone who is bigger or older involves a child in sexual activity by using their powers over the child or taking advantage of the child's trust. Often children are bribed or threatened physically or psychologically to make them participate in the activity. (DCD, 2006)

The information from the department goes on to mention using a child for prostitution or pornography, and exposing children to the sexual activity of others. It does not include the specifics of what activity is considered child sexual abuse, as do other definitions like that of the Department of Human Services, Victoria. That service says sexual activity can include 'fondling of the child's genitals, masturbation, oral sex, vaginal or anal by a penis, finger or other object' (DHS, Vic., 2006).

The definitions highlight the perpetrator's use of their power in developing the relationship and they remove any suggestion that the activity is morally acceptable even when supposedly sought or desired by the child. A child is too young to be able to give consent. The definitions focus on contact sexual abuse rather than on non-contact abuse, and do not cover the full range of non-contact abuse, such as spying on children without their knowledge while they are in the bathroom and bedroom; nor do they cover that form of non-contact abuse referred to as grooming.

Grooming (Corby, 2000) is the process by which perpetrators prepare children for sexual abuse by breaking down their inhibitions through strategies like talking of sexual activity, acting out sexual activity without actually doing it, and playing covert and overt sexual games. Such behaviour is a common prelude to sexual abuse. However, those who are inexperienced in the area may not recognise it as such. Understanding about such behaviour has developed from research on perpetrators who have described what they do to engage the child in order to build up a secret sexual relationship without using physical force. Oprah Winfrey's campaign against child sexual abuse has produced considerable material about grooming—what it is and what parents and professionals should watch for (van Dam, 2001; Winfrey, n.d).

In one of the cases in the first Family Court study (Brown et al., 1998), a father took photographs of his young daughter while she was naked. This may seem harmless—indeed, it certainly can be so. Yet this father took photographs of his naked nine-year-old daughter with a wedding veil draped behind her as background on an isolated beach in the company of three adult men and no one else while telling his daughter they were playing 'the secret wedding game'. This game is not harmless; nor is the father's behaviour merely 'inappropriate'. It is a way of the father breaking down the child's inhibitions regarding sexual activities with the father and other male adults, through playing games with sexual overtones with the child and the male adults in the presence of the supposedly trustworthy and protective father. It binds the child to secrecy in an apparently harmless game that is actually grooming activity carried out by the father and the other adult males as preparation for sexual abuse. Of interest is the fact that the Interpol website which devotes considerable attention to grooming uses the example of parental separation to show how opportunities for grooming occur and how it proceeds to actual abuse (Interpol, n.d).

EVIDENCE OF ABUSE

A complication of child sexual abuse is the difficulty in gaining evidence that it has actually occurred. Unlike physical abuse, sexual abuse often leaves no clear evidence of its occurrence. As Jenny (1996) points out: 'A high proportion of children with well-documented [sexual] abuse will have normal physical examinations'. The activity is carried out in secret, usually with only the perpetrator(s) and the victim present. While paediatricians have tried to build conclusive tests, none has yet emerged, as the famous fiasco in Cleveland, England, showed. In the aftermath of Cleveland, where over-zealous doctors and social workers removed over one hundred children allegedly abused sexually by parents, although no one had made a formal allegation, the chairperson of the inquiry, Lord Justice Butler-Sloss, pointed out that a medical test of unknown reliability was relied on excessively, and that the professionals should have given more credence to the voice of the children (Butler-Sloss, 1988). Strong physical evidence, such as a sexually transmitted disease or internal injuries in a young child, or other evidence of the events like videos, photos and descriptions from perpetrators' diaries, is not common.

Thus the determination of child sexual abuse, and all other forms of abuse, requires a full forensic investigation, not merely the carrying out of one or two interviews with the child by an expert such as a psychiatrist, a social worker or a psychologist. Child protection services investigating sexual abuse will interview the victim, the family members including siblings and the alleged perpetrator, and will seek a medical assessment. They will also gather evidence from other services, such as schools, child-care centres and family doctors. Many child protection investigations are carried out in the company of police, who will assist in interviews with the child and video the interview for later use in court. The notion that Gardner (1987) put forward of a risk assessment tool for the use of one professional to test the allegation (see Chapter 1) is clearly insufficient to gather the full and detailed information required to determine what has happened.

Could a risk assessment tool have determined whether a paternal uncle was sexually abusing his twelve-month-old niece when he was found putting his hands under her nappy on several contact visits while he was alone with her, as in one case in the first Family Court study? No, a full child protection investigation would be best placed to investigate this problem.

Given that the most important source of evidence in investigating sexual abuse is likely to be the actual account given by the victim, what is the reliability of a child's account of such events and, in particular, how old might they be before their recollection is trustworthy? Do children lie about such matters and, if so, in what circumstances might this happen?

The older the child, the better their recollection tends to be. However, children as young as three can give clear accounts if approached properly (Saywitz and Goodman, 1996). Young children do not necessarily have poor memories, nor are they particularly suggestible as many believe (Oates, 1996). Nevertheless, their accounts will be heavily influenced by the way they are approached. Saywitz and Goodman suggest that the best approach for professionals when interviewing children is to use specific questions because questions framed in this way retrieve clearer, more numerous and more detailed memories. The younger the child, the less productive are open-ended and undirected approaches. While some children will suppress memory of the events—especially children under seven—the fact that the events were traumatic does not mean all children will suppress them, as the traumatic nature of the events means some children will remember them in exact detail. Furthermore, while children may suppress memories for a short time, most remember at intervals, even though they may forget again.

INTERVIEWING STRATEGIES

Problems in obtaining reliable information can occur if the forensic interview is not conducted in a way that is congruent with a child's development—for example, young children may be unable to put a date to an event, or identify details of a person's appearance such as their height, or give details of surroundings. They may not understand all the questions in the way that adults mean them, and in such circumstances they may not say so. They may answer the question to the extent that they understand it, although the answer may not be a response to exactly what the adult thought they had asked. Hence the need for simple questions, repeated questions, questions to test understanding, familiar language and familiar tasks in comfortable surroundings with a supportive interviewer. By the age of ten, most children can understand the aim and the process of a forensic or investigative interview. Nevertheless, the material gained from interviewing a child is only as good as the competence of the interviewer who undertakes a very difficult task that now includes an increasing number of specialised interviewing techniques (Saywitz and Goodman, 1996). There are now many good manuals (Wilson and Powell, 2001), and even kits with video guides (Toth, 2004) to assist in interviewing children about possible sexual abuse.

Many of the professionals who interview children about alleged abuse in the circumstances of residence and contact disputes in family law proceedings have some training in this work. Others do not. Even those who are educated appear to make common mistakes. Hay's (2003) work, with children who had experiences of being investigated in relation to allegations of child abuse in the context of family law proceedings, suggests that children see the common mistakes as being professionals' failing to explain clearly to the child the purpose and the process of the interview; not clarifying the child's meaning and understanding; not appreciating how fearful the child may be, especially if they are on their own with the professional or if the professional introduces the alleged abusive parent without warning; not indicating that the child is free to stop the interview if distressed or free to leave the room; not offering a supportive and empathetic approach; and—possibly the worse error—indicating that certain answers are not acceptable or giving other hints that the interviewer has a particular bias (Hay, 2003; Mudaly and Goddard, 2006). Professionals must approach the child respectfully and sympathetically

DELAYS AND CHANGES IN TELLING OF THE ABUSE

Some professionals believe that if the child has not told anyone about the abuse at the time, it cannot have happened. However, research with adults from the normal population shows that half of those who reported suffering abuse as a child told no one about it until they told the researcher (Cawson, 2002). Of those who do tell, most delay disclosure for some time at least. Professionals find this confusing: why did a child who was old enough to tell delay speaking of this? When children do tell, they tell their mothers most often. Very young children disclose more frequently accidentally than as a deliberate act (Berliner and Elliot, 1996).

Some children tell about the abuse but then deny the disclosure later, or become very tentative and uncertain about it, leading professionals to wonder whether they lied originally. Some 8–22 per cent of children were found in a number of studies to recant allegations that had been shown by other evidence to be true (Briere and Elliot, 1994). This is thought to have occurred because of pressure from the perpetrator or from family members, or due to a perception of negative effects on the victim or on their family from the disclosure. For example, in one case the mother of the seven-year-old victim of sexual abuse, substantiated by the child protection service and the police, that had been inflicted by her paternal uncle while she was on contact visits to her father, said:

> Her uncle's therapist has rung me to say that her uncle is bitterly ashamed and he is having treatment. Her father says he and her uncle do not need her to speak up about it in court to make him stop. Her father says please don't let her go to court.

The mother said she felt under extreme pressure from her former husband and his family to stop the child from giving evidence in court in order to ensure smooth family relationships.

All of the difficulties mentioned in gaining unambiguous and conclusive evidence as to the sexual abuse of children demonstrate why such allegations are regarded with suspicion in family law proceedings. Such allegations—made as they are within a community that tends to deny the existence of such abuse and within a dispute where other motives can be suggested for the allegation, and by children whose age, way of telling and responses in interviews give rise to doubts—are very difficult to accept. At the same time, family law proceedings are a likely forum for the resolution of such allegations, for a parent will break the partnership to protect the child if they are offered no other way to do so.

CAUSES OF CHILD ABUSE

It is not easy to explain why child sexual abuse of any kind—let alone within the family—occurs. In the past, we saw children as the cause of their own sexual abuse, depicting them as being sexually provocative and encouraging the behaviour that followed. Statements made by a recent governor-general of Australia, in defence of the way that he (as a church leader) managed allegations in his diocese of the sexual abuse of children in church institutions by suggesting the child instigated the sexual activity, fall into this category. Such explanations disregard the fact that so many children who are sexually abused are too young to entice an adult into sexual activity, and that it is the adult rather than the child who has the power in this situation. Also, we have seen mothers blamed as the cause of the sexual abuse, either because they failed to protect their child from a presumed ever-present threat of sexual abuse or because they failed to protect their menfolk from fabricated allegations of sexual abuse (Myers, 1996; Humphreys, 1997).

Today we see the causes of child sexual abuse as being complex, with no single factor as the over-arching cause of all child sexual abuse (Corby, 2001). We understand that there is a constellation of causes, and that the constellation is not the same for all types of sexual abuse, for all child victims or for all perpetrators. Different constellations of causes drive different perpetrators to different victims and to different forms of abuse. Ironically, the differences emerging in these constellations of causes for the various types of abuse and groups of victims allow the adherents of all of the various factions propounding different causes to be—at least to some extent—correct.

Domestic violence

Inflicted more often on female partners, domestic violence is closely associated with sexual abuse—and indeed, with all types of child abuse (Brown et al., 1998, 2002b; Cawson, 2002). The mechanisms by which the association occurs are not fully known. Domestic violence demoralises and imprisons the affected partner; it can hide accompanying sexual abuse of the child or children, and make it difficult for the partner to break free if they do discover such abuse. Domestic violence appears to reverberate in a family and lead to abuse between the children and between them and their parents, producing a very chaotic family environment that is hard for the parent being victimised to manage and to escape.

Interaction of risk factors

None of these approaches deals with the complexity of causes and the different constellations of causes that appear to produce different types of perpetrators, victims and abuse. A better framework is to see the abuse as arising from the *interaction* between a number of risk factors on the one hand and a number of protective factors on the other (Kaufman and Zigler, 1987, 1989). Using this approach, it is possible to appreciate that there are factors which may cause sexual abuse that interact with factors which may mitigate against abuse, and these factors can be both societal and individual. Thus factors commonly associated with abuse—like poverty, unemployment, criminality domestic violence, a parent's mental illness, imbalances in power between parents and between parents and children, and a past history of abuse—can come together in constellations for certain individuals and families. In the absence of protective factors like social supports, social integration, employment, intellectual competence, and physical and mental health, the risk factors can lead to abuse.

This approach focuses explanations of cause on the risk factors without seeing them as immutable forces that cannot be resisted. It explains the variety of causes and the differences in the constellations of causes in different groups of perpetrators and victims.

MARITAL PARTNERSHIP AND PARTNERSHIP BREAKDOWN AND DIVORCE AS RISK FACTORS

It is clear that a risk factor for child sexual abuse is the marital partnership; paradoxically, the breakdown of that partnership is also a risk factor. Marital partnerships—legal and de facto, where the parents are the biological parents or otherwise—do lead to the sexual abuse of children; sadly, some parents are the source of the sexual abuse of their own children.

Parental sexual abuse is the least common of all sexual abuse of children, and it represents some 5 per cent of the total child sexual abuse reported (Cawson et al., 2001). Parental sexual abuse is perpetrated mostly by fathers and within the group of fathers is a disproportionate number of step-fathers, legal and de facto. In addition, the marital partnership brings with it another group of perpetrators of sexual abuse: those family members who live in or who are associated with the marital partnership—that is, siblings, step-siblings and half-siblings and, wider afield, uncles and grand-parents. This latter group is a larger group of perpetrators of child sexual abuse, representing some 15 per cent in all. Of particular concern is the recent growth in sibling sexual abuse (Rayment-McHugh and Nisbet, 2004), which has been reflected in the residence and contact studies. In all of these circumstances, the discovery of intra-familial sexual abuse may bring the marital partnership to an end and the family may proceed inex-orably to family law proceedings. This is especially likely when the sexual abuse is denied by the person alleged to be inflicting it, and partnership separation seems the only way of protecting the child. In the hundreds of cases reviewed in the Family Court studies, only one father admitted the abuse on his own initiative. Some admitted it during investigation, but many denied it in the face of convincing proof.

In some families, the sexual abuse occurs after marital separation—even some years after divorce. A number of studies suggest that separation and divorce leave children more exposed to sexual abuse than when they live in two-parent families. Wilson (2002a) has explained findings like these through a review of a large number of studies on children whose parents have separated or divorced. She maintains the studies show that sexual abuse of female children occurs more commonly after separation than in intact families, no matter what post-separation family arrangements are made. She suggests that the loss of the quantity and quality of supervision afforded by two cooperative parents produces a vulnerability that in turn leads to opportunity for, and the actuality of, abuse. Wilson believes that it is such an integral part of parental separation and divorce that judges should consider it when making all residence and contact orders for children, and that judges should give warnings to parents even if no explicit allegation has been made.

PERPETRATORS

The perpetrators of child sexual abuse, both from within and outside the family, are far more commonly male than female. Child sexual abuse studies show that over 90 per cent of perpetrators are male (La Fontaine, 1990; Finkelhor et al., 1990a). The pattern is the same for child sexual abuse within the context of residence and contact disputes, with 91 per cent being male and 9 per cent female (Brown et al., 1998, 2001).

Those who have been substantiated as the perpetrator by the child protection service when sexual abuse is alleged in residence and contact disputes are most commonly fathers (73 per cent), then step-fathers (9 per cent), grandfathers and grand-step-fathers (9 per cent), step-mothers (4.5 per cent) and mothers with a cousin and with the child's older sibling (4.5 per cent). Fathers' perceptions that they are unfairly singled out as the accused perpetrators of child sexual abuse (Tolmie and Kay, 1998) are not valid. In these circumstances, fathers represent the vast majority of perpetrators of sexual abuse. Nevertheless, 27 per cent of the perpetrators are not the biological father of the child, and in this group there is a disproportionate representation from step-fathers as well as from step-mothers.

Fathers' perceptions of being unjustly accused are correct in some respects, however, as fathers are also the persons most often alleged to be the perpetrators of sexual abuse in this context. At the same time, fathers are not the most likely of all accused to be substantiated.Some 36 per cent of fathers accused are not substantiated as the perpetrator by the child protection service.

Mothers are the least likely to be accused; the only mothers who were accused were substantiated, but they had carried the abuse out in the company of other males, which has been suggested to be the typical way that women are involved in the sexual abuse of children (La Fontaine, 1990). However, by way of contradiction, in the Magellan study a step-mother who had sexually abused her two step-sons acted alone (Brown et al., 2001). All studies indicate that it is never safe to make assumptions as to who the perpetrator may be.

VICTIMS

The gendered nature of sexual abuse extends to the victims. Victims of child sexual abuse are more commonly female, with the female-to-male ratio being 7:3 (Finkelhor, 1986) although some suspect that the incidence of male victims may be higher as boys have been found to be even less likely than girls to report abuse because of the fear of being labelled homosexual (La Fontaine, 1990). The gender breakdown of the victims of sexual abuse in residence and contact disputes is the same as in child sexual abuse in other contexts, with girls being the more common victim (Thoeness and Pearson, 1988; Hume, 1997; Brown et al., 1998, 2001). The average age of the victims is very young—four years in the first Family Court study and eight years in the second (Brown et al., 1998, 2001).

One event of sexual abuse predisposes children to further events of abuse by the same perpetrator, and sexual abuse by one perpetrator predisposes children to abuse from other perpetrators. The abuse of the children who were being sexually abused while the marital partnership was intact did not stop when the partnership broke down. For most—80 per cent—it continued on contact visits; hence the move of the non-abusing parent to seek orders in family law proceedings for supervised contact or no contact.

The short- and long-term outcomes for the victims of intra-familial child sexual abuse are serious, more so than for the child victims of sexual abuse from outside the family. The impact of sexual abuse from a parent or step–parent is more severe because of the feelings that such abuse engenders in the child.

Initial and long-term effects include fearfulness, withdrawal and depression, hostility and aggression, low self-esteem, guilt and shame, running away from home, poor school performance, poor relationships with peers, inappropriate sexual behaviour and sexual disturbances, and further victimisation as children and adults. While we do not know whether the age of the victim, the gender of the victim and the duration of the abuse affects the severity of the impact on the victim (Corby, 2001), we do know that the closeness of the family relationship between the victim and the perpetrator, the existence of violence accompanying the abuse and the degree of family support for the victim as a response to the abuse affect the outcomes for the victim. It is sobering to reflect that the outcomes for the victim of child sexual abuse in this context are more serious than in others, and this leaves the professionals with a considerable responsibility for the child's continuing well-being.

RESIDENCE AND CONTACT ARRANGEMENTS FOR VICTIMS OF CHILD SEXUAL ABUSE

The impact of the abuse on the child needs to be taken into account for parenting arrangements following parental separation, divorce and family law proceedings when allegations of sexual abuse of the child have been made.

When the abuse has been substantiated, it is clear that the child needs to be protected from further harm and to be supported by the family to minimise the harm already inflicted. Children who have suffered such abuse will usually need assistance from mental health professionals. Today, an increasing number of specialised treatment centres exist. The impact of the abuse on the child implies that the perpetrator cannot become the residential parent, as the child would not feel safe and supported—and indeed, they could not be protected from the real likelihood of further abuse. Neither will the child be safe in contact arrangements that leave the perpetrator alone with the child, despite what the perpetrator may argue. Hence the frequent recommendation for supervised contact that allows the perpetrator who is the parent of the child to have a relationship with that child.

Even professionally supervised contact has its drawbacks for the child, and these may overcome any of the advantages such contact may provide. If the sexual abuse was accompanied by violence, either to the child or to the protective parent, the strength of the professional staff at a contact centre may not seem to be sufficient to the child to make them feel safe. The tension of this doubt and the ensuing fear for the child seem to offer little advantage to the child, especially as contact centre arrangements are usually only available for short periods of time. Evaluations of contact centres show they are of reduced value for children who have suffered abuse (Sheehan et al., 2005).

When the abuse has been neither substantiated nor the allegation found to be false, the child still needs to be protected and supported. In such situations, allowing the alleged perpetrator to be the residential parent is too fraught with danger for the child to be recommended. The fact that the abuse is not substantiated does not mean it has not occurred. In these circumstances, professionally supervised contact for a period of time may be desirable as it allows for ongoing monitoring that may reveal whether or not the risk is real. However, a perpetrator may be able to persist through such a period and then inflict further abuse when the period of intensive supervision is over.

Some of the answer to this difficult problem lies in the attitude of the child to the alleged perpetrator, what the child thinks they may gain despite the risks and how the child might be kept safe. Learning the child's views is necessary in order to know the child's wishes and how best to keep the child safe. In one case, the father—the residential parent on account of his wife's brother's sexual abuse of the two children and the mother's unwillingness to protect the children from her brother—agreed to the children having day-long contact with their mother each week, once they were old enough to use a mobile phone to ring him if there were difficulties. He knew the two children wanted regular contact with their mother if they could be protected from her brother.

THE ATTITUDES OF SOCIO-LEGAL PROFESSIONALS TO CHILD SEXUAL ABUSE

The denial surrounding child sexual abuse remains strong, even today. For many years, it was noted that professionals working with families where there was child abuse tended to deny it even though it was clearly evident. The many different reasons advanced to explain this behaviour fall under the umbrella of professionals acting unconsciously to protect themselves from the trauma of the victim's abuse and from their own difficulties in dealing with the impact of that trauma on the children and on themselves, and the difficulties faced in assisting the children. Summit (1983) suggests professionals accommodate to the sexual abuse and so ignore it. Dingwall (Dingwall et al., 1983) believes professionals use the rule of optimism to deny it, hoping it will all work out in the end. Parton (1991) believes it throws us into a moral panic and leads to over-intrusive actions. Stanley and Goddard (2002) suggest the perpetrators take the professionals hostage, and Kitzinger (2000) thinks that we cannot cope with it because it is about sex.

No matter what the psychological defence mechanism may be that professionals use to protect themselves, it is clear that professionals often do not wish to believe the abuse is occurring, and that they adjust their thinking to avoid it even when they are the very professionals designated to deal with it.

One strategy for the better management of the professionals' feelings is for them to learn as much about the problem as possible. They can then learn to dismiss the popular myths that have protected them from the existence of child sexual abuse, such as the myth that it doesn't happen because mothers make it up or the myth that children provoke their own abuse. Another strategy is for professionals to learn to articulate their feelings about child sexual abuse and about the members of the families they work with when it occurs. Professionals need to review regularly how their feelings are impacting on their work with each family as they encounter them.

CONCLUSION

The presentation of the intra-familial sexual abuse of children is atypically high in the context of parental separation and divorce, and family law proceedings. It is a cause of parental separation and divorce and, at the same time, parental separation and divorce leads to its further occurrence. Of all the kinds of child abuse, it alone seems to be growing—suggesting that family law proceedings will increasingly become the forum in which the issue will be debated and resolved.

Intra-familiar abuse is the most difficult of all kinds of abuse for family law professionals to manage for it is hard to detect and hard to understand, its perpetrators deny it, their victims deny it, the community denies it, and it has serious and long-lasting effects on the victims. In Chapters 6, 7 and 8 there will be discussion as to the ways family law professionals may deal with such abuse.

5

OTHER FORMS OF CHILD ABUSE

Just as intra-familial child sexual abuse has a particular profile in the context
of parental separation and divorce, so do the other forms of child abuse.
Some—like abduction—occur only in this context. Others—like neglect—
occur rarely. Some forms—like attempted and actual homicide and familicide—appear with a different face. Only one form, physical abuse, occurs
similarly in all contexts.

It is important for professionals in the family law services to be knowledgeable about the other forms of child abuse and to be confident in their
knowledge—especially with regard to those forms that are unique to this
context, as these forms have received little attention to date. Moreover,
professionals need to be aware that underlying the other forms is the
potential existence of severe parental violence to the children, to the other
parent and sometimes to professionals as well. Such violence tends to be
downplayed by parents and professionals alike, who interpret it as a fleeting
aspect of the dying partnership rather than as a real risk to the children,
the other parent, family members and others. For example, what might in
other circumstances be described as attempted murder is interpreted
as child abuse or domestic violence, and what might otherwise be seen as
child abuse is minimised and ignored. Downplaying, though common, is
inappropriate: both threatened and actual violence to the children, the
parent, other family members and professionals must be taken seriously.
Allegations should not be ignored or treated lightly; rather, they should be

investigated and, because of the potential danger to the children and other family members, carried out very carefully. Excuses from any source that obstruct or delay interventions should not be accepted. All intervention should be documented.

This chapter will present what we know of the remaining types of child abuse. All of these forms of child abuse are considered together because they seem to bear a relationship to each other, to have common causes and common patterns of perpetrators and victims—unlike intra-familial sexual abuse, which tends to stand alone. The chapter will present the issues these types of child abuse raise for professionals in the family law services, and once again propose some ways for professionals to protect children from further harm.

COMMUNITY ATTITUDES TO OTHER FORMS OF CHILD ABUSE

As with child sexual abuse, there is controversy over the extent to which communities have protected children from the other forms of abuse inflicted by the family. The conventional view is that the English-speaking world, along with Europe, tolerated the physical abuse of children by their parents until the nineteenth century (Gillham, 1994). However, Corby (2000) has disputed this view, drawing our attention to the fact that parents were prosecuted for the physical abuse of their children in England from the thirteenth century, in Europe from the sixteenth century and in the United States from the seventeenth century. Furthermore, he does not accept the common view that families are treating their children better as living standards improve. He thinks the physical abuse of children by their parents is increasing with the spread of urbanisation and its fractured families living in fragmented communities that provide less support and less scrutiny.

Bearing out Corby's views is the fact that concern for children suffering from physical abuse, neglect and abandonment by their parents arose in Australia at the beginning of European settlement because families—especially convict families—had few physical resources for the care of their children. Colonial governments had to intervene, organising and funding charitable child welfare organisations (Clark, 1979a, 1979b). When the position of families worsened as a result of the social and economic dislocation of the gold rushes, New South Wales and Victoria introduced legislation to protect children from physical abuse, neglect and abandonment.Abandonmentand neglect, rather than physical abuse, were the critical issues for the politicians of the day (Brown, 1982).

The services established by the early legislation, the industrial schools and the formalised governmental funding of the charitable organisations were unable, however, to overcome the child welfare problems.The services could not deal with the social turbulence of the rapidly changing colonial life. Towards the end of the nineteenth century, the increasing numbers of young children abandoned by their families in the expanding cities of coastal Australia,together with discoveries of babies murdered by fraudulent foster families,led to the emergence of the child rescue societies.These societies sought to stamp out child abuse by extending child welfare legislation, and by opening agencies for the children and their families. The agencies employed case workers to offer assistanceto the families and, if that failed, the workers were empowered by legislation to remove the children and place them in residential care, often administered by the same organisation.The child rescue movement proposed a specialisedjurisdiction for abused and neglected children, and Children's Courts were established in Australia within each state's legal system from early in the twentieth century (Sheehan, 2001).

From these beginnings, the current services—state-based government and non-government child protection services funded by the state governments—grew in numbers and strength in each state and territory during the twentieth century. Eventually, following international trends, the state governments made the reporting of physical abuse, neglect and sexual abuse to the child protection services mandatory for specified professionals. In 1969, South Australia introduced a requirement for the mandatory reporting of child abuse by doctors and in 1974, Tasmania did likewise. Subsequently, other states introduced mandatory reporting that covered a wider range of professionals, such as doctors, nurses, social workers, psychologists and teachers—a list that varies a little from state to state. New South Wales introduced mandatory reporting in 1977, followed by Queensland in 1978, the Northern Territory in 1983, Victoria in 1993 and the Australian Capital Territory in 1997.

Alone among the Australian states,Western Australia did not introduce mandatory reporting, except by the staff of the Western AustralianFamily Court. Instead, that state substituted protocols or guidelines for certain occupational groups for the reporting of the maltreatment of children (AIHW, 2004). Parents and professionalsinvolved in family law proceedings where there have been allegations of child abuse have argued that using protocols rather than mandating reporting has allowed the child protection service to sidestep an investigation when a report is made (Hay, 2003). Regardless, Western Australia has confirmed its stance with its acceptance of the findings of its last inquiry saying it believes mandatory reporting does not prevent child abuse or improve the care of abused children (Harries and Clare, 2002).

The desire of one state to occupy a unique position in child protection policy undermines attempts to produce a national policy with uniform standards of provision for families. Australia's child protection system is scattered around the various states, and is also split between the states— through state child welfare legislation—and the Commonwealth—through Commonwealth family law legislation. The consequent fragmentation of child protection legislation, policy and practice causes extreme confusion for professionals. It highlights a major structural problem: that there is no one clear and appropriately designed set of services to manage child abuse and child protection issues in the context of parental separation and divorce, and family law proceedings. Instead, there is a confused and contradictory patchwork of services whose dimensions and details are unclear to all.

THE PUZZLE OF REPORTED INCIDENCE

The fracturing of service provision has also led to confusion about trends in the reported incidence in Australia of the other forms of child abuse. In the previous chapter, trends in the reported incidence of child sexual abuse in Australia and internationally were discussed. Looking at the trends in the reported incidence of the other types of abuse, Australia has experienced the same increases in reported incidence of these types of abuse as have other countries in the post-Kempe era. However, the peaking of reported incidence and the slight decline in notifications that has taken place in the United Kingdom and United States has not yet occurred here (AIHW, 2004: 5).

Reviewing this difference in greater detail than in the previous chapter, it appears that the difference is not caused by a time lag that means Australia is experiencing the same events but a little later; rather, it is seen as stemming from the variations in legislation, policy and practice from state to state

(AIHW, 2002).The national picture of substantiatedcases (possibly a better indicator than notified or reported cases) shows that the trends in the states are contradictory. Substantiationrates are decreasing rapidly in Tasmania,and decreasing less rapidly in New South Wales, but they are increasing in all other states and territories apart from the AustralianCapitalTerritory, which shows no change at all.As a result, we are unsure about what is taking place. The AustralianInstitute of Health andWelfare thinks the national reported incidence of notifications and substantiationsis distorted by the differences in the policies and practices of reporting, investigating and disposing of cases between the states and territories, as well as by the frequent changes in the policies of each state in recent times (AIHW, 2004: 5).

Whatever the causes, the contradictions underline the need for profes-sionals working with families where there are child abuse allegations in the context of parental separation and divorce to understand that policies and practices are significantly different from state to state, and that they are currently changing quite frequently.

PATTERNS IN REPORTED INCIDENCE OF OTHER FORMS OF CHILD ABUSE

When we look at patterns in the occurrence of the different types of abuse reported in Australia, we are handicapped by a distortion caused by the international practice of reporting child abuse in four separately constructed categories.This practice obscures the overlap between various types of abuse that we now know occurs in reality. It is important to remember this when listening to and interpreting a person's account of what has happened to them and their children.

Physical abuse and *neglect* are the two forms of child abuse that are consis-tently reported most frequently to the state child protection authorities.The proportion of *physical abuse* is similar from state to state, although it does range from a low of 24 per cent in Queensland to a high of 52 per cent in Tasmania,where it is said to be altered by the way that state counts all abuse in either one or the other of only two categories (AIHW, 2004: 5). Generally, physical abuse hovers around 30 per cent—a little higher than the international figures of 25 per cent (Kolko, 1996). *Neglect* varies from a low of 19 per cent in New South Wales to a high of 43 per cent in Queensland; however, the Northern Territory, South Australia and Western

Australiaalso have rates almost as high as Queensland (AIHW, 2002). Rates for neglect in these states may be increased by the impact of their higher levels of low income earners in their populations. Internationally neglect represents approximately 11 per cent of all reported abuse (Hart and Brassard, 1993).

Emotional abuse is reported less consistently and less reliably; the variations are very great. Some states and territories use it frequently as a category: Victoria and the Australian Capital Territory have substantiated rates of 43 per cent and 41 per cent respectively. Other states use it rarely—such as Tasmania, where it is 2 per cent. It has been suggested that the incidence of emotional abuse is high where the child protection service accepts a wider range of notifications (AIHW, 2004: 5), or where it is difficult to substantiate sexual abuse, so emotional abuse is substantiated instead (Brown et al., 1998). Certainly each state or territory uses this category very differently.

PATTERNS OF ABUSE IN THE CONTEXT OF PARENTAL SEPARATION AND DIVORCE

The abuse reported to family courts is not reported or recorded in the four categories used by the child protection services, but instead in the words of the family members or professionals describing the actual experiences. Thus it is not possible to make an exact comparison of the incidence of each type of abuse across the two contexts. Nevertheless, it is possible to make some comparisons and to inform professionals of the difference in patterns of incidence of the various forms of abuse from one context to another.

Looking at physical abuse alone, the incidence of substantiated abuse seems at first glance to be similar to that of the state child protection authorities. In the study where the cases came from a sample of all cases involving abuse allegations in an eighteen-month period, physical abuse was the most common single form of abuse at 18 per cent. However, physical abuse was involved in a further 33 per cent of the reported cases of abuse, thus taking the total of all physical abuse to a much higher incidence than that reported to the child protection authorities (Brown et al., 1998). The same trend was evident in the study involving the Magellan program, where cases were drawn from a selected sample of reported physical and sexual abuse. Here, it was the second most common single form of abuse, at 9 per cent after sexual abuse—but again it was involved in a further 23 per cent of abuse (Brown et al., 2001).

Thus the state child protection authorities' practice of separating all types of abuse into categories may artificially deflate the incidence of physical abuse that they describe. Alternatively, there may actually be a higher incidence of physical abuse in the context of parental separation and divorce due to the numbers of couples separating on account of domestic violence.

Neglect, on the other hand, is uncommon in the context of parental separation and divorce, representing only 3 per cent as a single form of abuse in both studies and involved further in only 11 per cent of other cases in the first study and 9 per cent in the second. Since neglect is characterised as a problem of the entire family, not of just one parent, it is unlikely to be identified as an issue by one parent or the other. Emotional abuse is even less common, not occurring at all in the first study and representing 2 per cent in the second study, with no further incidence in multiple forms of abuse (Brown et al., 1998, 2001).

An examination of the reports of abuse expressed in the words of family members and professionals in residence and contact disputes shows that multiple forms of abuse or multi-type abuse are the most common form of abuse in this context, representing 45 per cent of all abuse in the first study and 34 per cent in the second study (Brown et al., 1998, 2001). Recent research on the prevalence of actual abuse indicates that the existence of multi-type abuse is more common than was previously realised (Cawson, 2002), but that its prevalence is low, at about 6 per cent. This is much lower than in the context of parental separation and divorce.

However, if the domestic violence identified in the Cawson studies (Cawson et al., 2001; Cawson, 2002) had been considered to be a form of child abuse, the findings of the incidence of multi-type abuse would have been different. The English study found that domestic violence played a significant role in physical abuse and emotional abuse in particular, but also related to neglect and sexual abuse. Of great concern—considering the frequency of domestic violence between separating couples in general, and especially between separating couples where child abuse was alleged— is the fact that the English study found domestic violence was associated with the most serious levels of abuse (Cawson, 2002). This assists in explaining why child abuse reported in this context is so often serious in nature.

REPORTED INCIDENCE OF ABDUCTION

The abduction of a child by one parent from another is unique to the context of parental separation and divorce. The event is not yet considered to be child abuse, although it is seen to cause psychological damage to between 30 and 80 per cent of the children who are abducted (Finkelhor et al., 1990b; Grief, 1998). In some cases, physical and/or sexual abuse takes place during the period of the abduction (Grief, 1998). It is often associated with domestic violence—as, for example, when it is used as an intimidatory tactic against the spousal victim. In a case discussed in detail in Chapter 8, the father abducted his young son to stop the mother reporting her suspicions about his sexual abuse of her daughter, his step-child. In this case, the mother was too frightened to report the child's disappearance to anyone.

Currently, abduction—being defined as a criminal offence—is reported to the police rather than to the child protection authorities. In the context of parental separation and divorce, there is little information as to incidence. In two studies of child abuse in residence and contact disputes presenting to the Family Court of Australia (Brown et al., 1998, 2001), it ranged from 1–5 per cent, with one of the abductions taking place in Australia and the others being abductions of the children overseas. In all instances, the abductions took place as the partnership disintegrated rather than after its end. Three of the children were not returned.

REPORTED ATTEMPTED AND ACTUAL HOMICIDE

We do not as yet know enough about the tragedy of the attempted or actual murder of children in the context of parental separation and divorce. In the first of the two Family Court studies, one parent had served a custodial sentence for the attempted murder of his child—an offence that had happened while the child was on a contact visit. The father carried out the attempt in the mother's presence while taunting her about being too far away to rescue the child.

The murder of a child by their parent following parental separation and divorce is, like abduction, not regarded as child abuse but as a crime—fortunately one that occurs rarely. The murder of a child in these circumstances is sometimes followed by the suicide of the parent who has committed the murder, and this sequence of events is termed *familicide*. Johnson (2002), one of the few researchers to study these sad events, suggests it happens to one family in Australia per year. She has found the deaths to be associated with prior child abuse and domestic violence, but she was unable to identify any indicator that might forecast the ultimate terrible outcome. In her research, all murders were carried out by the children's father, but in one subsequent case the murders were carried out by the children's mother.

SEVERITY OF ABUSE

A number of factors point to the severity of these other forms of abuse in the context of parental separation and divorce, thereby contradicting the myth that abuse in this context is neither real, nor—if it *is* identified—serious. The most common type of abuse is multi-type abuse, and it occurs more commonly in this context than in others. Moreover, the link between child abuse, domestic violence and the severity of abuse suggests a greater degree of abuse, as in this context domestic violence was commonly associated with the occurrence of the other forms of child abuse. Another link pointing to increased severity of abuse—that between the criminal histories of parents and severity of abuse—exists in this context, with both Family Court studies showing an incidence of maternal and especially paternal criminality well above average.

DEFINITION OF PHYSICAL ABUSE

Professionals need to be aware of precisely how the other forms of abuse are defined, and especially how they are defined in each state jurisdiction where the investigation and intervention take place.

Physical abuse is used as a broad term to cover the events that occur when a child suffers physical harm from a parent, another family member or from someone else in the role of the child's caregiver. The definition given below is used by the Western Australia Department of Community Development, and is typical of the definitions used by Australian and overseas child protection services. It has been selected for presentation because, as was the case in the definition presented for child sexual abuse, it is the most detailed definition used by government departments in the

Australian states and territories. Child physical abuse is defined as occurring when:

> a child is seriously hurt or injured by an adult having the custody or care of a child resulting in the non-accidental form of injury or harm. It can also be the result of putting a child at risk where he or she is likely to be injured. Actions such as hitting, shaking, punching, burning, leaving a very young child in a car can result in injuries such as cuts, bruises, burns, welts, dehydration, haemotomas and even death. (DCD, 2006)

The definition focuses on a parent's or a caregiver's physical ill-treatment of a child that has happened or is likely to happen. It does not mention harm suffered from disciplinary punishment, as does the definition used by the Department of Human Services in Victoria (DHS, Vic., 2006). Since parents in Australia may use corporal punishment to discipline their children, there is no clear line that must not be crossed, leaving unclear the boundaries of what is regarded as parental discipline and what is seen as physical abuse.

To deal with the fine line between parental discipline and physical abuse, some suggest the abuse be graded according to the severity of the injuries and the damage left behind, the duration of the attack, whether it happened once or repeatedly and, if repeatedly, how often it happened and over what time period (Bifulco and Moran, 1998). Documenting the abuse in this way is advisable anyway, for both accuracy and reliability. Community beliefs as to what is and is not acceptable in terms of severity, duration and frequency are used as standards. The specific mention in the definition of bruises, cuts and burns gives an indication of what the child protection service considers to be evidence of physical abuse. The physical abuse described in the Family Court studies (Brown et al., 1998, 2001) included bruising, burns and fractures. Some were the result of extreme discipline, like a four-year-old being tied up and placed in a cupboard as punishment; some were from an explosion of rage, like a three-year-old being hit repeatedly on the arms and body, leaving bruises; and some were the effects of torture, like forcing a six-year-old to drink something that would make him ill.

Munchausen syndrome by proxy can be seen as part of the spectrum of physical abuse, but it is more customarily defined separately although physical abuse is one of its consequences. It is a secretive type of abuse, where the perpetrator seeks to convince medical authorities that their child is ill. It is defined as occurring when 'a child presents with an illness that has been fictitiously produced by a parent, typically by a mother' (Corby, 2001). The abuse is seen to be both the symptoms of illness that the parent is producing, and the investigation and treatment to which the child is then subjected for their non-existent illness. Children who have suffered from it describe a sense of abuse that is wider than both the symptoms and the investigation and treatment for the supposed illness—more a sense of neglect and emotional abuse. It is thought to be rare (Gillham, 1994; Corby, 2001). Its diagnosis is controversial, since events in England (see Davis, 2005) have suggested that some children are diagnosed without adequate investigation, resulting in some parents wrongly being convicted of their child's murder (Davis, 2005). It is usually detected through covert surveillance in hospital wards (Southall et al., 1997).

Munchausen by proxy presents occasionally in the context of parental separation and divorce, and family law proceedings; in the first and second Family Court studies (Brown et al., 1998, 2001), the incidence was 2 per cent. All victims were pre-school girls who had many hospital admissions for illnesses that could not initially be diagnosed, and in all cases the treating doctors at specialist children's hospitals had concluded that the mothers were responsible for the symptoms.

DEFINITION OF NEGLECT

Neglect, while low in incidence in this context, does still occur. It is fundamentally an absence or omission of care. The definition used here is taken from the Department of Community Services in New South Wales, and its wording is almost identical to that used in definitions of neglect in all Australian states and territories and elsewhere. Neglect is defined as occurring when there is:

> continued failure by the parent or caregiver to provide the child with the basic things needed for his or her proper growth and development, things such as food, clothing, shelter, medical and dental care and adequate supervision. (DOCS, NSW, 2006)

This definition covers neglect broadly and, while giving some details, it does not say what level of food, clothing, medical attention and supervision is required. Being an absence of care, neglect is hard to assess and Stevenson (1998) has noted the difficulties social workers experience in assessing neglect.

This definition does not deal with the issue of different cultural standards of family care, a problem exemplified by the treatment of Indigenous children by the Australian child welfare authorities in the past. Australia embraces many different racial and ethnic groups, each with a somewhat different point of view. In one case in the Family Court studies (Brown et al., 1998, 2001), a residential father born overseas was assessed as neglecting his children because he did not obtain a continuity of schooling for them. They attended school, but spent so little time at any one school that they had been assessed as being unable to learn. He had received little schooling in his home country, and his time in Australia had given him no sense of the value of education. Different cultural backgrounds may explain different standards, but they do not remove the necessity for the child to be offered as many opportunities than other children in Australia.

Behaviour not previously regarded as neglect is emerging as important in the context of parental separation and divorce, especially in family law proceedings. This is behaviour that surrounds implementing contact arrangements post-separation and divorce. For example, neglect may include driving a car with a child as passenger while the driver has been drinking or is under the influence of drugs, driving a car without using a child's seatbelt, or leaving a child unattended in a car for more than a short amount of time. These fall under the absence of care and shade into a disregard for the child's physical safety.

DEFINITION OF EMOTIONAL ABUSE

While emotional abuse is thought of as an inherent part of all abuse, it has now been given its own category to cover those situations where no other abuse occurs and to more clearly identify the emotional abuse that accompanies other abuse. Some have termed it psychological abuse and others emotional abuse. One researcher has attempted to make a clear distinction between these two terms, and to have them accepted as two distinct forms of abuse (O'Hagen, 1993). However, they are still used as interchangeable terms. Again the definition used in Western Australia is presented, as it is the most comprehensive one used in Australia and is also very similar to those used overseas. Emotional abuse is defined as occurring when:

A parent significantly harms a child's development or when they cause the child's behaviour to be disturbed. This can be due to persistent coldness or rejection by the person who has the custody or care of the child. Constant threatening or scaring a child, putting a child down are all examples of emotional abuse. (DCD, WA, 2006)

This definition is broad, and gives examples of what it includes as abuse; however, the questions of how often and how severe the actions would need to be in order for them to be classified as abuse remain unclear. As can be seen in the Australian annual statistics on child abuse as presented earlier in this chapter, there are such great variations in the use of this category that it seems almost meaningless.

FORMS OF CHILD ABUSE SPECIFIC TO PARENTAL SEPARATION AND DIVORCE

Some new forms of child abuse are emerging that are specific to parental separation and divorce. They have not yet been defined as particular categories of child abuse, but instead have been placed within the existing categories. Nevertheless, they deserve consideration here and further attention in the future.

A parent's abuse of their child at the point of handover or changeover, when one parent is handing the child over to the other as part of the contact arrangements or orders, is a form of child abuse that occurs only in the context of parental separation and divorce. Such abuse has been identified as physical abuse, and as being associated with domestic violence taking place at the same time (Hester and Ratford, 1997; Kaye et al., 2003a). However, it can include emotional abuse as well. It was identified as a form of abuse in the first of the Family Court studies (Brown et al., 1998, 2001) and then measured in the second study. In the latter study, 3 per cent of families reported changeover abuse so severe that the contact orders of the court could not be carried out (Brown et al., 2001).

Contact centres have been designed to deal with this issue. In an evaluation of one of the new Contact Orders pilot programs (now known as the Parent Orders program), abuse at handover was one of the most common types of child and parental abuse among the families ordered to use the service (Brown and Smale, 2006). Categorising this behaviour is difficult, as it has elements of physical and emotional abuse of the children, of the parent to whom the child is going and of any other family members who are present at the time. For example, in one of the families in this new study, each time the father returned the child to the mother he shouted at the child and the mother, pulled the child back into the car and then pushed him out repeatedly and ran up and down the street verbally abusing his former spouse, her new partner and her parents.

Another form of abuse that takes place only in the context of parental separation and divorce is contact abuse—that is, any kind of child abuse that occurs while the child is on a contact visit with the non-residential parent. Some may see it as child abuse in another setting rather than as a separate kind of abuse; however, it has distinctive features that suggest it could be considered a particular form of abuse.

The distinctive features include the fact that the child is in a particularly vulnerable position, in the care of one parent only, because of the parental separation. Often the child is the only child in the care of the parent, and is very young. The events of the separation may leave the contact parent poorly disposed towards the child and lacking in empathy towards them. Moreover, the contact arrangements may include other people who have no concern for the child's welfare; sometimes the contact parent leaves the child with other family members and does not know what actually happens in their absence. The Family Court studies showed that half of the abuse originated after the separation and that most of this took place on contact visits. Of considerable concern was the fact that sexual abuse with multiple perpetrators took place only on contact visits.

CAUSES OF THE OTHER FORMS OF CHILD ABUSE

We have suggested that child abuse arises from a constellation of factors that interact with each other in different situations. This perspective suggests looking at each type of abuse separately to discern the constellation of factors around each form. Nevertheless, there are common threads in the causes of the other forms of child abuse as they are discussed here. These are domestic violence, parental mental illness, the abuse of the parent as a child, poverty, and parental separation and divorce itself. It is clear that all of these threads, when woven together, endanger the welfare of the children.

Physical abuse has long been associated with poverty (Gillham, 1994; Cawson, 2002), but certainly not every parent who is poor harms their children physically. Another explanation is that all abuse in childhood leads to later poverty as an adult (Frederick and Goddard, 2004). Yet another view, that physical abuse results from parents using the extreme end of the parental discipline continuum (Strauss, 1994), has been contradicted by research showing that parents who physically abuse their children do so while disapproving of what they are doing (Creighton and Russell, 1995; Smith et al., 1995). The causes of physical abuse remain elusive, but some factors—like parental mental illness and a history of the parents' physical abuse—seem significant.

At the same time, domestic violence is frequently associated with the physical abuse of children by both their fathers and their mothers, even when the mother is a victim of domestic violence (Brown et al., 1998, 2001; Cawson et al., 2001). Domestic violence appears to reverberate around a family and lead to abuse between the non-abusive partner and the children, among the children, and between them and their parents. Similarly, parental criminality is associated with physical abuse, as is unemployment (Brown et al., 1998, 2001).

Neglect has also been related to poverty, but the link is now regarded as an indirect one (Stevenson, 1998). Today, poverty is seen as leading to a number of other events like parental mental illness—especially maternal depression—that in turn can lead to neglect (Berliner and Conte, 2003). Another insight into the link may be the finding that neglect often follows a structural change in a family, such as parental death or separation (Bifulco and Moran, 1998). Parental separation is known to cause depression and to divert a parent's attention from their children as they mourn the loss of their partner and former way of life (Rodgers and Prior, 1998). Furthermore, poverty may follow separation and divorce for short periods of time for men and for long periods of time for those women with residence of their children.

As emotional abuse is a more recently established category, knowledge about the causes is scanty. The most overtly hostile emotional abuse from parents, like attacks on the child's pets or possessions, seems related to domestic violence (McGee, 2000), and to a desire of the parent to dominate the child. Other emotional abuse is related to the personality of the parent, but no widely held specific theory exists and the literature pays little heed to causes and far more to intervention (Hart and Brassart, 1996).

The causes of abduction are not clear. In the scanty research on abduction, it has been suggested that one parent takes this action when they have no respect for the other parent, and when they think the other parent has done or will do something that affronts their views of proper parental care

(Grief, 1995). However, the Australian research (Brown et al., 1998, 2001) did not identify such triggers. In one case, it happened before the separation in an attempt to stop the separation and prevent an investigation into allegations of child sexual abuse. In the other cases, it was to stop the mother having any contact with the children by removing them from her care and from an Australian jurisdiction that gave her an opportunity for parenting orders to be made that were favourable to her. Certainly, in these cases, there was evidence of an extreme disregard for the other parent.

So little is known of actual or attempted homicide that no causes are clear. Johnson (2002) could not identify any common causes except to say that prior child abuse and domestic violence were associated with the events. In addition, she drew attention to another common factor: a psychological trait of the male parent that meant they could not see their wives and children as separate from them. When the wives and children left, the men became angry beyond control and murdered or tried to murder the children and often the wives as well.

On the few occasions where the parent attempting homicide has been the mother, they have tended to be mentally ill and to believe they were saving the children from a terrible life (*Weekend Australian Magazine*, 23–24 October 2004).

Domestic violence is a common causal thread in all forms of child abuse. Research internationally shows the prevalence of domestic violence when child abuse occurs as ranging from 30–50 per cent (Stark and Flitcraft, 1985; Pagelow, 1990; Cawson et al., 2001; Edelson, 2002). It is a significant factor in all the various forms of child abuse in the context of parental separation and divorce (Brown et al., 1998, 2001), and it occurs in 40 per cent of cases. As discussed previously, domestic violence is likely to lead to parental separation and divorce and to continue afterwards, so its presence and its link to child abuse in this context are obvious.

Domestic violence is now seen as moving from being a *cause* of child abuse to being an actual *form* of child abuse because of the way that child abuse is viewed as an inevitable consequence of domestic violence, from the child experiencing the violence directly, through a deliberate or accidental act of the parent, from the child's witnessing the violence or from the surrounding atmosphere in the family of violence and control. In one unreported judgment, the judge wrote that, despite claims to the contrary, he was unable to see how the children would have been unaffected by their mother being punched and thrown around in the next room, then pushed through a wall, followed by the arrival of an ambulance and the police (Brown et al., 1998). At present, some state child protection services define domestic violence as child abuse, such as in New South Wales, and others define it as a risk factor for child abuse, such as in Victoria.

PARENTAL SEPARATION AND DIVORCE AS A CAUSE

There are many indications that the other forms of child abuse are associated with parental separation and divorce. However, no one has assembled a comprehensive and detailed picture of the nature of the links between these forms of abuse on the one hand and parental separation and divorce on the other. The first step towards producing the picture is to integrate what is known; however, that is not as simple as it might appear to be.

Child abuse has been presented as arising from a constellation of factors that interact with each other in various situations. Parental separation and divorce are one such factor. However, parental separation proceeds through stages over time; it is not just one isolated event. We know that some of the notified child abuse arises before parental separation, and also that separation does not usually bring it to an end. We know it continues during contact. We know also that abuse can begin afterwards. It may be that the causes of child abuse in this context are different for abuse that originates before and abuse that originates after the split.

We know that, in some 10 per cent of families making allegations of child abuse subsequent to parental separation, the abuse has led to the separation. However, there is no information as to the role that sexual abuse—as distinct from other forms of abuse—plays in the partnership breakdown in families where abuse occurred before the separation. We know something of the relationship after the breakdown, as we know that children from families where separation and divorce have taken place have a higher risk of physical abuse and neglect. This appears to be true both for those families where parents do re-partner and where they do not. We are not sure of the reasons for this association; however, stress, mental illness and poverty are consequences of separation and divorce for both men and women, and physical abuse and neglect are linked to these factors. Furthermore, neglect is related to changes in family structure, such as separation and divorce. It would seem that, after separation, these problems may be accompanied by physical abuse and neglect.

PERPETRATORS AND VICTIMS

The perpetrators of the other forms of child abuse in the context of parental separation and divorce are virtually all family members, as is the case for abuse in other contexts (Cawson, 2002). However, the gender balance of the perpetrators that exists in other contexts is not repeated in this one. Fathers, as opposed to mothers, are the most common perpetrators in the other forms of child abuse before and after separation and divorce, whereas in other contexts it is mothers. Using the data from the Magellan study (Brown et al., 2001), and excluding all cases of sexual abuse, among the substantiated cases of child abuse, some 45 per cent of the perpetrators were fathers acting alone, 13 per cent were fathers acting with other family members (most commonly their own parents), 6.5 per cent were fathers and mothers acting together, 16 per cent were mothers, 3 per cent were maternal grandmothers, 3 per cent were siblings, 3 per cent were step-mothers alone and 3 per cent were step-fathers alone. Recent findings (Cawson, 2002) show the most frequent perpetrators of other forms of abuse in other contexts being mothers (49 per cent), fathers (40 per cent), step-fathers (5 per cent), and step-mothers (3 per cent). This is most likely because of mothers' greater role in the discipline of children. However, the high incidence of domestic violence and its association with fathers rather than mothers would be the reason for the greater role of fathers in these forms of abuse before and following separation and divorce.

Also surprising is the greater incidence in this context of girls as victims, for they have been seen as the more usual victim of child sexual abuse rather than the other forms of abuse. However, some three girls to every two boys were found to be the victim of other forms of abuse. The average age of the children has always been young—an average age of four years in the first Family Court study and eight years in the second (Brown et al., 1998, 2001).

EFFECTS OF ABUSE

All the other forms of child abuse have short- and long-term effects for the children, but these are not as clearly demonstrated as the effects of intra-familial sexual abuse because of the difficulties in singling out the abuse as the only cause of the ill-effects. Many of the other types of abuse take place within an atmosphere of poor-quality emotional parenting that may also be an important contributing factor to the negative effects. (Corby, 2001). The effects that have been noted are poor emotional and social development, such as difficulties in relating to peers and poor school performance, mental illness, drug-taking, criminal behaviour and poor employment subsequently Domestic violence alone, or associated with physical abuse, has been associated with child fatalities. The cessation of domestic violence and provision of support to the children reduce the negative impact on the children. However, if any further domestic violence occurs—even one incident—the child loses any gains made through supportive programs (Cavanagh and Hewitt, 1999). The impact of physical abuse must be similar.

ARRANGEMENTS FOR RESIDENCE AND CONTACT

Reflecting on the various forms of abuse presented in this chapter, it is argued that most of them pose a danger to the child in any circum-stances—let alone in the vulnerable circumstances that follow separation and divorce when only one parent is present at a time. Physical abuse in its various forms, especially when linked to domestic violence and a criminal history, is the form of abuse that is most threatening to the child's physical and emotional welfare. This profile of abuse—physical abuse plus domestic violence plus criminal convictions—is common in the context of parental separation and divorce, and such a profile indicates that the abuse may have been severe, and may well remain so in the future.

Separation does not end the abuse. After separation, one partner—more often the child's mother—will raise questions as to whether contact between the child and the parent who is the perpetrator of the abuse should take place. Clearly the severity of the previous abuse will be a factor in the decision. Also, the extent to which others are implicated in the abuse will need to be considered. Often age is considered to be a factor, on the basis that a very young child will be defenceless; however, older children are not necessarily protected by their age. Sometimes, when severe damage has occurred, the question of contact still arises because of the hope that the perpetrator might change and because of the ideal of all children having the opportunity to benefit from having a relationship with both parents. Sometimes the perpetrator does change, but the results of studies of treatment programs to overcome physical abuse and domestic violence suggest this is not a very common occurrence (Corby, 2001).

When considering the best interests of a child, we know that children do recover from physical abuse and domestic violence. However, it seems that recovery takes place when there is no further contact with the violent parent: even one further episode of violence counteracts the benefits of treatment programs (Cavanagh and Hewitt, 1999). Thus supervised contact is sometimes seen as a way of preventing any further violence. To ensure the child's safety, supervised contact needs to be provided by professionally staffed and managed contact centres that will monitor closely each episode of supervision. Such centres are extending their services beyond facilitating contact and many offer counselling and parenting services. However, even if one gains a place in a professionally staffed centre, it may not assist the child. A recent review of the contact centres federally funded in Australia showed that, where domestic violence or child abuse had occurred, the children did not benefit from supervised contact through a centre (Sheehan et al., 2005).

Sometimes, when a parent has a history of repeated physical abuse—especially combined with domestic violence and an inability to see the damage that this causes their child—no contact will be the most successful option for the child. Some of these parents will accept consent orders of no contact or supervised contact because of the high likelihood of not gaining contact, or because they fear the effects of having this material introduced into court (Brown et al., 2001). The report from the child protection is vital in these negotiations.

ATTITUDES OF SOCIO-LEGAL PROFESSIONALS TO THE OTHER FORMS OF CHILD ABUSE

The other forms of child abuse do not evoke the distaste that child sexual abuse does. At the same time, they do provoke a strong reaction from the professionals. A common reaction is fear—fear caused by threats of violence or actual violence, including intimidatory tactics. Without professionals realising or intending it, these fears—mostly hidden due to seeming unprofessional—influence their professional intervention.

One strategy for dealing with this issue is for professionals to learn as much about abuse in this context as possible so they can accurately observe what is happening, interpret the observations, then assess and document the situation. Such knowledge gives precision and strength to setting out the professionals' view of what is happening and what they think they should then do. All details of the abuse and the families should be documented— in specifics, not in generalities. This material will be the basis for all future actions.

This includes knowing of all possible threats—blatant and subtle—that people might present, and to consider the circumstances under which they are more or less likely to happen. Obviously, if a parent tries to hit a professional, they are more likely to see this as a clear attack, recognise the danger and take action. However, such actions have been observed in court scenes in residence and contact disputes and dismissed as the naturally heightened emotions of the dispute rather than acknowledged as presenting some danger to everyone. In other scenes observed, the threats or indications of violence are more subtle: raised voices, not raised hands; positioning to glare and stare rather than to shout; barricading oneself with furniture and files to obstruct the access of the supervising police; joining protests outside the court and naming professional staff in the protest. These threats are not always recognised for what they really are, but instead are regarded as one of the costs the professional must pay.

Even if professionals ignore such actions, they will still be affected by them. They need to be acknowledged and their impact appreciated. Furthermore, actual threats must be more than acknowledged—they must be explicitly noted, considered and actions for protection planned. The context of parental separation and divorce makes for a threatening work-place for professionals: the clients are highly stressed; the actual events in which the professionals are participating are further stressful for the clients; many of the clients have histories of violence to their spouse, to their children, to other family members and to professionals; some have histories of criminal offences. Client violence is not professional failure, but an issue of ensuring occupational safety.

CONCLUSION

While it is difficult to place the other forms of intra-familial child abuse together for consideration, these forms have some close linkages. In some respects, the other forms of child abuse may seem easier to manage than child sexual abuse: they are more obvious; they are easier to detect; secrecy is not so strongly maintained;the perpetrators are less inclined to deny their blame; the abuse seems closer to conventional behaviour and easier to comprehend; and there is more hope that intervention may bring about improvement.

However, a current debate in family law policy suggests that the picture has become more complex because of the conflict between the ideal that a child should maintain their relationship with both parents and the need to protect the child from further harm (Graycar et al., 2000). In the following chapters, ways in which children can be protected in family law proceedings are discussed.

6

MANAGING FAMILIES AND THEIR PROBLEMS

Professionals working with families where child abuse allegations have emerged in the context of parental separation and divorce argue that they experience difficulties with these families that far exceed the usual client problems in both number and nature. The difficulties appear to lie in three distinct areas affecting clients and the professionals, and also in their interaction. The first is the broad problem that the families share: the parental separation and divorce. The second is the particular problem they are experiencing: the allegations of child abuse. The third lies not in the clients' problems but in the services system available to deal with them: the family law socio-legal service system, which struggles with providing a clear and appropriate—and therefore an effective—response.

While each of these areas has its own complexities, the interaction of the three areas generates an even greater complexity that leads to tensions and frustrations for clients and professionals alike. The problems caused by the parental separation and its impact on family members are exacerbated by the allegations of child abuse and their impact on family members—all of which is, in turn, aggravated by families and professionals seeking solutions from a service system that is not designed to deliver them. Consequently, the families and professionals experience considerable tension as they work together to resolve the issues.

Such tensions are illustrated by the actions of one Sydney legal practitioner who, when confronted with the consistent disregard of a domestic violence order he had obtained for his client on account of her ex-husband's physical attacks on her and the children post-separation, wrote to the ex-husband's solicitor saying: 'Tell that arsehole you represent, Mr John X, to ...' Not unexpectedly, the reply to his letter was similarly phrased.

This chapter aims to deepen professionals' understanding of how to manage these tensions by examining a number of issues that emanate from the first and second areas—the family's separation and divorce experience and the child abuse allegations experience—and the interaction that takes place between these two areas. In contrast to the previous chapter, where the issues emerged from particular cases and where they were discussed in relation to the case, these issues will be discussed in more general terms, and recommendations will be made as to how to deal with them. The issues that arise from the third area, the family law socio-legal service system, will be examined separately in Chapter 7.

THE IMPACT OF DIVORCE ON FAMILIES AND FAMILY MEMBERS

When parents separate and seek a divorce, the services warn them of the serious impact divorce has on all family members. Many services suggest it is the worst emotional experience most people have in a lifetime. Further-more, separation and divorce are not a single event as this description implies, but a series of events that take place over several years with each event having its own impact that adds to the impact of the subsequent events. Thus the so-called worst emotional experience of a lifetime is a number of experiences taking place over a long time (Hetherington and Kelly, 2002).

IMMEDIATE IMPACT ON FAMILY MEMBERS

The most difficult period is usually the first two years after separation, when both parents and children are accommodating to the shock of a compre-hensive and possibly unsought change (Wallerstein and Kelly, 1996; Hether-ington and Kelly, 2002). During this period, almost all parents are noted to be extremely angry with each other (Wallerstein and Kelly, 1996). Whatever the precise circumstances of the separation, their expectations as to their future lives have been profoundly disappointed, their hopes have been dashed, their investment in their partner has disappeared and trust has gone. They see their future as uncertain. At this point, parents are unable to maintain a clear and consistent stance as to their feelings for each other, and they are volatile both in general and towards each other. The enormous changes parents have to make at this early stage, combined with the intensity of their emotions, place considerable pressure on them. They are far more likely to become ill—physically and mentally—than previously. Although whoever makes the break—more commonly women than men today—functions better immediately than the one who is left behind, this short-term advantage does not necessarily last (Jordan, 1996).

For the first twelve months after separation, parents of all kinds and in all situations have been found to provide less warmth and care to their children than they did previously (Wallerstein and Kelly, 1996; Hetherington and Kelly, 2002). Obviously the parents become extremely preoccupied with managing their own feelings and their socio-economic changes at this time. Unfortunately, during this time children actually need more care than usual. Children of all ages find separation hard to understand and the changes hard to manage (Wallestein and Kelly, 1996; Smart et al., 2001). During this period, children are distressed and tend to show anxiety and stress. They have difficulties with their social functioning, such as at school and with friends. Their distress in turn affects their parents, who are already having difficulties of their own.

As time goes by, the situation improves for both the parents and the children of most families. Some research notes improvements after the first two years (Wallerstein and Kelly, 1996), and certainly some six years after the separation most family members are coping quite well. Nevertheless, a substantial minority of both parents and children are not. Among parents, some 30 per cent fail to cope (Hetherington and Kelly, 2002). This non-coping group is described as falling into two categories: those who are rootless, insecure and unhappy—and mostly male; and those who are overwhelmed and liable to depression and substance abuse—a group which includes both male and female members. Among children, a similar minority—some 30 per cent—is not coping (Rodgers and Prior, 1998). Whether this is due to the fact that, in some families, the pattern of reduced care persists beyond the initial two-year period, leaving the children more vulnerable to risk and to stress, or whether there is another explanation is not yet clear. Parental separation and divorce bring many changes, and it is not clear which changes bring about which specific consequences (Rodgers and Prior, 1998).

Thus, while the impact of parental separation and divorce is severe for all family members in the short term, with parents and children being highly emotional, intensely angry, anxious and erratic in their thinking, for a sizeable group of parents and children (albeit the minority of family members), these feelings last longer and they grapple with them for an extended time.

THE IMPACT OF THE CHILD ABUSE ALLEGATIONS

In addition to grappling with the separation, some families must contend with the problem of the child abuse allegations and with the climate of violence that so often surrounds them. Some 30 per cent of all marriages in Australia fail because of domestic violence (Stanton et al., 2000). In partnerships where child abuse allegations occur, an even higher proportion feature domestic violence; in these families, the child abuse and the domestic violence are the most common single cause of the failure of the partnership.

In the Magellan project, for example, some 44 per cent of fathers and some 21 per cent of mothers exhibited violence towards their spouse. The surrounding violence was more extensive than this description suggests, because in some 30 per cent of these families the parents had experienced violence from their own parents, siblings or other relatives. Another component of the violence was the children's violence to their parents. Some parents—8 per cent, of whom most were mothers—experienced violence from their children, in some cases so severe as to warrant hospitalisation. In one family, two young boys of eight and ten broke their mother's ribs when she tried to break up a fight between them and their two younger brothers (Brown et al., 2001).

Moreover, such violence travels beyond the home. Some 30 per cent of parents had been violent to people outside their immediate family during the period of the separation and the dispute, most commonly to child protection staff and to other family law socio-legal professionals (Brown et al., 1998, 2001).

Thus many of these parents—more often fathers, but also mothers—are not just extremely angry, but are violent—to their children, to their spouses, to other family members and to professionals. Family courts internationally have experienced violence from clients, and the Family Court of

Australia is no exception. Four public attacks on the Family Court and/or their staff have taken place in New South Wales resulting in two deaths. In Victoria, one has taken place, resulting in no injuries to anyone except the perpetrator. It may seem surprising that such crimes have occurred, but a high proportion of families where child abuse allegations are made in the context of parental separation and divorce have histories of criminal offences. The proportion of parents with a history of criminal offences ranges from a low of 2.9 per cent among mothers at the Melbourne Reg istry to a high of 25 per cent among mothers at the Dandenong Reg istry (a registry of the court located in an outer Melbourne suburb with a low socio-economic profile in a dying industrial area), and from a low of 39.5 per cent among fathers at the Melbourne Reg istry to a high of 50 per cent among fathers at the Dandenong and Canberra registries (Brown et al., 1998, 2001).

IMPACT OF THE ALLEGATIONS ON THE SUBSTANTIATED PERPETRATOR OF THE CHILD ABUSE

No one has systematically questioned those who are ultimately substantiated as the perpetrators of abuse about their reaction to the formal making of allegations against them. Some evidence suggests that such allegations increase the level of post-separation anger (FLPAG, 2001), presumably because the allegations—even when known by the perpetrator to be correct—are seen as a challenge to their ongoing control of the family. At the very least, the perpetrator might imagine that a formal allegation brings with it the threat of the loss of either the residence of, or contact with, the child and possibly loss of contact with the spouse as well. More of the substantiated perpetrators of abuse than not are perpetrators of domestic violence, with the most common type of domestic violence in this context being episodic battering, a severe type of violence used as a way of obtaining control (Brown et al., 1998). If the perpetrators have ruled their family through domestic violence and child abuse in the past, they may believe they can continue to do so in the future. They may seek to continue the violence after the separation, and go to extreme lengths following the allegations to demonstrate that this is so. For example, following such allegations, one father set fire to the family home where all the children's clothing and toys had been left when the mother fled the home.

As these parents are from all socio-economic classes and from all cultures, there is no one form or single pattern in the expression of their anger or violence at this stage. One father attacked his ex-wife's parents and a shopkeeper while the parents were out shopping, broke the windows of his former wife's flat on many occasions and stalked his child's paediatrician for six months.The range of aggressive reactions noted (Brown et al., 1998, 2001) include verbal and physical attacks on former spouses, on other family members, on passers by, verbal and physical attacks on professionals and their property, and destruction of other property. It is important to recognise that such behaviour—while understandable—is not acceptable, and it is dangerous for family members and professionals alike.

Once the abuse is substantiated by the child protection service, the perpetrators become motivated to negotiate in relation to their dispute Until this happens, they show little preparedness to do so (Brown et al., 1998). Delaying investigation delays potential post-separation cooperation; delays in investigation prolong post-separation violence.Thus the Magellan program set up the requirement in the first hearing for the making of an order for a referral to the child protection service for an investigation of the allegation and a report to the court within a month.This step, which used the expert authority of the child protection service in the investigation of and reporting about the allegations, proved to be effective in setting up a framework for negotiation, and some families negotiated a resolution at this stage (Brown et al., 2001). Furthermore, where families did not resolve the dispute at this stage, the substantiation provided a framework against which negotiation could eventually take place (Brown et al, 2001).

WORKING WITH SUBSTANTIATED PERPETRATORS

Clients who are substantiated perpetrators require skilled intervention, including knowledge of the best strategies and knowledge of the impact of such clients on professionals so that the strategies can be used to full effect.

The strategies advocated for dealing with such clients are numerous, but the efficacy of many remains untested.The simplest strategies are those used in marketing: expressing empathy with the client; demonstrating a motivation to work on the problem with the client; and promptly address-ing the issues the client raises (Brown and Smale, 2001). This means obtaining information from the client about the issues of concern. The professional needs to identify with the client the priority issues, and to maintain focus on them, avoiding 'red herrings'. The professional must remain calm, and speak clearly and quietly.

Additional useful strategies are giving frequent explanations, moving slowly and quietly, speaking without emotion, breaking off at times to reduce tension, and reflecting contradictions calmly if they occur (Forrest, 2002). As these clients are not highly motivated to assume responsibility for their problems, the explanations given should state and restate the professional's role and goals and the limitations to these. These explanations should be used as boundaries and as a framework to guide the interview, and they should be maintained throughout. A new model for working with clients who have not voluntarily sought services, developed by Trotter (2004, 2006), is relevant to working with these clients, as they feel the services they are using are not of their own choice. In this model, which has been used to good effect in child protection services, the professional uses the framework of a clear explanation of roles and goals, a collaborative problem-solving approach, and the maintenance of a constant monitoring and reinforcement of pro-social or law-abiding values. The model has the advantage of being research tested and of being explained in great detail in both theory and practice. Recently this model has been given another component to adapt it for use with parents in major conflict over their children's parenting. In this approach, a focus on the children is used whereby children's views in general and in particular instances are sought and placed before the parents throughout all intervention (Brown and Smale, 2006).

Working with substantiated perpetrators is a high-risk activity for professionals, according to the occupational health and safety experts, as both the tasks being undertaken and the clients being served are considered high risk or 'hot' (Mayhew, 2000), and likely to generate the sort of tension that erupts into violence in the workplace. The tasks are seen as 'hot' because they involve face-to-face contact with clients about problems of their own violence that may not be conceded. The clients are seen as 'hot' because they are in a state of emotional distress from the marital breakdown and from the allegations of abuse. Furthermore, the clients have a history of violence—to children, spouses, other family members and professionals. Some will have aggravating problems like drug abuse and mental illness as well.

The view from occupational health is that only a comprehensive framework of containment will ensure a safe working environment for client interaction with the professional.The framework includes offices without opportunities for violence: with easy exits, alarms and other security support, and no furniture or other items that can be used as weapons. It is also important to ensure that waiting times for clients are not long. The framework incorporates training for all staff in prevention of violence, such as not excusing any hint or threat of violence; not being alone in your office suite with a client; keeping your home and work identity separate; training for staff protection; and debriefing if violence should occur (Mayhew, 2000).

IMPACT OF THE CLIENT AND THEIR VIOLENCE ON THE PROFESSIONAL

Most professionals understand that a client who has been violent may provoke in them unprofessional feelings, feelings of distaste, disapproval and rejection that can interfere with their aim of giving a professional service to the client. They understand that they should remain neutral and objective in their attitude to the client, and not let any distaste they feel for such a person influence what they do. They may also understand that they need to know what emotions violence and the abuse of children arouse in them, and how they can move past such feelings to work with the client. Many will recognise also that their feelings may be stronger than anticipated because of personal experiences that are reawoken by the client's past and present behaviour. Professionals finding themselves in such situations will often know that they should examine their feelings, and most will believe they can manage well if they do this.

However, few professionals appreciate that they can also have more subtle and elaborate reactions to these clients. Research has shown there is an interaction that occurs between professionals and the perpetrators of the abuse that causes the professional to discount the severity of the perpetrator's violence to the child and their violence to any others in the family or in the community experiencing the abuse, including themselves, (Stanley and Goddard, 2002). It is suggested that the client uses actual or implied violence in the professional–client relationship to disempower the professional and to remove any threat the professionals intervention might bring. Professionals find themselves caught in a dilemma or conflict that they find difficult to resolve. They find that it is impossible to admit either the client's real intentions or the fearful and immobilising impact that the client's implied or actual violence is having on them. To do so would run counter to their professional education and their expectations of their professional self. Clients like this are not part of any professionals image of their clientele. Being frightened as a professional is not part of any professionals image of themselves. Summit (1983) suggests that professionals defend themselves by accommodating or adjusting to the violence; Howitt (1993) believes they minimise and discount it; Stanley and Goddard (2002) suggest that professionals become hostage to it and are powerless in the face of it. In other words, via one mechanism or another, the professionals deny the actual violence and its impact on them and anyone else.

Such information comes from the child protection services, where the clients are traditionally economically disadvantaged. In the context of parental separation and divorce, where child abuse allegations have been made, the families are not so disadvantaged. Possibly the threats to the professionals in this context are more frequent and are even stronger when they occur.

All propose that the professional has to recognise and admit the existence of such clients, and to recognise and admit the impact such clients have on them. Protection that allows professionals to work with these clients derives from the framework the occupational health and safety experts advocate, and it means ongoing recognition, support and supervision from the workplace for these issues. Workplaces that do not admit such possibilities damage professionals and cause further defensive avoidance of the problem of violent clients (Morrison, 1994). The professional must document implied and actual threats, and report threats and incidents to their organisation and to the police.

IMPACT OF UNSUBSTANTIATED ALLEGATIONS ON THE ALLEGED PERPETRATORS

All parents who are faced with a formal documented allegation of child abuse will feel anxious and afraid. They will worry about their ability to combat such an allegation, about what the process entails and about whether they can endure the emotional distress of the investigation when their distress is already high due to their separation. They will be afraid of the outcome of the allegation for their children and for themselves. Already angry over the separation, they will feel even more angry at the accusations and at the accuser. Any remnant of trust between the parents may now be destroyed.

We know little of the experience of being investigated, but what we know shows it to be extremely unpleasant (Howitt, 1993; FLPAG, 2002; Hay, 2003). The accused feels an extreme sense of powerlessness, viewing the former partner and the court authorities as having taken control of their own and their children's lives (Hay, 2003). For some parents, it seems that the former partner has been able to extend their oppression and abuse beyond the partnership and that there is no protection anywhere against indefinite abuse; they see the authorities as acting together with the former partner in maintaining the abuse (Hay, 2005). The sense of powerlessness is continued by the later realisation that, as an alleged but unproved perpetrator, they have not been found innocent—just not proven to be guilty. They feel they have an unjustifiable stain on their character that cannot be removed (FLPAG, 2001). Since investigations reveal only a relatively few allegations to be clearly false, with the majority of those not demonstrated to be true classed as unsubstantiated, (Brown et al., 1998, 2001), for those accused in these circumstances and not found guilty, there is a sense that the threat from the allegations is never removed. The anger about this is considerable, and lasts for a long time.

WORKING WITH ALLEGED PERPETRATORS WHERE THE ALLEGATIONS ARE NOT SUBSTANTIATED

Working with alleged perpetrators where the abuse has not been substantiated means working with clients who feel anxious, frightened and disempowered, and thus depressed about the possibility of their success in anything they do to protect themselves or their children. The position they find they are in, under the shadow of an unjust allegation, gives rise also to considerable anger.

These clients need clear explanations as to the role of the professional and the goals of any actions the professional is taking. They need empathy and a demonstrated commitment to working on the problem, promptly, calmly and quietly. Anger and depression make people deaf, and explanations may need to be repeated frequently—especially since their position is somewhat surreal.When the allegation has come as a counter-blow from a violent spouse, the situation becomes a nightmare for the accused perpetrator, and their sense of powerlessness and despair is even greater. These clients need considerable support, and often need additional assistance from a counselling service.

At the same time, some of the alleged but unsubstantiated allegations are possibly true—even if they are, as yet, unable to be proven. Professionals are then working with clients whom they suspect have abused the children. This is very difficult for the professionals,who feel obliged to try to protect the children and the other parent without any real authority to do so. Because professionals in such situations often feel they must hurry to rescue either the children or the other partner from the perpetrator's as yet unsubstantiated abuse, they are tempted to overstep the authority of their role and expertise (Corby, 2000). They must resist such a temptation and proceed carefully, putting in place any protection they can.

IMPACT ON THE PARTNER MAKING THE ALLEGATIONS

When allegations of child abuse occur in the context of parental separation and divorce, they are usually instigated by one or the other parent, rather than by a professional from an agency or by a friend or other relative. Making an allegation against one's former partner or a member of their family has a particular impact.

Approximately half of all allegations concern abuse that began before the partnership ended—abuse that forms a major component of the termination of the partnership.When the allegations arise in this way, the partner making them is trying to solve a problem with which they have lived for some time but which they can no longer endure. Leaving the partnership is one step towards stopping the abuse, but another—that is, making the allegations—is needed to ensure the abuse does not continue during post-separation contact. In some instances,the parent will have been advised to take this action by the child protection service (Brown et al., 1998, 2001; Fehlberg and Kelly, 2000).

Any parent who discovers the other parent may be abusing their child suffers guilt that this has happened and anxiety about the best action to take.Their expectations about what will happen after the allegation is made are often incorrect, however. The parent making the allegations will be surprised to learn that the allegation does not automatically stop contact with the alleged perpetrator, but that the possibility of abuse has to be investigated by the child protection authority. Some parents find their allegation is not taken seriously by their particular state protection authority, and that it is dismissed by the authority and subsequently by others—including other agencies and relatives (Brown et al., 1998; Fehlberg and Kelly, 2000; Hay, 2003). At this point, parents can be quite shocked, as they had no idea how the service system would deal with such allegations, or that there could be any ill-effects from making them. Parents report discovering that they have become very isolated at this time, and that they need considerable support (Kaye et al., 2003a). Some parents suffer retribution from their spouses over the allegations and, with the investigation process, both they and the professionals are at risk.

However, the most severe retribution reported—murder and suicide—does not generally come after allegations of abuse have been made in relation to a residence and contact dispute. While research is sparse on parents' post-separation murder of their children and/or spouse, and possible subsequent suicide, the violence generally seems unrelated to any actual dispute, but rather to the violent partner's sense of their own situation (Johnson, 2002). Such parents see the separation and/or the divorce as being beyond their level of tolerance, and as requiring them to punish their spouse. Retrospectively, such partners are seen as suffering from mental illness; however, they were not generally regarded in this way previously.

While about half of the allegations are made about abuse that has taken place before the separation, the rest are made after the separation—sometimes many years later. In some instances, the intervening years have led to new living arrangements that have produced the abuse, such as in one family where a child who was four at the time of divorce was found to have been abused four years later by the teenage son of her new stepmother. In other instances, a parent or other relative closely associated with the child does not begin to abuse the child until after the separation, either because of increased opportunities or for other personal reasons.

WORKING WITH THE PARENT MAKING THE ALLEGATIONS

Despite the views of Gardner, a parent making such allegations is not doing so lightly, but rather taking a serious step to protect their children. The frustrations they experience when the services do not seem responsive to the problem, the isolation they experience and the (often justifiable) fear of retribution make them very vulnerable and in need of considerable support.

When the parent making the allegations has been the victim of domestic violence, their anxiety and fear will be even greater. Many such parents are so overwhelmed that they become depressed, disorganised in their thinking and apparently unable to plan for themselves. In these situations, they will need long-term counselling and support. Many professionals cannot imagine how vulnerable such clients are. For example, one male solicitor—knowing how vulnerable his client was to the threats of her violent former partner—made sure he was with her at all times while they were attending a hearing in the Family Court. However, he did not think about this when she went to the toilet, so her former spouse seized this opportunity and followed her into the empty ladies toilet, where he threatened her and the children to force her to withdraw the allegations, stop the dispute and return to him.

IMPACT OF THE ALLEGATIONS AND THE PROCESS OF INVESTIGATION ON THE CHILDREN

Children are already distressed by their parents' separation. When allegations of child abuse are added to the mix, the children become more distressed, especially when the Family Court proceedings take place. The numbers of children experiencing severe emotional distress in these circumstances are high (some 29 per cent) and their distress is manifested as depression, extreme anger, great anxiety and sometimes as suicidal feelings even in very young children (Brown et al., 1998, 2001). There are many reasons for this distress. They include fears about future contact with the alleged or actual perpetrator, fears about each court event, fears about the outcome of the court proceedings, a sense that they are powerless, that they are not believed or what they say will be disregarded, and fears that the outcome of the court proceedings will not justify the costs to them of their disclosures (Hay, 2003). The only information about children's experiences of residence and contact disputes where child abuse allegations have been made (Hay, 2003) paints a sad picture of the children, as the legal processes fail to accord them any respect or protection.

WORKING WITH CHILDREN WHO ARE THE ALLEGED VICTIMS
OF FAMILY ABUSE

Children whose parents have separated and/or divorced, including those involved in family law proceedings, have put forward their views as to how they wish to be treated by professionals(Smart et al., 2001; Hay, 2003). They wish to be seen face to face, not spoken about behind their backs. They want clear explanations as to the professionals purpose in seeing them, expressed in plain language They want to be told exactly what will take place in interviews and at court. They do not want to be tricked or persuaded against their will. They appreciate the truth, even when it is not palatable. They believe that some professionals approach them about the abuse from a starting point of disbelief, and want them to deny it, which makes them feel they are not being respected or protected. Even when the abuse is substantiated, they comment that professionals do not fully understand what was done to them, how it was done and what it has meant to them. Consequently, the professionals show little understanding of their vulnerability and fears (Hay, 2003). They feel that they are on trial over the abuse, and that the legal process—supposedly about them and their care—keeps them on the edge of events (Hay, 2003). This perception of the disempowerment of children by the legal process has been identified as affecting children in all court jurisdictions (ALRC, 1997). The children see themselves as more rational and resolute than the professionals realise, and they believe they should be treated with respect and as capable individuals.

The children want far more support than they receive. They look to their parents for support, but the pressure on their parents is very great and often the children need more support than the parents can provide (Hay, 2003). Much of the intervention that takes place does not have a support element for the children. Thus it is desirable to find a way of providing support—as, for example, through a counselling agency that will accept children as clients, one that will understand the impact of the parental separation, the abuse allegations, the legal processes and any actual abuse.

OTHER FACTORS

There are a number of factors that add to the complexity of the separation and divorce combined with the allegations of abuse and the difficulties for the professional in dealing with them. These include ethnic and racial diversity, intellectual disability and mental illness.

Australia is a nation comprising many different racial and ethnic groups. However, the former Chief Justice of the Family Court of Australia has argued that family law processes have not taken account of cultural diversity until very recently (Nicholson, 2003). In 1999, the Family Court conducted an audit of its responses to cultural diversity and found that the court had no bridges to its services for clients from non-English speaking countries, no signs in community languages other than in English, few multi-lingual staff, few interpreters, no links with non-English speaking communities, no staff training in cultural sensitivities, no booklets in languages of the recent groups of immigrants and more. As a result, the court has introduced Arabic and Chinese translations of the Family Court book that explains court processes, begun staff training in cultural sensitivity, and introduced translator software on the Family Court website (Nicholson, 2003).

The families who have come to the court with child abuse allegations in residence and contact disputes reflect the full extent of Australia's ethnic and racial diversity. Depending on the registry involved, some 6–22 per cent of parents were born overseas in non-English speaking countries (Brown et al., 1998, 2001). The representation of overseas-born people is similar to that found in the general population. This may be surprising to those who are of the view that child abuse is a problem of certain cultures only—it is not, and it exists worldwide.

There are a number of issues related to working with families brought up with different cultural norms and different societal institutions encountered by professionals working in the family law service system. The most obvious is that of language, where the client's English is poor and communication is difficult. Even when a client's English seems adequate, a term or expression may be misunderstood, as concepts are not the same in all cultures—even at an apparently simple and indisputable level. Thus asking about a person's family may cause confusion because the term 'family' may mean one thing to the professional and another to the client. All language, including common terms, has to be made clear, and it may be necessary to repeatedly question and define the terms being used. This may become more difficult when an interpreter is required. Accredited interpreters have been advocated by non-English speaking groups as the best to use in such circumstance (Nicholson, 2003). However, there are no interpreters who specialise in working in family law settings, so the problem of differences in understanding and experience in family law legislation and services may be substantial for any client.

Furthermore, there may be differences in each culture's approach to parental separation and divorce. Australia's family law legislation, with its no-fault provisions, emphasis on negotiation, equal treatment of both genders and priority given to the child's best interests, is regarded as advanced internationally The supporting family law service system is complex and unusual in both its sophistication and its fragmentation.It is a secular system, and is not integrated with any religious system.There can be misunderstandings and clashes between what has been customary and what is required now. A client who has come to Australia as an adult may have no friends or relatives who understand the system and who can help bridge the gap. Thus it is often necessary for such clients to be provided with additional support.

Another major issue for professionals is gaining an understanding of the meaning of the alleged abusive behaviour in another culture so that the behaviour can be properly assessed,its meaning understood, and intervention planned. Professionals ask repeatedly: is the behaviour of the parent typical of parenting in that culture or is it atypical and abuse? Is it abuse in the other culture, as it is in Australia?What meaning does the behaviour have for the parent who is alleged to have inflicted it? The issue is not that abuse should be excused because the parent does not regard it as such. Cultural norms are not able to override human rights that have been expressed in legislation, and there is legislation in every state defining what constitutes child abuse in the Australian culture.

However, the meaning of the behaviour is important in determining what to do about it. It is important to know the details of parenting behaviour in the parents' culture of origin, as they may still be part of that culture if they are living in a network of families from their original homeland.What does parenting in that culture imply about any particular behaviour of these parents, what are the different approaches taken in that culture and what has been the parents' prior experience in that culture? Mostly these doubts arise over physical abuse and neglect because the cultural norms in these areas seem to be more diverse.

Indigenous parents face particular problems regarding allegations of child abuse in the context of parental separation and divorce (Kaye et al., 2003a). They mistrust state child protection services more than other groups because of the history of the removal of Indigenous children by state child welfare authorities; consequently, they are less likely to take such problems to any legal authority, including the Family Court of Australia. At the same time, research (Stanley, 2003) has revealed widespread parental abuse of children in Indigenous communities, especially child sexual abuse accompanied by domestic violence. Indigenous women are calling for action from male and female Indigenous people to overcome a culture of male violence that oppresses women and children (Fair, 2003).

Due to the fear Indigenous women have expressed about the consequences of their speaking out and taking action over their own and their children's abuse, the position of Indigenous people making allegations of child abuse in this context was reviewed (Brown et al., 2001). Few parents making such allegations were Indigenous: only some 2 per cent of mothers and 4 per cent of fathers were Aboriginal or Torres Strait Islanders (Brown et al., 2001). These families used specialist Aboriginal legal services, and this type of service may have been the reason they were able to use the family law service system at all. Their families were more dispersed across the various states than other families, so they had some difficulties in using a national service that relies on supporting state services. Nevertheless, their disputes were resolved at very early stages in the program (Brown et al., 2001).

Another group that requires a special approach is parents with an intellectual disability Society's attitude to those with an intellectual disability has changed. Once seen as unable to live independently, to partner and to parent, they are no longer seen in such a negative light. Many with an intellectual disability live in the community independently, partner and parent.

Child protection services have feared that intellectual disability will be a drawback to parenting, and have attempted to determine whether this is in fact so. Intellectual disability does appear as the fourth in ranked order of six characteristics associated with parental abuse (Allen Counsulting Group, 2003). Considering the lower incidence of parents with intellectual disability, it may be a more prominent characteristic than is currently presented. Certainly, some 7 per cent of mothers in Project Magellan were identified by their legal representative as being intellectually disabled. It is interesting that no fathers were so identified, although courtroom observations suggested otherwise.

Problems do occur for these clients because of the speed of courtroom decision-making. When the professionals have sufficient time to canvass the full range of options with the clients, they are better able to manage decision-making in family law proceedings. When new options arise in the formality of hearings and people have to decide quickly, they can make poor choices. They can agree to arrangements that they cannot carry out. For example, one mother with an intellectual disability agreed to find someone to drive her 150 kilometres each alternate weekend to ensure that the children, split between her and the father, were together each weekend. Ultimately she could not carry out this arrangement. Such clients need careful preparation and support, and do not do well if pushed to a speedy decision.

Those parents with mental illness also need additional assistance Today, mental illness is more common—or at least more commonly recognised—but less crippling. Treatment is more successful, often without long hospitalisations. People with a mental illness live in the community to a greater extent than previously.

Parental mental illness or psychiatric disability has been identified as being associated with child abuse. After domestic violence, it is the second highest of the six ranked characteristics of parents who abuse their children (Allen Consulting Group, 2003). It is associated with all types of abuse, but particularly with neglect (Cawson et al., 2001).

Such clients have special problems and difficulties, making them vulnerable in many ways. On the one hand, they are vulnerable to scapegoating and stigmatisation from the other parent and their legal representatives, and on the other they may have an illogical perception of events and of their children's needs. They may be inflicting abuse without understanding what they are doing. For example, one parent in the midst of a bout of severe depression, who had his daughter of five on an overnight contact visit, could not appreciate his former partner's distress at finding him unconscious from an overdose, with the child sitting beside him, when she came to pick up the daughter the next morning. People with mental illness may be well enough to work on the issues lying between them and the other parent at one time but not at another time, and the disagreements may wander along without resolution. They may be unreasonable in their relationship with professionals, but not be aware of this. They may feel as if they are being persecuted and the professional and other family members may feel similarly.

Strategies similar to those used with clients who are violent can be used successfully here; such strategies provide a framework to protect the mentally ill and to maintain focus on resolving issues. They require empathy, a demonstrated motivation to work on the problem, a collaborative approach to the problem, clear explanations of the role of the professional and what goals can and are being tackled, and a calm, quiet and neutral approach. It may seem illogical to propose such strategies for those who may not be reasonable themselves, but other strategies are not successful. It is important to maintain focus on the problem to be dealt with. Using another person as a support—someone who is trusted and who can explain and reinforce information—is very useful. Keeping meetings short also helps. One parent with a long-term mental illness who maintained that his wife abused him and their only child was prepared to accept throughout all his family law proceedings the support of a federal police officer. The policeman spent the proceedings explaining and interpreting the legal events to the father. Psychiatric disabilities are not fixed and unchanging; the person's mood and understanding can vary considerably. If a parent maintains a consistently unreasonable approach, it is better not to persist but to attempt another meeting in the hope that the next one will bring an improvement.

A particular problem is that such parents are one of the two most common sources of allegations of abuse that prove to be incorrect. At the same time, they may be abusive themselves. They can make repeated notifications with no basis in fact over lengthy periods of time. It is tempting to avoid the issue, hoping that when the person recovers, the allegations will stop. They may indeed stop, but then start again. The allegations they make must be addressed promptly, as is the case with all others.

A final group of parents to consider are those with substance abuse problems. The incidence of those with such problems is growing extremely rapidly and some 26 per cent of mothers and some 41 per cent of fathers in the first Family Court study (Brown et al., 1998) were identified as having substance abuse issues, with rather more being due to alcohol than to drugs. Somewhat oddly, this group did not stand out as clearly needing additional help in that the issues identified in the court as the priority problems were those of violence and mental illness rather than substance abuse. This may have been because the substance abuse was more often from the use of alcohol rather than drugs, and problems of parenting while using drugs were not flowing to the Family Court. Instead, they flowed to the Children's Court, where such parents have been noted to frequently be (Sheehan, 2001). Occasionally, when both parents had drug-abuse problems, grandparents sought the residence of the children against the wishes of their own children. One of the most difficult issues arising here was the scattering of the locations of grandparents, parents and children among the different states. The poor coordination between state child protection services became a great problem in working with these families (Brown et al., 2001).

CONCLUSION

Working with parents and children when child abuse allegations have been made post-separation and divorce can be very difficult. The reasons are not mysterious: all family members are the captives of the devastation of parental separation and divorce, and of the anger and volatility that they produce. The allegations of abuse bring further distress and tensions. Many of the families have histories of other family violence, domestic violence and sibling violence, and many family members have been violent to people outside the family. A climate of violence surrounds many of these families.

Working with clients who are perpetrators of violence, some of which is inflicted on the professionals, is very difficult—especially since there is little recognition of this element in the work. The cloud obscuring the violence in these families has handicapped development of strategies for working with them. However, there are strategies to use, beginning with a recognition of the existence of the violence in these families, extending to comprehensive general prevention policies in the workplace and including education and support of the professionals by their employing organisation.

Other factors can compound the difficulties of these families, including the wide ethnic and racial diversity of parents in the community and the issues of intellectual disability psychiatric illness and substance abuse.

7

MANAGING THE FAMILY LAW
SERVICE SYSTEM

When professionals in this area seek services for their clients, they find themselves lost in a maze of fragmented—even contradictory—services (FLPAG, 2001). The family law socio-legal services system has grown since the introduction of the first family law legislation without any overall direction or integrating policies. As a service system, it has no consistency and no transparency—and therefore no ease of use. Even professionals need guidance to navigate it and wring benefits for their clients. In addition, it was not designed to confront and resolve child abuse allegations and, while it has attempted reforms to meet this new social problem, it does not do so well.

The purpose of this chapter is to identify the problems of the service system and to present strategies for professionals to use to overcome these problems. Professionals know the system is unresponsive to their clients' needs, but they do not know the exact nature of the problems or why they have developed; they may also not know that the problems are system-wide. Thus they struggle to devise successful strategies to overcome the problems and remain very dissatisfied throughout the process.

THE FAMILY LAW SOCIO-LEGAL SERVICE SYSTEM AS A MAZE

When the Family Law Pathways Advisory Group (FLPAG) was constituted by the Commonwealth Attorney-General and the Commonwealth

Minister for Family and Community Services to create a road map for the integrated development of the family law socio-legal service system, it became clear that the many flaws in the service system had brought it into disrepute (FLPAG, 2001). The service system had not been designed as a whole, but added one service at a time by different sponsors from government and non-government bodies at local, state and federal levels. All the organisations had different goals, different forms of management, different structures, different procedures, different ranges of discipline groups, different communication patterns and different language. The major commonality was their client group—those who had experienced partnership breakdown and divorce—although some services had no focus on partnership breakdown, while others did. Few had any recognition of the way the system impelled clients to move from one organisation to another for assistance, and few had any awareness of the impact one organisation had on another or on the system as a whole.

THE CORE OF THE SYSTEM

The core of the system was identified as the Family Courts of Australia and Western Australia. These two family court systems operated side by side because Western Australia had stayed outside the coverage of the Commonwealth family law legislation, preferring to adopt its own—identical—legislation. Moreover, the Family Court of Australia, covering the remaining seven states and territories, exhibited through its many local registries around the nation differences in processes and outcomes from place to place. It did not have a nationally consistent approach (Kimm, 2005).

The core included an additional set of jurisdictions, the Magistrates Court in all states and territories (except Western Australia), since preliminary hearings concerning children can take place in any state Magistrates Court under the Commonwealth family law legislation. In 2000, the Federal Magistrates Service was added to the core of the system (Bryant, 2000), fragmenting it even further. However, with the appointment of the Honourable Diana Bryant, the former Chief Federal Magistrate as the new Chief Justice of the Family Court of Australia upon the retirement of the Honourable Alastair Nicholson, the two services are moving together to establish a combined family law registry with shared services, one file and one form, though with two separate courts (FCA, 2005). The Family Court and federal magistracy are supported by the federal police force, which ensures compliance with its orders, and order and protection for family members in court hearings. The state and territory Magistrates courts are supported by the state and territory police forces.

Supporting the core are the eight state and territory legal aid commissions that are empowered to fund parents' and children's legal representation in family law proceedings. This assistance required by the high cost of litigation in the Family Court, is provided on a means and merit eligibility, according to the means of the litigants and the merits of their case, and it is provided in the form of grants to the litigants' private legal representatives or through the allocation of one of the commissions' own employed legal practitioner to the party concerned. The state legal aid commissions provide legal representation for children in family law disputes at the request of the Family Court. The legal aid commissions are guided by the policies of their funding body in family law disputes—that is, the Commonwealth Attorney-General's Department—but, despite Commonwealth policy guidance, the legal aid commissions' family law services vary from state to state. Some, though not all, provide services such as information and referral, counselling and mediation. In addition, there are generalist community legal centres providing information and advice, and specialist community legal centres for women and for Aboriginal and Torres Strait Islanders, providing information, advice and legal representation. Adjoining these services are the private practices of solicitors and barristers, many of whom are specialists in family law.

Standing close to the core, in its shadow and as an alternative to court proceedings, are the community-based mediation services for those involved in family law disputes. These services may be part of another general mediation service, part of a counselling service or of a community legal centre, or they may stand alone. Usually they aim at excluding clients with family violence problems, but they cannot be certain that they have done this, since exclusion rests primarily on the self-reporting of violence by the family members. In the past, their services have been used by few people involved in family law disputes, and their long-term potential has been questioned. Criticisms have been made because of power imbalances between the mediating partners, the difficulty in dealing with family violence including child abuse, their inability to deal directly with children, their need for clients who are articulate and have well-developed language skills, and an absence of tight regulation (McCoy, 2005; Batagol et al., 2006).

However, Commonwealth government policy released in 2004 in a discussion paper titled *A New Approach to the Family Law System* (Attorney-General's Department, 2004) has proposed 65 new family relationship centres across the country, offering post-separation parenting services including information, advice and dispute-resolution services such as mediation. While it will not be compulsory to use such services, it will not be possible to proceed to the Family Court without first attending such a service or an equivalent private practitioner service, or obtaining an exemption from using such a service in the case of domestic violence and/or child abuse. With the opening of these new centres in July 2006, the flaws detected in the small amount of current community-based mediation may become more obvious and serious in their consequences.

THE COMMONWEALTH FINANCIAL BENEFITS AGENCIES

Standing alongside the core of the family law socio-legal service system are two large national agencies providing financial benefits for family members following parental separation and divorce. One is Centrelink, which provides a range of financial benefits under Commonwealth legislation for individuals and families, including payment to sole parents for their own support and for that of their children. Centrelink provides information, counselling and referral to a wide variety of other social services. It employs a large staff of social workers for this purpose. Centrelink has long been a first port of call for parents after separation.

The other national agency is the newer Child Support Agency (CSA), operating under its own Commonwealth legislation, through which payment for the support of children of parents who have separated and/or divorced is determined. If the parents cannot reach a private arrangement for the financial support of their children post-separation, one or the other parent can apply for an assessment from the Child Support Agency and pay privately according to that assessment or have CSA channel payments from the payer—usually the male non-resident parent—to the recipient—usually the female resident parent. That agency also provides information and referral, with a policy of ensuring the client is properly hooked up with the suggested additional service.

The Child Support Agency has been criticised ever since it began in 1988. The agency has been attacked for large payer debts and its methods of working with those who pay as well as with those who receive payment. It has been able to improve its work by reducing payer debts, by instituting better links with other agencies, especially Centrelink, and by using a more proactive mentoring relationship with payers in the first year. Criticisms of its assessment methods and the formula by which it determines payments have been addressed by a Commonwealth inquiry that has proposed a new formula that will give more consideration to payers who are supporting children from subsequent families and to payers on higher incomes. The new formula will also recognise the higher costs of older children and take the recipient parent's part-time earnings into greater account (Ministerial Taskforce on Child Support, 2005). These recommendations will be phased in during the period 2006–08.

COUNSELLING AGENCIES

Scattered around these services are the national non–government agencies that provide separation and family relationship counselling, like Relationships Australia, Anglicare and Centacare. To these should be added state and local non-government agencies that provide similar services, but whose geographical range is more restricted. There are also the private practices of the therapeutic professionals—counsellors, psychiatrists, psychologists and social workers. In addition to providing therapy to family members, their staff may be used as experts to give evidence in family law proceedings in court of their assessment of a parent or child's functioning on behalf of that parent or a child, or be appointed by the court as a court expert for the same purpose.

The original Commonwealth family law legislation did not make provision for family violence as an issue in parental separation and divorce but, as already discussed, family violence has emerged as a major factor in partnership breakdown, both as a cause and a consequence. Thus a number of specialist services relating to the various kinds of family violence have been established and become part of the service system. These include women's refuges and domestic violence resources centres that are aimed primarily at assisting women. These services are usually local non-government services, but each type is linked together in statewide networks. Many domestic violence centres have adopted a policy development approach, and undertaken research to support new perspectives and new programs in family violence.

In addition, there are many non-government generalist services that have added some family violence programs. Furthermore, local community health centres take on supporting roles for families with and without family violence when they are dealing with parental separation.

SERVICES FOR CHILDREN

Few of the services discussed above are targeted at children. Some that do provide for children are specialist child abuse assessment and treatment centres, like the Melbourne-based Centre for Child Abuse sponsored by the Australian Childhood Foundation and the Gatehouse Centre sponsored by the Ro yal Children's Hospital, both of which have been established in the last fifteen years and which are increasingly used by families where child abuse has occurred in the context of parental separation and divorce (Brown et al., 2001). When families in the study used those services for their children, the children appeared to be less distressed by the child abuse and/or other family violence, and by the court proceedings (Brown et al., 2001). Another service, the national Kids Help Line, provides a telephone information, referral and counselling service directly to children without any parental involvement. The greatest proportion of children making contact seek help with family relationships and a further group seeks assistance because of child abuse (Kids Help Line, 2004).

Children's contact centres are emerging as a focus of a number of Commonwealth-funded service innovations. These services were designed to allow contact to take place for parents who were separated and who could not manage the contact changeover or the contact period without safe professional supervision. They are open on a number of nights a week and at weekends. Parents apply to use them, usually because they have received Family Court orders requiring contact or handover to be carried out only under professional supervision. If the parents and children meet the centre's requirements and the centre has a place, the child will be booked in to attend at certain times, and all contact between parent and child will take place under the watchful supervision of trained centre staff. The centres have security arrangements, and have inside and outside play areas and play equipment to allow some normalcy and enjoyment. Staff will assist the parent during the contact visit.

Contact centres face limitations in that their funding is not intended to cover a child for long periods of supervised contact, and there are questions as to what can be achieved in short periods of time. There are also indications that, while contact centres benefit many of their client children, they do not benefit all the children. Those children for whom contact has been ordered and forcefully implemented—most of whom have suffered child abuse and/or domestic violence—have been found not to gain from the experience (Sheehan et al., 2005). A new program, the Parent Orders program, covering a small number of contact centres in each state, has introduced additional services for parents and children where there are contact problems—services that provide parents and children with group and individual support, education and mediation. A new development is the inclusion of the children in group support, individual counselling and mediation (Gordoncare, 2005).

The emergence of these new services affecting children has prompted service providers to consider the extent of the children's involvement in the services. Should the child be involved at all, and if so in what way? Services have settled on a continuum of child involvement ranging from no involvement, but an expressed concern and focus, to an involvement termed 'child inclusive', where the child is involved in some way, to what is termed 'child directed', where the child is treated as a self-directing client similar to an adult (Strategic Partners Ltd, 1998; Grimes and McIntosh, 2004). The contact centres are child focused, some community-based mediation services are child inclusive and the Kids Help Line is child directed, as the children have the responsibility for initiating and using the service.

STATE CHILD PROTECTION SERVICES

The primary agencies to assist children and families with child abuse, the state child protection services, are designed to deal with child abuse but not especially in the context of parental separation and divorce. In fact, state child protection services have been accused of ignoring child abuse in this context for many years (Brown et al., 1998; Parkinson, 2003). Since child protection is a state rather than a Commonwealth responsibility there are the eight state and territory child protection services to which allegations of child abuse in any context, including parental separation and divorce, can be reported when it occurs. All states except Western Australia have mandatory reporting of child abuse. These services have had substantial service failures in recent years. In 2003, services in New South Wales, South Australia, Western Australia and Queensland seemed on the verge of collapse, leading to governmental inquiries in each of these states. Since then, the New South Wales, South Australian and Queensland services have been reformed—dramatically so in the case of Queensland, with its new and unique Department of Child Safety begun in 2004. Despite the failings of the service in Western Australia, little change has been noted.

Linked to the various state child protection services are the Children's Courts, specialist courts within the state Magistrates Courts. These courts make protection, care and guardianship orders for children, and views as to their adequacy are generally mixed (Sheehan, 2001), though they are consistently negative in relation to children where the child abuse has emerged in the context of parental separation and divorce (Fehlberg and Kelly, 2000). The state child protection services are supported by the state police forces, which may investigate child abuse allegations jointly with the child protection service and undertake consequent criminal prosecutions. In New South Wales, a new alliance between the child protection services and the police has resulted in some trial joint child protection and police teams (Cashmore, 2002; Morrison, 2006).

LOBBY GROUPS

There are a number of lobby groups in the service system providing advocacy services for various interests: those representing fathers, those representing mothers and, unfortunately, just a few representing children.

The most vocal—and, it has been argued, the most powerful (Smart et al., 2001)—are the men's groups, a development seeking to promote fathers' interests in the light of changes to their position subsequent to the more relaxed divorce laws and the international children's rights movement. In Australia, the Men's Rights Agency, Equality for Fathers, Dads Against Discrimination, Dads in Distress and the Lone Fathers Association represent fathers. They are active in public debate, make many submissions to inquiries and attend public consultations frequently (see, for example, the list of submissions and consultations for the last three Commonwealth inquiries into aspects of family law, 2001–2005: (FLAPG, 2001; House of Representatives Standing Committee on Family and

Community Affairs, 2003; Attorney-General's Department, 2004). It has been suggested that these groups do not have a large membership, but rather are directed and supported by a few committed individuals in each organisation, some of whom are women, and a shifting group of newly separated men (Kaye and Tolmie, 1998a). Most operate within the law, and any person who has attended a Family Court registry will have observed members of these groups outside registries criticising processes and individuals within the courts. Some attending court find this intimidating. One group, the Blackshirts, has been prosecuted in Victoria for its members' harassment at homes of individual women who were separated or divorced (McCoy, 2005). None of these groups rivals the UK group, Dads 4 Justice, in terms of publicity stunts, as, for example, their alleged plan to kidnap Prime Minister Tony Blair's youngest child.

The men's groups direct professionals to issues about fathers post-separation, believing these issues will not be tackled without their pressure. Considerable evidence exists to suggest that fathers are ignored as parents (Fleming, 2003). However, the denial by many of the groups (Flood, 2005) of the extent of domestic violence by husbands against their spouses, and their similar denial of fathers' abuse of their children, detract from their argument (Kaye and Tolmie, 1998a).

On the other side stand the lobby groups supporting mothers. They comprise the women's legal centres, of which there is usually at least one in each state, and the domestic violence centres and centres against sexual assault, which are linked in loose state and federal networks. There is also the Aboriginal Family Violence Prevention and Legal Service, the Women's Information and Referral Exchange (WIRE), the Australian Centre for the Study of Sexual Assault and the Australian Domestic and Family Violence Clearing House. By way of contrast with the men's groups, they are a collection of agencies led by professionals—by legal practitioners, social workers, psychologists and social science researchers. They do not focus as much on the broader problems of post-separation parenting, as the men's groups do; instead, they are concerned with the narrower issues of violence and abuse before and after separation, and the consequences of this violence for women and their care of the children.

The women's lobby groups have been successful in having the Commonwealth government address family violence through the Commonwealth program of Partnerships Against Domestic Violence. This program has channelled considerable funding into services and research. However, the proposed changes in family law that are presented in Chapter 2 have been interpreted as a sign that the men's groups have gained the ascendancy with the Commonwealth government, and as a result the new legislation has been greeted gloomily by women (Alexander, 2005). There are only a few groups representing children in family law disputes. Two of the best known are the Council for the Single Mother and Her Child, and Bravehearts. They were not originally established to take the position of children in family law disputes where there has been child abuse or domestic violence, but their concern for children has led them to lobby for children's interests in these situations. As an individual, Professor Freda Briggs has been a tireless activist for children subject to parental abuse and involved in family law proceedings. State bodies advocating for children have ignored children who are abused in this context, and the federal body for child abuse research, the National Child Protection Clearing House, has similarly ignored this group of children, always preferring to look at the children who come into the state child protection systems. See, for example, the Clearing House 2005 bulletin, again covering only children in the state child protection systems (Bromfield and Higgins, 2005).

FUNDING

The family law socio-legal service system is not funded from a single source, but rather fuelled from many sources, with any one of its components possibly receiving funding from many sources simultaneously with consequent program boundary problems. The greatest amount of funding comes through allocations from the Commonwealth government. The Commonwealth government funds Centrelink and the Child Support Agency separately and directly. The Commonwealth government funds the Family Court of Australia, the federal police, the state legal aid commissions for family law matters, community legal centres and most of the non-government agencies providing mediation, information, referral and counselling services, including the new family relationship centres. It funds these services through the Commonwealth Attorney-General's Department, and also funds some specialist domestic violence services and child contact centres through the same department. Some family counselling funding, including parent education funding, comes through the Commonwealth Department of Family and Community Services and Indigenous Affairs.

The various state governments fund the child protection services, the state courts and the state police, as well as some of the counselling services provided by state and regionally based non-government services.

Clients fund themselves through payment for legal representation, the costs of legal proceedings additional to legal representation and payment for counselling and mediation services.

Clearly the power to direct the service system that might come from the provision of most of the funding for this system is in the hands of the Commonwealth government. However, because it provides this funding through various pieces of legislation to many different organisations, and because this funding merges with funding from other sources at the organisational level, its power is fragmented—just like the service system itself. Nevertheless, a new direction is discernible as the Commonwealth government gradually draws more services into the service system to form a more comprehensive system that is moving away from reliance on court and adversarial legal strategies.

PROBLEMS OF A SERVICE SYSTEM THAT HAS BECOME A MAZE

Describing the service system shows how complex it has become. The national consultation with those who have attempted to use it showed that users did not understand the system and that it did not meet their expectations (FLPAG, 2001). Clients see the system in terms of their own problems, and do not understand that its generality and its absence of a focus on the particular problems that occur in this context mean that it cannot work for them in the way that they require (Hunter et al., 2000; Hay, 2003).

While the generalist nature of the service system reflects and may be derived from the generalist nature of the Commonwealth family law legislation, and the procedures and services set up by the courts administering that legislation, the movement that occurs in service development from general to specialised services has not occurred to any extent in the family law service system. The potential leader of that system, the Family Court of Australia, has largely failed to develop specialised court programs designed for particular client problems or for particular client groups. One size has been supposed to fit all.

Consequently, clients feel the service system does not relate to them and they become frustrated and angry at the system. This is reported constantly

(FLPAG, 2001). Some clients believe the service system punishes them for the fact that their problems do not fit easily into the generalist services with their generalist procedures for client problems, no matter what they are (Hay, 2003). The gaps in the service system increase clients' feelings of anger and frustration about the system not meeting their needs. When a client does find one of the few specialised services, it is rarely comprehensive and so is unable to take them to the conclusion of their problems. No matter what the state of mind of the clients before they begin to move into and use the service system, the nature of the system itself is highly likely to lead to deterioration in their adjustment as they use it.

NO SPECIALISED SERVICES FOR CHILD ABUSE ALLEGATIONS

As the service system has no specialised services to address child abuse within the context of parental separation and divorce, there is no particular place in it for families to go. While some parents and some children attempt to address the problem by seeking assistance from the variety of services on the edge of the family law service system—such as medical practices, health centres, hospitals, schools, pre-schools, child care centres and sexual assault centres—these agencies and their staff have no place to send these families subsequently They are likely to recommend a number of possibilities, none of which will be entirely satisfactory for none will be a specialist service focusing on child abuse in the context of parental separation and divorce (Dessau, 1999).

Some agencies will refer family members to the most obvious source of help, the state child protection service. These services cover all types of child abuse, and are the most obvious agency to deal with this problem. However, the services have no special expertise regarding child abuse in the context of parental separation and divorce. Unfortunately, when such clients are referred to it, the service often gives them a low priority. It may undertake only a superficial investigation and report that the abuse has not been substantiated. These words mask the real meaning of events—that is, that the service has had a quick look and decided not to proceed further, although it has no evidence as to whether or not abuse has occurred (Hume, 1997; Brown et al., 1998; Family Law Council, 2003).

When it does pursue an investigation of child abuse in this context, and substantiate the allegations, the child protection service may not take further action, but instead expect one parent to take action independent of it by going to the Family Court of Australia.The service believes this is the best pathway it can recommend to ensure that the parent perpetrating the abuse does not have contact with the child (Fehlberg and Kelly, 2000).This group of clients—the so-called protective parents—are seen by the child protection service as being capable of asserting their children's interests, and being able to resolve the problem without child protection help. In addition, the service sees the Family Court as the more relevant service when the abuse is placed in the context of separation and divorce—more especially because of its ability to make parenting orders for longer periods of time. Some child protection staff see families making allegations of child abuse at this point as being more difficult to work with than other families, and as having less serious abuse issues—although the evidence of the pattern of abuse and the profile of the parents do not support most of these assumptions.When the myths of the fabrication of abuse allegations in this context are added to the other assumptions, the clients are regarded as less in need of their services (Brown et al., 1998, 2001).

Even when the allegations are taken seriously, investigated and substantiated, the links between the child protection service and the court are not strong, despite the existence of the protocols that have been developed in most states over the last ten years to improve coordination (see Chapter 3). Some family courts do not take child protection reports substantiating abuse as seriously as the child protection service expects, and do not give protecting the child from further abuse the emphasis the child protection service wishes (Hay, 2003). Family courts give the child's best interests, rather than the child's safety, the higher priority, and the difference between the objectives of the two jurisdictions leads to difficulties between the two organisational domains. Furthermore, the most recent family law legislation's emphasis on joint parenting and on the child maintaining contact with both parents is said to have allowed a further diminishing of concern for the child's safety (Graycar et al., 2000).

In the past, the relationship between the state and territory child protection services and the Family Court was confused, as each jurisdiction was able to act independently and without regard to the others. However, the development of *protocols* to set in place policies to smooth out conflicts between the two organisations has encouraged a joint approach. Despite this, the sequence of events does not always happen as planned, and conflicts and gaps between the two services do occur (Fehlberg and Kelly, 2000; Brown et al., 2001).

Until recently, had the family decided to go to the Family Court, rather than to a child protection service, in order to seek orders preventing the alleged perpetrator from having contact with the child, they would have discovered that the court did not distinguish this problem from other issues surrounding marital breakdown and divorce. It had not put in place a specialised service for child abuse allegations. As a court presiding over marital breakdown and divorce, it took a wider view of the child's parent-ing arrangements than looking only at the abuse. The court had to be guided by the legislation that specified the need to consider the child's best interest as the paramount principle of decision-making—not the child's safety or protection from abuse, as many families imagined. Child abuse was taken into account, but it was not the only factor to be considered. Moreover, the court encouraged parenting orders made by consent, and this often seemed inappropriate to parents who were seeking a determination of whether the child had been abused and, if so, what the plan should be for the child's future protection.

NEW SPECIALISED SERVICES AND PATHWAYS

As a result of mounting dissatisfaction with the service system, a few pioneering services have now been created to improve the way the system deals with child abuse. The new services have not developed from an across-the-system approach, but rather from changes to the parts of the system where innovation is able to occur.

The Magellan program

The Magellan program—the first specialised Family Court program dealing with child abuse allegations in the context of residence and contact disputes to be designed and implemented internationally—was introduced into the Family Court of Australia as an experimental program in the Melbourne and Dandenong registries of Victoria in 1999 under the lead-ership of the Honourable Justice Linda Dessau. The experimental program was built on previous research undertaken by the Family Violence and Family Court Research program in conjunction with the Family Court.

The program was based on a number of principles which included an inter-organisational approach, a focus on the children, prioritising early intervention, a judge-led and tightly managed time-limited approach, court-ordered expert assessments including both a child protection investigation and a court family report, publicly funded legal representation for every child, and a multi-disciplinary court team.

The program's trial was highly successful. The time taken on average for each case was halved, the number of hearings was also halved, the number of cases going through to a full trial fell by two-thirds, the rate of breakdown of orders fell by one-third, and the number of highly distressed children fell by more than three-quarters. The legal aid costs also fell, despite the removal of caps on legal aid expenditure per party and the appointment of a legal practitioner for each child in the program. Clients and professionals were very satisfied with the program and sought to make it permanent. Subsequently, in 2001, it was rolled out around Australia, beginning with Adelaide. The last state to adopt it was New South Wales, where it began as a pilot project in one Sydney registry in October 2005.

Being grounded in the previous research, the new program was custom built to address residence and contact disputes where there were child abuse allegations. The program comprises four court events, all of which are held on the same day of each week. The first court event, or hearing, is a preliminary mention presided over by the judge with the senior counsellor and registrar present. The judge explains the program and makes a number of procedural orders, as well as interim orders if required. At this hearing, the judge orders the appointment of a legal representative for the child and a child protection investigation, a report of which is to be returned to the court within five weeks. The report and the file are made available to the legal practitioners one week before the next hearing, and the report is made available to the parents at the same time.

The second court event is held seven weeks later if the case has not been resolved. At this time, the judge receives the child protection report and orders a report from the court counsellors assessing the family's functioning to be completed and returned to the court in seven weeks. Legal practitioners and parents are given the report one week before the next hearing, expected to be in ten weeks' time.

The third court event is a pre-hearing conference led by the registrar and with the senior counsellor. The family, their legal advisers and other professionals, such as staff from the child protection service, meet at the informal conference to discuss views, reports, common ground, options and ongoing concerns. The fourth court event is the trial, or final hearing, which takes place ten weeks from the pre-hearing conference and which is conducted in the same way as all trials in the Family Court.

The Magellan program has maintained its achievements since its intro-duction, and is being considered for an extension by a widening of the eligibility of its cases of child abuse. It is an example of a more inquisito-rial approach in that the judge takes greater control than in the past, and uses a pre-planned series of steps, including reports from experts, to take decision-making forward.

The Columbus program

A related program, Columbus, was introduced into the Family Court of Western Australia in 2001. Unlike Magellan, it was not based on prior research from the Family Court of Western Australia, but on the experi-ences and views of the court staff as to flaws in the court processes for managing family violence that they argued were given validation by the research of the Family Violence and Family Court Research Program (Kerin and Murphy, 2003; Murphy and Pike, 2003). The Columbus program went further than Magellan, as it sought to include families where there were allegations of spousal abuse as well as allegations of child abuse. Columbus also sought to test the use of less adversarial processes. The program, while targeting families where there were allegations of child abuse and domestic violence, did not incorporate any formal process to investigate the allegations by any source outside the court, such as the child protection services or the police.

The program comprised a series of multi-disciplinary court conferences offered on the basis of the individual needs of the case as each case presented. When any residence and contact case presented at its first court hearing, it was scrutinised for evidence of spousal abuse, child abuse or any other risk of harm to the child. If any was detected, the case was then offered the opportunity to proceed into the Columbus program.

The case then moved to a diversionary process of case conferences managed by a registrar and a counsellor that was tailored to the needs of each case. This process continued until consent orders could be achieved; if they could not, the case reverted back to the usual court process and proceeded to trial. The program was not as time-limited or as discrete a specialisedprogram as Magellan. It did use an inter-organisationalapproach in the sense that the Western AustralianLegal Aid Commission provided a legal representative to each child and some non-government agencies, such as Relationships Australia, were involved too, but there was no formal incorporation of the child protection service and the police.

The aims and processes of the two programs are somewhat different, so it is not possible to make direct comparisons, but the early research (Murphy and Pike, 2003) has suggested Columbus is a promising program that can assist more families, where violence has been alleged, to build 'more stable contact and residence regimes' than has been the case in the past. At this stage, it appears that the average number of court events required to achieve these outcomes is high—more than five—and, as the events are individualised conferences of some hours, each event is expensive in terms of court resources. The final results of the evaluative research built into the program should show more conclusively how successfulit is. However, both the Magellan and Columbus programs represent new concepts that have been specifically designed to deal with child abuse in the context of parental separationand divorce, and thus offer the possibility of better outcomes for the children and their families.

Other programs

For some years, the Family Court of Australiahas been investigatingother family violence strategies to better manage residence and contact disputes where domestic violence is alleged. In 2003 it issued a report (Family Violence Committee, 2003), and it has now introduced a screening and risk assessmentpilot project in the Brisbane Reg istry. Following evaluation, it will consider a national rollout of the program (FCA, 2004–05). In addition, it has introduced a family violence staff training program (FCA, 2004–05). Hopefully these strategies will improve the court's management of domestic violence, for—as already discussed—domesticviolence plays an increasing role in parental separationand divorce (Stanton et al., 2000), and domestic violence and child abuse are closely interrelated and commonly occur together. The court has tended to simplify the various strandsof family violence when they coexist, tackling only one or none at all (Brown et al., 1998). Thus a program for child abuse allegationsneeds to be buttressed by a program for domestic violence for the full protection of the children.

A number of other programs that link one service to another to produce a more coordinated approach have been established in the wake of the Family Law Pathways Advisory Group's report (FLPAG, 2001). One example is the *common assessment tool*. This was proposed in the report as a way that services could adopt a more consistent approach to their client so that every client—no matter where they entered the family law service system—would receive the same screening for potential problems and then, on the basis of that screening, be offered further relevant services. Every service would use the same core assessment framework, although each service might add components of its own. Relationships Australia and the Child Support Agency adopted a common assessment tool and, within it, established a link between the two agencies so that a client could be immediately referred while on the phone to the other agency. It has been described as a 'hot link', and it gains an immediate and relevant additional service for someone who needs it.

STRATEGIES FOR MANAGING THE MAZE

While the service system is developing more programs with a coordinated approach for families where there are problems of child abuse—either through a number of agencies sponsoring joint programs or through agencies interrelating through coordinating mechanisms such as protocols, common assessment tools, hot links and others—the professional is still left with the task of managing a service system that resembles a maze. Thus professionals have to create pathways for their clients and manage the clients along those pathways—two very real challenges.

To create pathways, professionals need to research and assemble knowledge about two things. They need to identify what the current system comprises, then they need to make a map of all the component parts—a map that places all the parts in relationship to each other, building up the whole. They need also to identify the particular range of needs of the clients who come to them, and the services the clients are likely to require in addition to their own. Using the map of client services and the identification of client needs, they can then make a conceptual path for their clients to those other services so that they ensure the clients will receive services for their full range of needs.

To make the conceptual path real for the use of clients, professionals develop informal relationships with relevant staff in those agencies that they have identified as part of their map. However, this frequently used strategy depends on a continuity of staff that cannot be guaranteed. It is preferable to make pathways permanent through developing formal relationships that will endure after current staff leave. If staff work at maintaining those relationships after they are established, rather than assuming that a relationship once formalised, does not need constant nurturing and reviewing, the relationship becomes a long-lasting, real pathway for their clients. It is possible that the family relationship centres may take on a role of identifying, mapping and developing service pathways, but in any event all service providers still need to do their own work here.

Once the pathways are created, the professional has to be able to walk the clients along the track. Assuming that a referral of a client from one service to another will work because a pathway has been built is incorrect. Walking the pathways means understanding the other organisation, what clients it works with, how it works with its clients, what goals it seeks for its clients, what internal processes exist in the organisation, and how it relates to other organisations and to other organisations' clients. To uncover such information about other organisations requires both the skill of moving outside the boundaries of the organisation where one is based and a flexibility of outlook—a tolerance of the ways other organisations and their component disciplines function.

Much has been written about inter-disciplinary relationships: it has been acknowledged that services would work much better for clients if the inter-disciplinary obstacle inherent in child protection could be overcome (Hallett, 1995). The same problems of inter-disciplinary relationships have also been documented in the Australian family law service system (Faulks, 1997), further complicating service provision. Faulks has depicted the latter as stemming from different professional goals supported by different training, different professional procedures, and ultimately different languages with consequent communication barriers. To overcome such obstacles requires a willingness to accept the legitimacy and utility of other disciplines, and to work on knowing about and understanding their actions, procedures and view points.

Walking the track requires a strong commitment to the client group, and the commitment fosters a perspective that allows the different professionals to work together. Assisting clients to walk from one service to another means more than just informing the client of the service. It means contacting the service about the particular client, ascertaining their eligibility for assistance establishing the client's need for and willingness to use the other service, interpreting the service, ensuring the client can connect with the services and checking that they have actually done this. It includes feedback about the relevance of the service, and the success or otherwise in making the connection. It may be that the family relationship centres will be the agencies that draw the maps for all clients and professionals, the agencies that create the pathways and walk clients along to the end of their particular track.

CONCLUSION

The family law socio-legal service system is a fragmented one that was not designed to deal with any family violence and certainly not with child abuse. As a result, using it is extremely difficult for families who expect better, and who become angry when they do not receive an adequate service. It then falls on professionals to make the service system work for their clients, and its contradictions, gaps, and confusion that give it a maze-like quality hinder professionals' efforts for their clients.

It is difficult for professionals to work together to create targeted and coordinated inter-organisational programs, like Magellan and Columbus, designed to deal with child abuse in this context. It requires special knowledge of inter-organisational dynamics and the tolerance, energy, expertise and experience to achieve such programs. Even setting up links between just two organisations is not easy. Family law professionals need to know the map of the service system, how to make pathways for their clients to use it, and how to help their clients walk those pathways successfully

8

CASE PRESENTATIONS: THE PROFESSIONALS' CONTRIBUTIONS

The problems that arise for families when child abuse allegations occur in the context of parental separation and divorce quickly push the families into the arms of the various professionals—the solicitors, social workers, psychologists, doctors, nurses, teachers and others, who work in the agencies that comprise the family law socio-legal service system. Yet there is no guide for professionals working with families struggling with problems of child abuse in this context. There is no advice as to how the professionals might assess their situations, no knowledge bank saying what strategies the professionals might consider for these families or, having made a choice of the preferred strategies, how they might implement them.

This chapter considers the strategies for professionals to use with families needing assistance with these problems. The chapter presents two cases that exemplify the families and their problems. After each case is presented, questions are raised about the contribution that a range of professionals might make and then they are discussed. The discussion begins with the over-arching issues for all disciplines, and then looks at the questions each professional confronts and what contribution each might make.

THE USE OF A COMMON FRAMEWORK

Many—if not most—families need the resources of a number of services staffed with professionals from a range of disciplines to help them manage their separation and divorce. When child abuse allegations are added to the family's problems, they will need more assistance—and in particular, assistance that recognises the inter-disciplinary and inter-organisational aspects of best-practice professional intervention at this time.

While families need inter-disciplinary and inter-agency collaboration, such collaboration is often missing—not because of the oversight of any one professional group or any one service, but because achieving inter-disciplinary and inter-agency collaboration is inherently difficult (Thoeness and Pearson, 1988; Brown et al., 1998; FLPAG, 2001). The Honourable Justice J. Faulks (1997), Deputy to the Chief Justice of the Family Court of Australia, has suggested problems of collaboration come from the difference in the perspectives of the various professions working in the services which make up the family law system. When the different professional perspectives are underlined by employment in the various services, the barriers to collaboration become even greater.

One way to overcome the differences is for each profession and each service to move to the use of a common framework or approach within the family law socio-legal service system. This means that each profession and each organisation would, within the confines of its organisation and its disciplines goals, use a common knowledge base and common parameters to guide its approach. No matter what the disciplinary background of each professional, they would use a common framework, derived from the emerging research-based specialised knowledge, to deal with families with these problems.

The common framework would rest on knowledge from the following areas:

- expertise in child abuse in the context of parental separation and divorce;
- expertise in domestic violence in this context;
- expertise in the relationship between the two forms of family violence;
- awareness of the potential for secrecy regarding family violence in the context of parental separation and divorce;
- expertise in the impact of such families on the professionals working with them;
- expertise in the legal context.

The common framework would rest also on the following intervention principles:

- maintaining a focus on the child;
- ensuring the child's immediate and long-term safety and well-being;
- ongoing collaboration with other services to achieve an integrated service for the children;
- using the authority of expertise within this particular legal context;
- using early intervention;
- using structured intervention;
- using timely and time-limited intervention.

CASE PRESENTATION AND DISCUSSION

The sample cases presented for discussion are fictitious—no family is real. However, the example have been compiled to demonstrate the common features found among the hundreds of cases reviewed in the several studies of residence and contact disputes where child abuse allegations were involved (Brown et al., 1998, 2001). Following each case, questions facing the various professionals about their possible contribution are identified and discussed from the point of view of the particular professionals who are relevant to resolving the problems of each family.

THE FIRST FAMILY

Marie and James Swinden and Samantha and Ben Swinden

Marie and James were aged 33 and 35 when James suddenly left his wife, their two children and their Melbourne inner city apartment. The two children were a girl, Samantha, aged six and a boy, Ben, aged four, who had just been diagnosed as having a mild intellectual disability. James was a high school teacher working at a school near the apartment, and Marie worked part-time in the evenings as a bookkeeper for a clothing business. When James left, he moved into a flat rented by Andrew, another teacher from the same school. Andrew's wife had recently left him, taking his two young daughters with her.

Marie was faced with immediate financial worries. She wanted to ensure that James continued to mind the children on the nights she worked, as her own parents lived interstate and could not help her. He agreed to having them overnight at the flat that he and Andrew shared on the three nights she worked each week. James was opposed to formalising the separation, and delayed any legal action regarding residence and contact or property.

Six months later, the principal of the school the daughter attended sought a meeting with Marie and James and raised concerns about the daughter's behaviour at school. She said the girl was very aggressive to the other children, yet was very anxious; she was showing great interest in the boys in her class, especially in their genitals, asking them if they wanted 'sex'. The principal suggested the parents consider the possibility of the child having been sexually abused.

At the school meeting, James denied there was a problem. He opposed Marie or the school taking any further action. His parents telephoned Marie to support his stand. Two weeks later, the principal had another meeting with Marie alone; the child had continued to behave in the same manner and she argued that if James would not cooperate she would have to notify the child protection service to investigate. Once again, when contacted by Marie, James opposed any action.

Over the next three weeks, Samantha became very unhappy about going to the flat and the school contacted Marie again to say the child was having even more trouble at school. This time Marie took her daughter to see her local doctor, seeking advice as to whether the girl had been sexually abused. After listening to Marie and examining Samantha, the local doctor told Marie that he did think there were some signs of sexual abuse and that he must notify the child protection service. Marie immediately went to a nearby family law solicitor for legal advice.

Issues for professionals

Here are two working parents who have separated but where there are no obvious problems except the ongoing care of a son diagnosed with a mild intellectual disability Although the parental separation has been almost twelve months in duration, neither parent has established any formal agreement in regard to the residence and contact arrangements for the children or in regard to property distribution. However, the daughter's school has raised concerns repeatedly about her possible sexual abuse. The school's pressing of its concern has propelled the mother into taking the child to the local doctor and to a meeting with a solicitor before the child protection worker arrives.

The problem-free appearance of this middle-class family may mislead professionals, encouraging them to discount sexual abuse as a possibility, fail to investigate it thoroughly, and look to some other explanation for the child's behaviour. This is because the family seems to be a well-functioning unit, except for the fact that the father left the family—rather suddenly—almost a year before. The father has rejected the possibility of sexual abuse, categorically denying the school's suggestion of a problem. The mother, too, has responded with disbelief. Thus professionals might reject the concern expressed by the school and question the school's interpretation of the child's behaviour. They might question the motives behind the mother's subsequent change of view and question her move to see her local doctor, the child protection service and a solicitor, wondering if she sees the allegations—while not initiated by herself—as a useful tactic for driving the father to formalise the financial and other support arrangements.

A series of issues will arise around the determination as to whether any sexual abuse has occurred. One issue is that sexual abuse is difficult to discern and to demonstrate to others. The difficulty of detection may be made worse by the very young age of the daughter, who may not be able to provide a precise picture of what has happened, when it happened and with whom it happened. Two further issues are whether the daughter has experienced any other form of abuse, and whether the boy has experienced any abuse too. If abuse of any kind is detected, the next issue will be who might be responsible for any such abuse. How, if at all, does the sexual abuse relate to the father's departure from the family? Might the perpetrator be the father, his flatmate, a friend or relative of either the father or the flatmate, or someone else who comes to the flat—or a group of these people? On the other hand, might it be someone who visits Marie?

Since James has rejected the possibility of abuse, he may be difficult to work with in identifying a perpetrator, assuming he is not involved in the abuse. His parents have rejected the possibility of such abuse, and they too may not be helpful. If he is involved in any way, as a sole or joint perpetrator, as the local doctor suspects, he will deliberately be obstructive, possibly hostile and certainly misleading to all those who contact him. An intelligent and well-educated person, he is equipped to meet this challenge.

If abuse is detected, both Marie and James will be confronted with its implications for the child's future care. Marie will still need child care to allow her to work at nights. Marie seems socially isolated, estranged from her former husband and his parents. She will need considerable support to work through a situation that may now escalate to one of significant conflict between herself and James and his family. She will also feel guilty and angry over what has led to this situation, and she may feel she has failed as a parent and be unclear and anxious as to how to deal with the many problems of this new situation.

If abuse is substantiated, there will be a need to provide assistance to the daughter. She is showing considerable distress, and any investigation will need to be carried out in a way that focuses on her safety and well-being, and allows her some participation in the decision-making that will take place. She will need support through the investigation and subsequently and her mother may not have the resources to provide as much support at this time as the child needs.

Questions for the professionals about intervention with this family

Within the common framework, each professional confronts the issue of developing the most appropriate intervention. In order to do this, they will need to ask and answer a series of questions.

Questions for the school principal

- If a teacher brought concerns to you about a child's behaviour that suggested child sexual abuse, what information would you seek from the teacher about the child?
- If you were then more suspicious about the possibility of sexual abuse, what further action might you take—for example, would you look for evidence of other forms of abuse, consult with the pre-school the brother attends, contact one or other or both parents, undertake other investigations, and/or contact the child protection service?
- How would you approach the parents? What would you say and would you bring anyone else to an interview with the parents?
- If the parents maintained that sexual abuse had not occurred, what would you do then?
- For how long would you delay contacting the child protection service if the parents did not take action?
- What plan for managing the child would you suggest after the child protection service investigated and did substantiate the abuse?

Intervention issues for the school principal

The school principal has intervened quickly by calling a meeting with both parents of the child after the class teacher brought her concerns about the child to the principal. The child's behaviour—anxious and aggressive, with language and actions showing knowledge of heterosexual behaviour that one would not expect from a child of six—is suggestive of possible sexual abuse. However, with the tendency of many professionals to describe the child's behaviour as some kind of disturbance exhibited in the area of sexual functioning, rather than as the more likely child sexual abuse, the school principal needs to find out from the class teacher as much as she can about the child's behaviour—at school, in the classroom and in the playground—as well as about the child's relationships in the family, to consider the best course of action. It is not suggested that the principal talk with the child herself, but rather try to establish just what the child has said to anyone else, like her class teacher. She could consult with specialist child sexual assault services or with any school social workers or psychologists to learn more about the signs about abuse.

The school principal has chosen to see the parents; some would not do so, but rather refer the child to the child protection service, knowing they are mandated to do so. Some school principals are also required to report the matter to a more senior manager in the education system in which they work. The school principal may think she does not have enough information to make a notification, believing that although a suspicion may satisfy legal requirements no action will be taken unless she has considerable evidence. The principal has chosen to see the parents alone, but a better strategy would have been to see them with another teacher. Two people may be needed to manage two possibly angry and uncooperative parents—one a teacher himself—in the interview. They may need to give support to each other and there would also be a witness to the events of the meeting. They should start with the fact that they are concerned about the young girl and that they are seeking to address her difficulties. Presumably they would share with the parents what the disturbances in her behaviour were. They may say that they feared she was being abused, although they would have to concede that it was not within their province to determine this. Thus it is desirable that they suggest a referral to the child protection service to undertake a full investigation.

Once the parents refuse to accept the school's concerns, the school principal is left with the problem of their refusal, their ill-will, and the worry of the child's welfare and that of the other children. On this occasion, the principal waits and tries again two weeks later when the child continues to show distress. It is common for professionals to wait, hoping that the problems will resolve. However, problems of child sexual abuse do not resolve of their own accord. Waiting worsens; delays cause deterioration. Early intervention gives the best hope of cessation of abuse and recovery from abuse.

Nevertheless the principal remains focused on the child and her problems, and tries again—this time varying her approach by tackling Marie alone. Marie, as the mother, is the least likely perpetrator and she is a suitable point of intervention. The principal has a clear objective, too: that of having the child investigated for sexual abuse by the child protection service. Yet, once again, she does not take this step. If she thinks that sexual abuse is a strong possibility she should do this; however, she tries to have Marie take this step. She may not know that the child protection service may give greater credence to a notification from her as a professional than to one from Marie who may be regarded as a mother seeking to gain an edge in a residence, contact and property dispute.

Questions for the doctor

- What investigations of the allegations would you undertake yourself?
- Would you send the child and mother to a specialist sexual assault centre for children for an initial investigation?
- How would you talk with the child? How would you explain your purpose and what would you ask her?
- Would you seek to see the girl's brother?
- What would you do about the mother's distress?
- Would you seek to see the father?
- Would you contact the school; if so, what would you say to the principal?
- Would you ring the child protection service if your consultation led to some evidence of abuse, or tell the mother to do so?

Intervention issues for the doctor

The local doctor will be confronted with a mother who may be distressed, who may know little about child sexual abuse, and who may be unclear about what action she should have taken in the past as well as what action she should take now, whatever conclusion the local doctor reaches. The mother does not know whether abuse has happened, who has done it if it has occurred and what she should do for the protection of the child in the future. The local doctor may have difficulty in both understanding her account of her problem and determining what she is seeking.

When Marie asks whether Samantha has been sexually abused, the doctor will have to consider whether to investigate personally or whether to refer Samantha to a specialist sexual assault centre or to a paediatrician. After all, the Gatehouse Centre for the diagnosis and treatment of abused children is nearby. This is a centre with specialist expertise in the diagnosis and treatment of sexual abuse, and support services for sexual abuse victims and their families. However, as the family GP, who has treated the child since birth, knows her history, and has a long-standing professional relationship with her, the doctor decides to investigate. A discussion takes place with Marie about Samantha's behaviour and what this may mean, with the doctor noting that Samantha's account of events is one of the most important sources of evidence. Unambiguous and simple questions put calmly to the child are the most appropriate approach to take with Samantha. The doctor needs to explain what will happen in any examination, giving consideration to Samantha's emotional state. Consideration must also be given to investigating Ben for possible sexual abuse.

Once a parent fears their child may be abused, the doctor's actions and notes may become part of subsequent court proceedings—either criminal or Family Court proceedings—and the doctor may be called on for a written report to a court and to give evidence. The doctor will also have to decide—depending on what is discovered—what should be done in relation to notifying the child protection service and how this should happen. The doctor needs to find out what has been done by any other professionals in relation to any possible notification, and recall that medical practitioners are legally mandated to report child abuse to the child protection service. There is a need to consider the support which might be available to Samantha and her mother, and also whether or not the possibility of Ben being sexually abused should be investigated. At this stage, the doctor may refer the family to the Gatehouse Centre for the investigation of possible sexual abuse of Ben and for ongoing support for both children.

The doctor decides, on the evidence of what Samantha tells him about her behaviour and staying with her father, that it is necessary to notify child protection, and explains this to Marie. The doctor also tells Marie he suspects the father is involved; however, the decision is to allow the child protection service to contact James.

Questions for the solicitor

- What facts would you seek from the mother?
- What evidence of abuse would you seek?
- Would you seek to see Samantha, and possibly Ben?
- Would you ask about suspicions/evidence of other types of child abuse?
- Would you ask about domestic violence?
- If domestic violence were mentioned, what would you advise the mother to do about it?
- What, if any, advice would you offer about the imminent arrival of the child protection service?
- What, if any, advice would you offer about the father's denial of possible abuse and his insistence on the children maintaining contact with him?
- What legal processes would you plan to set in train for this mother?
- Would you contact the doctor who had seen the child locally and/or the child protection service once they had contacted the mother?

Intervention issues for the solicitor

The solicitor Marie has chosen is one who is experienced in family law work. Marie has been able to see him almost immediately after her and Samantha's visit to the doctor. By now, Marie believes there is a growing likelihood that her daughter has been sexually abused, and she is even more worried as to what exactly has happened, when it has happened, where it has happened and who has done it. She knows the children are with their father and his friend several nights a week, and she suspects this has provided the opportunity. She feels betrayed and guilty about her own parenting failure. She is very angry with him, his parents and herself. She feels she must take immediate action to stop all contact between Samantha and her father. She expects that the solicitor will assist her to do this. She has brought Samantha with her, envisaging that the solicitor will speak with her, as did the local doctor, even though she is so young.

The solicitor will want to explore the facts of Marie's crisis, what the school has said and done, who has said and done it, and what the doctor has said and done. The solicitor will want to know the events of the separation, the post-separation arrangements for residence, contact, child support and property settlement, and what—if any—legal processes have been set in train. He will seek information from Marie about the details of the abuse, and any evidence supporting a conclusion of abuse. He will ask Marie about her observations of Samantha's behaviour to add to the information she has given him from the teachers and the local doctor. He will also ask about Samantha's understanding of what is happening.

He should ask Marie about domestic violence, because of its association with child sexual abuse, using questions about specific abusive behaviour rather than general questions. This family may look to be an ordinary middle-class family, but domestic violence may be present. This exploration may not be easy as Marie is upset, does not always understand what is being said, and has come without any friend or relative to support and interpret for her. Marie is adamant that the solicitor must stop the father seeing Samantha and probably also Ben.

The solicitor will explain that there are a number of interventions or orders he can seek, but that it is not a simple matter of stopping James seeing the children. He will explain his role as a solicitor acting on behalf of Marie, and point out that he cannot see and represent Samantha, as he is Marie's solicitor, but he can apply to the Family Court for orders for a separate representative for both children. Marie's solicitor does know that, at six and four years of age, the views of both children might not be given much weight by the court, but they should be obtained and presented. This can be done through a separate representative or through a court-appointed expert presenting their views.

If he discovers there has been domestic violence, the solicitor will advise seeking an intervention order (or equivalent) against James for the protection of Marie and the children by making an application to the state Magistrates Court. He will try to respond to Marie's concern about contact arrangements, although the child protection service has not yet investigated. He can suggest an application to the Family Court for her to seek residence of both children, and to provide for contact only under conditions that will safeguard the children in the short term—conditions like contact during the day under professional supervision. At this stage, there is no evidence that Samantha wants no contact at all, just that she does not want to stay overnight. However, as more information becomes available on her views, on the abuse and its impact, such arrangements may have to be changed.

Marie has told him of the notification to the child protection service, and wonders how they will fit into the problem. He will advise her to cooperate with them, inform them he is her solicitor and ask them to contact him. He will explain that it is possible that child protection might wish to take legal action themselves to protect Samantha, and Ben also if he is found to have been abused as well. In that case, the service would make an application to the state Children's Court. There are technical questions of jurisdiction between the Family Court and the Children's Court, and parallel proceedings cannot take place. Usually proceedings in the Children's Court would take precedence over proceedings in the Family Court under the protocols put in place in most states.

Seeing how distressed Marie is, and wondering how distressed Samantha is too, the solicitor would consider referring Marie to a local counselling service that could provide short- as well as long-term support. If domestic violence were involved, he would also consider a referral to a specialist domestic violence service. He may consider alternative dispute resolution services for the residence and contact questions, but with the unresolved question of the children's sexual abuse and other family violence this would not seem appropriate at this stage. He will be seeking a medical report from Samantha's doctor to support Marie's application for no contact, and he will ask the doctor for this.

Questions for the child protection worker

- What would you say about your role when you arrived to visit the mother?
- What would you say to the child, who is present, as to your role?
- What information would you seek from the child and the mother?
- What would you say to the child if she denied any sexual abuse?
- What would you say to the young brother, and would you investigate the possibility that he too had been abused?
- What evidence would you seek to determine that domestic violence was or was not involved?
- Would you seek to see the father?
- Would you contact the father's parents, his flatmate, and/or the flatmate's ex-wife?
- Would you contact the child's school, the brother's kindergarten, the family's doctor and/or the mother's solicitor?

- Would you want to know what the mother's solicitor had advised and what his plans were?
- Would you refer either child to a specialist sexual assault clinic?
- Would you refer the family for counselling at a community-based agency?
- Would you give a view as to what legal action the mother should take?

Intervention issues for the child protection worker

The child protection worker will find a family that is different from many families referred to the service. Both parents work in skilled occupations; both have comfortable accommodation; neither has a history of social problems; both are articulate. Marie is now more knowledgeable about her own and her child's position as a result of visiting the doctor and the solicitor, but she is very distressed. Indeed, she is very angry with her husband, blaming him for causing the problem with his departure, as her increased knowledge suggests she has a serious family problem. However, Marie may not know much about the role of the child protection service, what the service might do and how it will do it. The worker will need to give Marie this information.

The worker will have to work with an angry, distressed and anxious mother in order to focus on whether or not the daughter has been sexually abused, whether or not she has suffered any other form of abuse, and whether or not she is at any risk of future harm. The worker needs to recall that female children seem to be at heightened risk of sexual abuse after parental separation, that children with any disability are at heightened risk of sexual and physical abuse, that sexual abuse takes place in all social circumstances, that such abuse may be accompanied by physical abuse and emotional abuse, and that no one may tell the truth for a variety of reasons.

The worker will seek to discover who might be the perpetrators of possible sexual or other abuse, having regard to the fact that the children are always in the care of only one parent at a time, that neither parent can scrutinise the other fully, and that a male is the most likely perpetrator but that occasionally females do sexually abuse children. The worker will seek information from Marie, the child, the child's brother, the local doctor and the solicitor, the school and from James, his flatmate and possibly James' and Andrew's friends. Possibly the reasons for Andrew's separation will need investigation.

During this process, the worker will have to deal with parents who were in the midst of a marital dispute—one sufficient to lead to their separation—before the issue of sexual abuse was raised. The marital dispute is not yet settled in any respect, and Marie for one cannot explain why it happened. She is very mistrustful of her husband, and very angry with him over the marital separation and now over the possibility of abuse. It has not occurred to her yet that the daughter may have been physically abused as well, that her son may have been abused too or that a number of perpetrators may have been involved. When she realises these possibilities, she will become more angry still. She may become insistent that the worker stops the father or any of his friends having contact with the daughter and the son immediately.

The worker will have to engage with James, who has rejected the possibility of sexual abuse and who may be unwilling to cooperate or at best be evasive. He too may be extremely angry with Marie, either because he thinks the abuse is occurring while the child is with her or because he is associated with the abuse and doesn't want the matter examined. The worker will consider whether James has any history of violence when challenged, as he will be by these events. The worker will have to consider what threat James poses to Marie and to the worker. When visiting James, the worker should take a colleague along or see him in the office.

The worker will have to interview both children; again, straightforward, simple and unambiguous questions will be best. Since the children may have been warned against telling—or even threatened—the worker will need to establish a relationship with them that allows them to trust the worker. The worker will need to explain her role to the children, the purpose of the interview, the sort of things the worker will ask them, how they should deal with her questions and what will be done with the information.

After an investigation, the worker will have to consider what action she might recommend to both parents if one or both children have been abused; such action might include making suggestions about adults' further contact with the child, depending on the severity of the abuse, who was involved, whether or not violence was involved, what effect the abuse had on the child, what commitment there was to change, how change might be effected, what measures would protect the child and for how long protection was needed. The worker can suggest the mother or father take action through making a residence and contact application to the Family Court— and indeed it appears that Marie has one underway already. That being so, the worker may recommend that Marie proceed with that application, and that she seek for the application to go on the Magellan list in that Family Court registry—that is, to the specialised court program that deals with child abuse allegations in residence and contact disputes.

The worker will have to consider what support or other services the children and their parents need during the investigation and immediately afterwards.

Case coordination

Initially the school principal must undertake the case coordination responsibility, as she has begun an investigation of the possible abuse. If she had made a notification herself, she would have undertaken some further case coordination as she continued to work with the staff in her school and with the child protection service while the investigation continued. In the longer term, she will want to remain in the group of agencies managing Samantha's problem as long as the child remains a pupil at her school.

Although the doctor and the family law solicitor are the next professionals to see the child and the mother, the problems pass quickly to the child protection worker, who will have the major responsibility for inter-disciplinary collaboration in the next period. The worker will work with the local doctor, the school and the mother's solicitor as she seeks to assess the allegations and to develop a plan for Samantha's care. Marie's solicitor will also need to work with the child protection worker and the local doctor to advise the mother as to what action she should take and to assist her to do this. At this stage, it is not known whether the family's problems will take them to any action in any legal jurisdiction, although this seems likely. If so, a series of further collaborative arrangements will need to be made.

THE SECOND FAMILY

Annie Fenton, Jason Grimaldi, Stacey Fenton, Adam Bryant and Anthony Fenton-Grimaldi

Annie Fenton and Jason Grimaldi were in a de facto relationship for two years when their son, Anthony, was born. Annie had two children, Stacey, aged eleven, from a short-term de facto relationship, and Adam, aged nine, from her marriage to Max, a member of the police force. She had left Max three years earlier because of his violence to her. Subsequently he remarried and moved to Caringbah, a southern suburb of Sydney, half an hour away by car from Annie's rented public housing home in Mt Pritchard, where she had moved from the refuge after leaving Max.

Jason had been a friend of her sister who lived nearby, and Annie had met him on his release from gaol, where he served a sentence for armed robbery. Jason too lived nearby, at his mother's home. He had been married previously but Annie knew little of this marriage. Jason and his family did not see his former wife or children. Jason's three married sisters lived nearby. Jason worked locally as a motor mechanic for a mate, but often left his employer for months at a time.

After Anthony was born, Jason took time off from work to help Annie. When the baby was three weeks old, Annie went to her daughter's graduation from primary school. At the graduation, Annie's sister told her there had been trouble when she was in hospital and that her daughter and son had run away to the aunt one night saying that Jason was hitting and punching them both, and arguing and shouting at them constantly. Annie noticed that both children were afraid of Jason and she spoke with Jason about this. She was surprised by his anger. He hit and punched her while she was holding the baby. He had hit her previously, but this was worse. Life at home deteriorated and Jason became violent to Annie and her older children, but not to the new baby. He did not return to work as arranged, but instead stayed at home, allowing her no time to herself except when he took the baby to his mother's for a few hours several times a week. Annie noticed that Jason had drilled holes in the floor of all the bedrooms and the bathroom, and a person could watch the rooms from under the house.

When the baby was six weeks old, Jason took him to visit his mother as usual but returned home alone, saying that he knew Annie wanted him to leave and if she forced him to leave he would make sure she never saw the baby again. He would not bring the baby back until she agreed he could stay. She agreed, but he did not bring the baby back for three days. Neither Annie nor her sister could locate the baby. When the baby was twenty weeks old, Jason went back to work. Life appeared to return to normal for some months until the children complained that someone was watching them from under the house during the day.

Then Annie's sister, without telling Annie, contacted Max, suggesting he should be concerned about Jason's physical abuse of his son. Max contacted the child protection service about Jason's violence to Stacey and Adam. He knew nothing of the baby's abduction. The child protection service arranged with the school to see the children there with the police. After the interviews with each child, the police telephoned the mother at home. Annie was out shopping but Jason was home. He pretended to be Annie's brother and took the message that the police wanted to see her. He did not deliver it but waited until Annie came home, then took the baby with him on a supposed visit to his mother but he did not return. When the police came, apparently unannounced, to the house two days later, Anne denied the accounts of Jason's violence that her children had given to the police. Subsequently the children denied their original allegations when seen again by the child protection worker at school. After ten days, Jason returned with the baby.

The police and child protection took no further action. Max spoke about seeing the solicitor who had assisted him in his divorce from Annie and asking him to make an application to the Family Court for residence of his son. Annie indicated she might agree to this. Max did make an application to the Family Court, but to Annie's surprise it was for the residence of both children on the grounds of their physical and sexual abuse by Jason that Annie had refused to stop. Annie panicked and went to the Domestic Violence Centre that had assisted her previously.

Issues for all the professionals

This is a family with many splintered relationships.Annie has children from three relationships,including a baby son with her current partner. They all live with her and Jason,who has a mysterious past marriage. At least one of Annie's past relationships has been fraught with domestic violence. The present one contains domestic violence affecting her and all the children, the physical abuse of two of the children, the possible sexual abuse of one of the children and the repeated abduction of the baby as a tool of control over the mother and her children. Jason's family is Italian in origin, and it is tempting to explain his history of criminal offences, his disappearances from his job and home and his abduction of his baby son as an aspect of his Italian heritage, as Max chooses to do.

Annie seems powerless to protect herself and her children. Although she and the children have experienced physical abuse from Jason, she has done nothing—presumably because Jason abducts their baby in order to maintain control over her and the children. Agencies have attempted to intervene, but Jason's threats regarding the baby have ensured that Annie and her children have pretended nothing is wrong. As a result, Annie's former partner, Max, a man of some power, is taking action through the Family Court to protect his son and his step-daughter, with whom he had lived for some four years.

A consequence of the domestic violence is concern for the current safety of the children, of Annie and of any of the professionals working with the family. Jason's strong desire for control will be challenged by Max's actions. Consequently, his violence may escalate. Should any precipitate action be taken towards immediate separation for the protection of the children and Annie, they may all be in more danger from Jason in the immediate aftermath of a sudden unplanned separation.

The threats to her baby seem to have overwhelmed Annie and, even if she can gain assistance it may not be effective. She was able to leave a past violent relationship by using the supportive services of a refuge to separate and to relocate with her children. Although she rebuilt her life, she entered into another relationship marked by domestic violence—and it appears to be an even worse one for her and the children. The question of Max's past domestic violence, how extensive it was, how it affected the children at the time, whether or not it takes place in his new family and whether he could cooperate with Annie over parenting should he gain an order for the residence of either one or both of the two older children needs consideration. So does the question of Max's intentions: does he really want to be the residential parent for one or both of the children, or is he seeking something else?

Engaging Stacey and her mother to determine what is really happening and to assess what, if any, protection is needed and can be gained for all the children and Annie will be difficult. Achieving an honest professional relationship with both Stacy and Annie is vital, but both will lose some of the better aspects of their life if they reveal the truth. Yet if they don't reveal the truth they may lose even more. It is important to achieve an honest professional relationship with both at the same time, for achieving an honest relationship with only one family member—even when they are a victim—has not been sufficient to resolve the problems. Obtaining honest communication with Max may be difficult, and it could well be impossible with Jason. Max may not wish to reveal his past domestic violence and Jason certainly does not.

The children must wonder how they can be honest with a professional without bringing themselves or the baby into danger. Where would they feel safe to live? What are the circumstances that they think would allow them to live with one or other parent or step-parent? What are their feelings about any association with Jason? Might the daughter consider living with Max so as to be away from Jason? How would they maintain a connection with their mother if they lived with Max? Should they be separated, how would they maintain any contact with each other? How might they wish to participate in making these decisions?

Finally, there are a number of issues around Jason as a father to his baby and a step-father to the two older children. Although the two oldest children may leave to be cared for by Max, they might return on contact visits to Annie, and the baby may feature as a method of controlling them and Annie when they are there. Jason has a criminal history, repeats a criminal offence in abducting the baby, shows no regard for the care of his partner and her children, and threatens Annie and the children with his violence. Should Jason and Annie not separate, Annie may not be considered a suitable residential parent for her daughter or her son. If Annie became the contact parent, should Jason have no contact, no overnight contact or only supervised contact with his step-children? If Annie and Jason were to separate, what parenting arrangements should be set up for him with his son?

Questions for the professionals

As in the last case, all the professionals will face a number of questions as they meet the different members of this family.

Questions for the Mt Pritchard Domestic Violence Centre worker

- Annie has been assisted by your service previously but you are new to her. What would you say about your role and that of the service now?
- She has told you that her current partner, Jason, is being accused of being physically and sexually abusive to her daughter and physically abusive to her son, and that she fears losing them to her former husband who was also violent to her. What information would you seek from her about Jason's treatment of her, his step-children and his own child?
- Having gained this information, would you see any or all of the children or Annie or anyone else as being in any danger from Jason?
- If so, what would you advise her to do about this?

- Do you think she has any power to implement solutions to her problems?
- Would you advise her to seek legal advice as well?
- Would you advise Annie to contact the child protection service or would you contact them yourself? Or would you avoid the child protection service as it was no help previously?
- You discover from Annie that Jason has abducted their son on at least two occasions and has threatened to do it again if she leaves him. What would you advise her to do about this?
- Would you contact Annie's sister?
- Would you contact any other family members?
- Do you think Annie and/or her children need other services?

Intervention issues for the Domestic Violence Centre worker

As Annie has been a client of this service before, it may seem unnecessary to explain the worker's role. However, the service may have made changes in service provision and an explanation of the worker's role is one way to open up Annie's concerns and set the boundaries for the relationship Annie may have considerable difficulty in engaging with the worker due to her feelings of disempowerment after two violent marital relationships and the current threats from Jason. Even if she can engage, she may have difficulty in being honest—she has learned over a long time to conceal the violence in her household.

Annie's past successful working relationship with the service and the worker's knowledge of domestic violence and child abuse, as well as their likely impact on Annie and the children, will be an advantage to the worker. The worker will know to ask specific questions about Annie's experiences, such as the details of all the violence, physical and emotional, and about control in relation to herself and her children, as well as about the possibility of threats to herself, to the children or to anyone else. The worker does not know how dangerous Jason is, and may be tempted to minimise his violence, but she will need to assess this, and her own vulnerability to his violence, as a basis for further action. She must collect all the information that she can, and when she does discover his threats, his disappearances with the baby, his criminal record, his time in gaol, his strong desire to control people and his surveillance arrangements, the information will indicate a high potential for serious violence to family members and to professionals. She may decide to contact child protection and the police to gain more information in assessing Jason's behaviour, and to discuss options in managing Annie's possible departure.

Gaining Annie's trust will be difficult, but the threat of losing her daughter—even all her children—may create such a crisis for Annie that she will be as motivated to change as she was when she left Max. Because the worker is part of the service Annie is most likely to trust—the one with the most expertise in her and her children's problems—the worker should consider that she and the agency will be the central pivot for all future action.

The worker will be faced with an urgent situation, but must nevertheless proceed cautiously. A simple rescue approach to Annie will not succeed. The worker will see the dangers for Annie and her children in staying with Jason, but she will need to assess how urgent the need is for implementing Annie's now expressed desire to leave Jason and how she might do this safely. She will know that, if Annie stays, she may lose the residence of all of her children: when information is presented to the Family Court by Max, as well as by any expert his solicitor commissions, by any child legal representative and by the child protection service, Annie may appear unable to protect any of her children, regardless of who her partner is. If she leaves, she and the children may face even more violence from Jason and she will also lose her home and her way of life.

The worker will also have to assess whether Annie should take any legal action now. Should she take an apprehended violence order against Jason immediately; should she see a solicitor to assist her with Max's application for residency of the two children; and should Jason's abduction of his baby be reported to the police? The most cautious action would be to bring in the services of a family lawyer for Annie, while the worker considers all options. Taking an apprehended violence order at an early stage might inflame the problem, although it would demonstrate Annie's willingness to protect the children from Jason. Reporting Jason's abduction of the baby and his threats to the police might also cause further problems unless it were done in such a way as to maintain Annie's continuing care of the baby and her own and the other children's safety.

Annie is fast approaching a family crisis, and the worker would be well advised to include Annie's sister in the forward planning. She has been a support to Annie and her children for a long time, and Annie will need her continuing concern.

Questions for the child protection worker

- As you and the police have already investigated a notification for two of the children in this family and encountered considerable frustration, what do you regard as the problems ahead in undertaking a second investigation that will be set in the context of a Family Court residence and contact dispute?
- What might your feelings be about this, and how would you deal with them—especially your views that this may be a divorce storm in a teacup and a no-win family problem?
- Max's comments convince you to investigate again. What would you do differently in an investigation this time?
- How might you approach the two older children this time?
- How might you approach Annie this time?
- How might you approach Jason?
- Max has told you of Annie's sister's role in the family; would you contact her?
- Max has told you his solicitor has obtained a legal representative for the two older children; would you approach this person, and what might you discuss with them?
- Would you check Jason's criminal record and gaol history?
- Max has told you he thinks Jason is dangerous and is involved in the Mafia; how would you investigate this?
- Do you think Annie, her children, other professionals or yourself are in any danger?
- Do you think you need to do anything about this?
- Do you think anyone in the family needs other support services; if so, what might be available?

Intervention issues for the child protection worker

The child protection worker, being based in one of the busiest child protection offices in Sydney, may feel disheartened by the report from the team leader of Max's second notification and his and Annie's sister's reported outline of the same problems investigated unsuccessfully previously. The worker may find it hard to plan the investigation free of feelings of frustration, even despair. The worker and the police officer had been sure from what the children said and from the school's accounts that Jason had physically abused them. Then their findings were obstructed by Annie's denial, followed by the children's denial. The worker may have thought that the approach and each interview with the child had been handled well and not understood what had gone wrong. The worker may wonder if the re-notification relates to Max's unsuccessful application for residence of his son when he and Annie separated. Maybe he is just angry with her for leaving or jealous of Jason and Jason's role in his son's life, and so is using Annie's sister to confirm his mischievous allegations. Since these children are quite old enough to speak for themselves, surely they knew what they were doing when they withdrew their allegations? Maybe their abuse was not as serious as the child protection worker and the police had originally thought; perhaps intervention was not justified.

However, the worker needs to counter any underlying pessimism with the knowledge that child abuse allegations arising in the context of parental separation and divorce are more likely to be true than false, and that children of divorced and separated parents are at greater risk from child abuse than are other children. The worker needs to consider also that physical and sexual abuse often coexists with domestic violence, and that the perpetrators of domestic violence can take physical and psycho-logical control of their victims. The worker knows that retractions by victims of allegations can happen as a result of explicit or implicit threats from family members, and retractions can indicate a greater level of family complexity than originally appreciated. Thus the worker might consider approaching the family less directly than previously, possibly beginning with Max and with Annie's sister, in order to find out the reasons for the denial of the abuse previously. The worker might also consider approaching the school to see what staff there know of the family since the first investigation.

Approaching Annie's sister should give the worker more understanding of Annie's situation, and possibly inform her of Jason's domestic violence, his criminal history, his disappearances with the baby and the threats he has made. This contact may lead the worker to meet Annie next, rather than approaching the children, as Annie's fear of Jason is silencing the children and little may be gained from the children as yet. However, the worker should appreciate that Annie may be suspicious of her, knowing the worker's power to take action about the future care of her children without her agreement and knowing the worker suspects she has lied previously. If the worker cannot find any way to engage Annie by explaining the worker's role, then it would seem important for the worker to see whether there was any service—like the Domestic Violence Service or Annie's solicitor—that she could trust and work with.

The worker is aware that Max has made seemingly outlandish suggestions about Jason's Mafia connections. These may seem untrue, but they do need investigation through the police force, and Max may be of use in guiding the worker through the information procedures of his employing agency. The infliction of child abuse is related to criminality and the more serious the abuse the more this is so. Details of his imprisonment would assist as well. Admittedly, it is difficult to learn anything about Jason; he makes every effort to be secretive. Jason's secrecy may obscure his potential danger to his family and to any professionals investigating him. Furthermore, if there is any suggestion that Annie will leave him and take his son, then family members and professionals will be in danger.

Ultimately, the worker will need to approach Jason, but should not visit him alone. The worker must appreciate that Jason has a criminal history which includes violence with a weapon. Jason may not cooperate, but attempts should be made to see if he would.

Questions for the legal representative for the children

- You have been appointed to represent Stacey and Adam, aged eleven and nine. Would you meet them face to face?
- What would you say to them about your role?
- What would you ask them regarding the possible abuse, noting that they had made allegations in the past but then denied them?
- What would you ask them about their preferences for their future parenting arrangements?
- What, if any, commitments would you make to them?
- What would you do if they were able to tell you of Jason's threats to abduct their baby brother?
- Would you see Annie and/or Max and/or Jason and/or Stacey's father, who is uninvolved?
- If so, what would you discuss with them?
- Would you contact the children's school, the Domestic Violence Centre, the police or the child protection services?
- Would you contact any other agency?
- Would you explore Jason's criminal history?

- Would you commission an independent evaluation of the children's family functioning?

Intervention issues for the separate representative for the children

The separate representative will be appointed from a panel of experienced family law practitioners who usually have had further training in representing children. The representative will see the children face to face, as they are clearly of an age appropriate for discussion of these issues. Seeing children face to face—even when very young—is always advisable so as to learn directly about them. The solicitor will know that Stacey and Adam may now be distrustful of any professional, and they may also be resentful about seeing yet another one. The solicitor will need to explain why she is seeing the children, her role in the legal process, and what the consequences of their representation may be. The children will usually meet the solicitor in her office to maintain a professional relationship and to avoid witnessing home events and conditions. Part of the professionalism in the relationship is a clear, warm and empathic style of communication, and language must be kept suitable for the children's age and level of understanding. As children do not know the intricacies of the legal processs, repeated explanations are desirable.

Since the children may be distrustful, and since they have made allegations and retracted them, the solicitor may prefer to rely on the child protection services account of their findings about the abuse. The solicitor may concentrate instead on determining the children's wishes as to their parenting arrangements, including the strength or otherwise of their relationships with their parents and step-parents. In the Family Court, the best interests of the child—a wider concern than the safety of the child—are the paramount concern in deciding their residence and contact arrangements. It is the separate representative's responsibility to prepare the case on behalf of the children, and to promote and protect their welfare rather than merely present their wishes as in the Children's Court. The representative will wish to discuss how they relate to their parents and step-parents, what they do with them, what they want to do with them, how the parents and they fit into their other activities, how they live in their home(s) and whatever else the children want to say. It is common to ask broad and open-ended questions about these matters, trying to elicit as much information as possible. It is also important to be receptive to what the children say, even when they say surprising or unwelcome things. And these children—especially Stacey—might say some unwelcome things. She might not want to live with her mother if it means she has to live with Jason, or she might not want to live with Max even if it means living with an abusive stepparent. Being eleven, she is old enough to have strong views and to maintain them regardless of contrary persuasion. This is a family that may evoke a strong reaction in the separate representative. The mother lacks an ability to protect her children, the step-father, Jason, is potentially dangerous to the family members and the professionals, and Max may not be a satisfactory father. The professional may feel angry with all the adults and dismiss what ability does lie with them.

The children's situation is difficult for them; they will have to weigh up their relationship with their mother and put it against their relationship with others and against their feelings of personal safety. The separate representative is likely to want to seek further material to assess the children's needs and how best to meet them, and may make inquiries of the school and the family doctor to obtain their written records of the children. Assessing the threat that Jason poses to the children is critical, and the solicitor will want to seek Jason's criminal record and even his record from the gaol. She will also subpoena the child protection service for its file on the children. The separate representative may find she needs more expertise in assessing the children's future care, and may seek orders for a court-appointed expert to undertake a further assessment to deepen the information available to her.

The separate representative would probably have seen the children's mother, as the children would be unlikely to travel without her, but she may not have seen any of the other parents. However, the child representative would seek to have the other parents and step-parents interviewed by the court expert and, given proper safety precautions, also interviewed with the children.

Questions for the expert evaluating the children's situation

- You have been asked by the legal representative of Stacey and Adam to provide an independent evaluation of the impact of the possible abuse of these two children by their current step-father and to make recommendations as to the future parenting arrangements for these children. What would you say to these children about your role?

- How would you deal with the fact that they have been seen now by the child protection service on three occasions, the police twice and their own legal representative once about this same problem?
- Would you see Annie and/or Max and/or Jason?
- Would you see them with the children?
- Would you see the baby with or without Jason?
- What evidence would you be seeking to use in any recommendation?
- Would you contact all the other agencies with which the family has been involved?

Issues for intervention of the expert

The evaluation expert will expect to interview the two oldest children as the primary source of information for the report about the children and the family's care of them. When interviewing the children, the expert has to treat them with respect, give them a full and understandable explanation of their role and actions, cover the confidentiality of information given, indicate an expectation of reciprocal honesty and trust, maintain the children's safety while making the report, and not make unfounded (and biased) assumptions about the possible abuse. The expert has to acknowledge the impact of what the children have endured through the past and present family turmoil, and especially how the children view seeing yet another professional. The expert needs to be careful about seeing the children with and without either parent, and needs to canvass this with the children first.

The court expert will want to see Annie and Max as the two possible residential parents; having done that, they will find they are confronted by alternatives that are difficult to assess for the children's future care. Max has a history of domestic violence to Annie, and this will have had an impact on the children. Annie has partnered two violent men. Careful delving into the impact of the past and present violence on the children and their relationships with the parents is essential, and will involve contacting many other people, such as the children's aunt, Adam's step-mother, the children's doctor, the children's school and any other services with which the children have contact. The expert may think they do not need to make so many collateral contacts, but in this family—with its history of overt and hidden violence—it is necessary in order to assess parent–child relationships. Contacting the domestic violence service and the child protection service will be a high priority, as well as seeking their advice about which other agencies to contact.

The expert may decide not to see Jason, as sufficient evidence about his treatment of the children may be available without the need to see him. On the other hand, the expert may want to meet with Jason personally. If so, it is important to consider whether this will threaten Annie and the children. The expert may feel some concern for Anthony, and will have to consider carefully any professional responsibility to him if evidence is found of Jason damaging relationships with his step-children.

Case coordination

The complexity of this family's difficulties will not be tackled successfully without ongoing collaboration between all the legal representatives, the child protection service, the domestic violence service, the police and the Family Court. All will have to remain in close contact, and the issue will be which professional should lead the collaboration. The answer isn't clear. No one agency has ongoing responsibility for the family as a whole, or even for any one of its members. In such circumstances, family members often prefer the collaboration to remain in the hands of an agency with a legal mandate for intervention, like the police, the Family Court or the state child protection agency. None of these agencies has authority for long-term monitoring, and the domestic violence service does not have a service focus around the children. The absence of a suitable long-term monitoring agency for these circumstances is a gap in the family law service system.

CONCLUSION

The cases presented, and the discussion of them from different professional perspectives in relation to parental separation and divorce, underline the need for professionals to make a full assessment of the problems presented to them. They must do so, and come to decisions about intervention, using their specialised knowledge of child abuse in this context. Unless assessment and intervention are built on the knowledge flowing now from rigorous research, the contribution of professionals will be poorly based and not as effective as it should be. Children caught in abusive families are mostly too young to take any action independently If professionalscannot intervene appropriately, the children are victimised again—by those who are supposed to assist them.

This book has argued that much of what has been accepted as fact about the nature and causes of child abuse in the context of parental separation and divorce has not been true and that, as a result, much of the professional intervention with families affected by this problem has been misguided and inadequate It has argued that sound research has recently become available, and from this the authors have constructed an integrated research-based body of knowledge for professionals working with the problems of child abuse within the jumble of the services termed the family law service system.

This book has undertaken a pioneering task. It has shown how children have been metaphorically and actually abused by professionals working in the family law service system largely because professional intervention has not been based on research-tested knowledge but on myth and misunderstanding. Consequently, professionals have tended to dismiss child abuse allegations in the context of parental separation and divorce. The book shows that child abuse in this context is real, that it is serious and it is damaging to the children involved.

The book has argued for a new understanding of child abuse in the context of parental separation and divorce based on the evidence of recent research: parental separation and divorce and child abuse are not coincidentally linked but causally linked and their link is a new social problem in post-modern society. Recognising that child abuse in the context of parental separation and divorce is a new social problem, the book seeks to offer the professionals of the family law service system improved intervention. It does this by being the first book to present the research now available for professionals to use to assist the children and their families with abuse in this context, and by weaving the knowledge into an integrated multi-disciplinary intervention framework. The framework is demonstrated by the discussion of the various professional roles in the case studies in this, the final chapter. The fact that much of the professional intervention in the family law service system for this problem is still based on myth (Hart, 2006) is troubling. This book is a step in a long journey to support children caught up in this family and societal problem.

NOTES

Chapter 2

1 The two main case reports in the Family Court of Australia matters are 'FLC'—Family Law Cases (CCH) and 'FLR'—Family Law Reports (Butterworths). These are cited with paragraph numbers. Quotations are cited with page numbers and details of the judge or court making the decision. Cases in the text itself are referred to by name and year only. Full citations appear in the separate list of cases. Family Court cases are also available online at <www.familycourt.gov.au>. Cases in the Federal Magistrates Court are accessible online at <www.fmc.gov.au>.

2 'De facto' literally means 'in fact'. These are heterosexual and same-sex couples who cohabit but are not formally married. Australia does not recognise same-sex marriages. De facto relationships are governed by federal law in respect of children's matters such as where children live, who children spend time with, and child support. De factos are governed by individual state law in respect of property division and 'spousal' maintenance In some states and territories, de factos are called 'domestic partners'.

3 National statistics on marriage and divorce are available through the Australian Bureau of Statistics (ABS). As there is no formal requirement to register or dissolve a de facto or domestic relationship there are no national figures. According to the 2001 Census, 5 per cent of cohabiting heterosexual adults defined themselves as 'de facto' couples; 0.01 per cent identified as

being in male same-sex cohabiting relationships and 0.08 per cent in female same-sex relationships. The census conducted in 2006 may reveal different figures.

4   The two federal courts—the Family Court of Australia and the Federal Magistrates Court—share the same registries, buildings and in-house primary dispute resolution services like counselling, mediation and conciliation. They have different rules, procedures, forms, fees, listings and judicial officers. A combined registry and streamlining of some procedures are being considered.

5   Section 60CA states that 'in deciding whether to make a particular parenting order in relation to a child, a court must regard the best interests of the child as the paramount consideration'.

6   Section 68R states that a court may make, revive, vary, suspend or discharge a contact order in family violence proceedings subject to certain provisions including the purpose stated in section 68N not to expose people to family violence.

7   The *Children, Youth and Families Act* 2005 has been passed in Victoria. It is expected to come into effect in October 2006. New section 162(1) contains exactly the same six grounds as in the *Children and Young Person Act* 1989. The other two grounds not detailed refer to abandonment by, and death or incapacity of, a parent.

8   'The seriousness of an allegation made, the inherent likelihood of an occurrence of a given description, or the gravity of the consequences flowing from a particular finding are considerations which must affect the answer to the question whether the issue has been proved to the reasonable satisfaction of the tribunal. In such matters, "reasonable satisfaction" should not be produced in inexact proofs, indefinite testimony, or indirect inferences.' (*Briginshaw v Briginshaw*, 1938: 362)

9   In civil matters in federal courts like the Family Court of Australia and the Federal Magistrates Court, this is in part reflected in section 140 of the *Evidence Act* 1995 (Cth), that reads:

(1)   In a civil proceeding the court must find the case of a party proved if it is satisfied that the case has been proved on the balance of probabilities.

(2)   Without limiting the matters that the court may take into account in deciding whether it is so satisfied, it is to take into account:
(a)   the nature of the cause of action or defence; and
(b)   the nature of the subject-matter of the proceedings; and
(c)   the gravity of the matters alleged.

Chapter 3

1   The Convention came into force on 16 January 1991.

2   In 1995, the legal aid bodies calculated that $6 million per annum nationally was required to fund the increase in the number of child representative appointments following *Re K* (1994). See also Keough (2000: 216–18).

3   In November 2004, the federal Attorney-General launched *Pathways for Children: A Review of Children's Representation in Family Law.* The report reviews earlier Practice Directions, papers and case law about the appointment and role of child representatives under the former section 68L of the *Family Law Act.* Many of these recommendations are now enshrined in legislation in the revamped section 68L and new section 68LA pursuant to the *Family Law Amendment (Shared Responsibility) Act* 2006.

4   One reason for the low media profile is section 121 of the *Family Law Act* which prohibits publication by any means of any proceedings under the Act without court approval (section 121(9)(g)). Such approval is rarely granted.

5   For example, the model in Victoria developed in 1992 is acclaimed and was followed in many states. See 'Protocol between the Department of Human Services and the Family Court of Australia'.

6   Project Magellan was established in-house in the Melbourne Reg istry of the Family Court of Australia in 1997. It was named 'Magellan' to reflect the creation of an internationally unique, innovative and exploratory project. The subsequent establishment of the Columbus program in Western Australia follows a similar theme.

7   Evaluations published in 2001 (see Chapter 7) of the initial pilot program of Project Magellan of 100 children's cases involving allegations of serious physical and/or sexual child abuse drawn from the Melbourne and Dande-nong registries in Victoria showed a reduction in time to reach final hearing from an average of 17.5 months to 8.7 months. The Magellan Procedures Manual of the Family Court includes cases management guidelines whereby Magellan cases ideally reach final trial and judicial determination within six months of a matter being designated as Magellan. This guideline is not always met.

REFERENCES

Alexander, R. 2002, *Domestic Violence in Australia: The Legal Response*, 3rd edn, Federation Press, Sydney.

—— 2005, 'Law Ignores the Reality of Split Families', *The Age*, 9 December.

Allen Consulting Group 2003, *Protecting Children: The Child Protection Outcomes Project—Final Report for the Victorian Department of Human Services*, VOHS, Melbourne.

Attorney-General's Department 2004a, *A New Approach to the Family Law System: Implementation of Reforms—Discussion Paper*, Attorney-General's Department, Canberra.

——2004b, *Pathways for Children: A Review of Children's Representation in Family Law*, Report, Attorney-General's Department, Canberra.

Australians Against Child Abuse 2002. 'What is Child Abuse? Definitions', <www.aaca.netlink.com.au/whatis/definitions.html>, accessed 20/2/02. This website has now been abandoned, as AACA has become the Australian Childhood Foundation, <www.childhood.org.au>.

Australian Institute of Health and Welfare (AIHW). 2004, *Child Protection Australia, 2002–2003*, 2004–2005, Australian Institute of Health and Welfare, Canberra.

Australian Law Reform Commission 1999, *Review of the Federal Civil Justice System*, Discussion Paper 62, ALRC, Canberra.

Australian Law Reform Commission and Human Rights and Equal Opportunity Commission 1997, *Seen and Heard: Priority for Children in the Legal Process*, Report No. 4, ALRC/HREOC, Commonwealth of Australia.

Bala N. and Schuman J. 1999, 'Allegations of Sexual Abuse When Parents Have Separated', *Canadian Family Law Quarterly*, vol. 17, pp. 192–243.

Batagol, B., Brown, T. and Kourdoulis, V. 2006, *Community Based Mediation in Family Law Report*, Law and Justice Foundation of NSW, Sydney.

Berliner, L. and Conte, J. 2003, 'Present State of Assessment and Treatment in the Field', a plenary paper presented to the 14th International Congress on Child Abuse and Neglect, ISPCAN, Denver, Colorado, July.

Berliner, Lucy and Elliott, Diana 1996, 'Sexual Abuse of Children', in John Briere, Lucy Berliner, Josephine Bulkley, Carole Jenny and Therese Reid (eds), *The APSAC Handbook on Child Maltreatment*, The American Professional Society on the Abuse of Children with Sage Publications, Los Angeles.

Berns S.S. 1991, 'Living Under the Shadow of Rousseau: The Role of Gender Ideologies in Custody and Access Decisions', *University of Tasmania Law Review*, vol. 10, pp. 233–55.

Bifulco, A. and Moran, A. 1998, *Wednesday's Child: Research into Women's Experience of Neglect and Abuse in Childhood, and Adult Depression*, Routledge, London.

Blanchard A. 1993, 'Violence in Families: The Effect on Children', *Family Matters*, vol. 34, pp. 31–6.

Briere, John, Berliner, Lucy, Bulkley, Josephine, Jenny, Carole and Reid, Therese (eds), 1996, *The APSAC Handbook on Child Maltreatment*, The American Professional Society on the Abuse of Children with Sage Publications, Los Angeles.

Briere, J. and Elliot, D.M. 1994, 'Immediate and Long Term Impacts of Child Sexual Abuse', *The Future of Children*, vol. 4, no. 2, pp. 54–69.

Briggs, Freda 1993, *Why My Child?*, Allen & Unwin, Sydney.

——1995, *From Victim to Offender*, Allen & Unwin, Sydney.

——1997, *Child Protection: A Guide For Teachers and Child Care Professionals*, Allen & Unwin, Sydney.

——2003, 'Child Sexual Abuse and Justice', a plenary paper presented to the Child Sexual Abuse: Justice Response or Alternative Resolution Conference, Australian Institute of Criminology, Adelaide, May.

Briggs, Freda with McVeity, Michael 2000, *Teaching Children to Protect Themselves*, Allen & Unwin, Sydney.

Bromfield L. and Higgins, D. 2005, *National Comparison of Child Protection Systems*, National Child Protection Clearing House, no. 22, Australian Institute of Family Studies.

Brown, Thea 1982, 'The Role of Local Government in the Development of the Social Services in Victoria, 1835-1975', PhD thesis, University of Melbourne, Melbourne, Australia.

——2003, 'Fathers and Child Abuse Allegations in the Context of Parental

Separation and Divorce', *Family Court Review*, vol. 41, no. 3, July, pp. 367–80.

Brown, Thea, Frederico, Margarita, Hewitt, Lesley and Sheehan, Rosemary 1998, *Violence in Families, Report No. 1: The Management of Child Abuse Allegations in Custody and Access Disputes Before the Family Court of Australia*, The FamilyViolence and Family Court Research Program, Monash University, Melbourne.

Brown, Thea with Sheehan, Rosemary, Frederico, Margarita and Hewitt, Lesley 2001, *Resolving Family Violence to Children, Report No. 3: The Evaluation Of Project Magellan, a Pilot Project for Managing Family Court Residence and Contact Disputes Where Allegations of Child Abuse Have Been Made*, FamilyViolence and Family Court Research Program, Monash University, Caulfield, Victoria.

Brown, Thea and Smale, S. 2001, 'Working With Angry Clients', unpublished paper, Department of SocialWork, Monash University, Caulfield East,Victoria.

Bryant D. 2004, 'The Future of the Family Court', the 3rd Annual Austin Asche Oration, Melbourne, <www.familycourt.gov.au>.

Butler-Sloss, Lord Justice E. 1988, *Report of the Inquiry into Child Abuse in Cleveland 1987*, Cmnd 412, HSMO, London.

Cashmore, J. 2002, *Evaluation of the Joint Investigation Team/Joint Investigation Responses Strategy*, report commissioned by Department of Community Services, NSW, NSW Police Force and NSW Health, written in conjuction with J. Taplin andV. Green, <http://pandora.nf a.gov.au>.

Cavanagh, Jo and Hewitt, Lesley 1999, *Through the Eyes of the Children: Families and Violence*, Southern Family Life, Melbourne.

Cawson, Pat 2002, *Child Maltreatment in the Family*, NSPCC, London.

Cawson, Pat, Wattam, Corinne, Brooker, Sue and Kelly, Graham 2001, *Child Maltreatment in the United Kingdom: A Study of the Prevalence of Child Abuse and Neglect*, NSPCC, London.

Charlesworth, Stephanie, Turner, Neville and Foreman, Lynne 2000, *Disrupted Families*, Federation Press, Sydney.

Charlow, A. 1987, 'Awarding Custody: The Best Interests of the Child and Other Fictions', *Yale Law and Policy Review*, vol. 5, pp. 267–90.

Chisholm, R. 2002, ' "The Paramount Consideration": Children's Interests in Family Law', *Australian Journal of Family Law*, vol. 16, pp. 87–115.

Clark, C.M.H. 1979a, *A History of Australia, Vol. 1*, Melbourne University Press, Melbourne.

——1979b, *A History of Australia, Vol. 2*, Melbourne University Press, Melbourne.

Community Care Division 2002, *An Integrated Strategy for Child Protection and Placement Sevices*, Department of Human Services, Melbourne.

Conte, Jon R. and Shore, David (eds) 1982, *Social Work and Child Sexual Abuse*, The Haworth Press, New York.

Corby, Brian 2000, *Child Abuse: Towards a Knowledge Base*, 2nd edn, Open University Press, Buckingham.

Corwin, D.L. 2002, 'An Interview with Roland Summit', in Jon R. Conte and David Shore (eds) *Social Work and Child Sexual Abuse*, The Haworth Press, New York.

Cox, P., Kershaw, S. and Trotter, J. 2000, *Child Sexual Assault*, Palgrave, Basingstoke.

Creighton, S. and Russell, N. 1995, *Voices from Childhood: A Survey of Childhood Experiences and Attitudes to Child Rearing Among Adults in the United Kingdom*, NSPCC, London.

Dallam, S.J. 1999, 'The Parental Alienation Syndrome: Is It Scientific?' in E. St Charles and L. Crook (eds), *Exposed: The Failure of Family Courts to Protect Children from Abuse in a Custody Dispute*, Our Children Charitable Foundation, Los Gatos, CA.

Davis, M. 2005, 'Baby Murders Mum Wins Right to an Appeal', <www. Mirror.co.uk> and <www.msb.com>.

Department of Community Development, Western Australia 2006, *Abuse and Neglect*, <www.wa.gov.au/Resour ces/Child+Pr otection/Abuse_and_Neg lect.htm>.

Department of Community Services, New South Wales 2006, *What is Child Abuse?*, <www.community.NSW.gov.au/html/child_protect/ abuse.htm>.

Department of Human Services, Victoria 1996, *Protocol Between the Department of Human Services and the Family Court of Australia*, DHS, Melbourne.

——2006, *What is Child Abuse?*, <http://hnb .dhs.vic.gov.au/children/cednav. nsf/childdocs/>.

Dessau, Hon. Justice Linda 1999, 'Children and the Court System', a plenary paper presented to the Australian Institute of Criminology Conference, June, Brisbane, <www.familycourt.gov.au/papers/html/ body_dessau.html>.

Dewar, J., Giddings J. and Parker, S. 1999, 'The Impact of Legal Aid Changes on Family Law Practice', *Australian Journal of Family Law*, vol. 13, pp 33-51.

Dewar, J. and Parker, S. 1999, *Parenting, Planning and Partnership: The Impact of the New Part VII of the Family Law Act 1975*, Griffith University, Brisbane

Dingwall, R., Eekelar, J. and Murray, T. 1983, *The Protection of Children: State Intervention and Family Life*, Blackwell, Oxford.

Doyle, Wyatt and Gail, Elizabeth 1986, *A Sourcebook on Child Sexual Abuse*, Sage, Beverly Hills.

Edelson, J.L. 2002, 'Studying the Co-Occur rence of Child Maltreatment and Domestic Violence in Families', in S.A. Graham-Bermann and J.L. Edelson (eds), *Domestic Violence in the Lives of Children: The Future of Research, Inter-*

vention, and Social Policy, American Psychological Association, Washington DC.

Fair, Vicki 2003, 'Following Black Footprints: Child Sexual Abuse in Indigenous Communities—Dynamics, Complexities and Solutions', paper presented to the Child Sexual Abuse: Justice Response or Alternative Resolution Conference, Australian Institute of Criminology, Adelaide, May.

Faller, K.C. 1998, 'The Parental Alienation Syndrome: What is It and What Data Supports It?', *Child Maltreatment*, vol. 3, no 2, pp. 100–15.

Family Court of Australia 2002–03, *Annual Report*, Canberra.

——2004–05, *Annual Report*, Canberra.

Family Law Council 2000, *The Best Interests of the Child? The Interaction of Public and Private Law in Australia*, Discussion Paper no. 2, Ausinfo, Canberra.

——2002, *Family Law and Child Protection, Final Report*, Children's Services Committee, Family Law Council, Commonwealth of Australia, Canberra.

Family Law Pathways Advisory Group (FLPAG) 2001, *Out of the Maze: Pathways to the Future for Families Experiencing Separation*, Commonwealth of Australia, Canberra.

Family Violence Committee 2005, *Family Violence Consultation Report*, Family Court of Australia, Canberra.

Family Violence Professional Education Taskforce 1996, *Family Violence: Everybody's Business, Somebody's Life*, 2nd edn, Federation Press, Sydney.

Faulks, J. 1997, 'The Languages of Help and Resolution', a plenary paper presented to the 25th Australian Association of Social Workers Annual National Conference, Canberra.

Fathers Rights Wikipedia 2006, <en.wikipedia.org/wiki/Father s'_rights>.

Fehlberg, B. and Kelly, F. 2000, 'Jurisdictional Overlaps Between the Family Division of the Children's Court and the Family Court of Australia', *Australian Journal of Family Law*, vol. 14, pp. 211–33.

Fergus, L. and Keel, Monique 2005, 'Adult Victims/Survivors of Childhood Sexual Assault', Australian Centre for the Study of Sexual Assault, *Wrap*, vol. 1, November, Australian Institute of Family Studies, Melbourne, Australia, pp. 1–6.

Finkelhor, D. 1984, *Child Sexual Abuse: New Theory and Research*, Free Press, New York.

Finkelhor, D. with Araji, Sharon, Baron, Larry, Browne, Angela and Peters, Stefanie 1986, *Sourcebook on Child Sexual Abuse*, Sage, Beverly Hills.

Finkelhor, D., Hotaling, G., Lewis, I.J. and Smith, C. 1990a, 'Sexual Abuse in a National Survey of Adult Men and Women: Prevalence, Characteristics and Risk Factors', *Child Abuse and Neglect*, vol 14, no. 1, pp. 19–28.

Finklehor, D., Hotaling, G. and Sedlack, A. 1990b, *Missing, Abducted, Runaway and Throwaway Children in the USA*, Government Printing Office, Washington DC.

Finkelhor, D. and Jones, L. 2001, 'The Decline in Sexual Abuse Cases', *Juvenile Justice Bulletin*, NCJ 186027, pp. 1–15, Government Printing Office, Washington DC.

Fleming, J. 2002, 'Just the Two of Us: The Involvement of Fathers in Building Stronger Families', *Developing Practice*, Winter, pp. 60–9.

Flood, Michael 2005, 'Fact Sheet 2: The Myth of Women's False Accusations of Domestic Violence and Use of Protective Orders, Comments from the Lone Fathers Association (Australia) Inc. on Review of Protective Orders Legislation, ACT', <www.ncsmc.org.au/docs/FalseAllegations DV. pdf>

Forrest, M. 2002, 'Working with Angry Clients', seminar, Department of Social Work, Monash University, Caulfield Campus, 24 May.

Frederick, John and Goddard, C. 2004, 'Does Poverty Cause Child Abuse or Does Child Abuse Cause Poverty?', a paper presented to the 15th International Conference, International Association for the Prevention of Child Abuse and Neglect, Brisbane, September.

Gardner, R.A. 1986, *Child Custody Litigation: A Guide for Parents and Mental Health Professionals*, Creative Therapeutics, Cresskill, NJ.

——1987, *The Parental Alienation Syndrome and the Differentiation Between Fabricated and Genuine Child Sex Abuse*, Creative Therapeutics, Cresskill, NJ.

——1989, *Family Evaluation in Child Custody Mediation, Arbitration and Litigation*, Creative Therapeutics, Cresskill, NJ.

Gardner, R.A. 2006, website, <www.rgardner.com>.

Gillham, Bill 1994, *The Facts About Child Physical Abuse*, Cassell, London.

Goldstein J., Freud, A. and Solnit, A.J. 1979a, *Beyond the Best Interests of the Child*, new edn, The Free Press, New York.

——1979b, *Before the Best Interests of the Child*, The Free Press, New York.

——1986, *In the Best Interests of the Child*, The Free Press, New York.

Gordon, M. 1991, 'Recent Supreme Court Rulings on Child Testimony in Sexual Abuse Cases', *Journal of Child Sexual Abuse*, vol. 1, pp. 59–71.

——1990, 'Males and Females as Victims of Childhood Sexual Abuse', *Journal of Family Violence*, vol. 5, no. 4, pp. 321–32.

Gordoncare 2005, *Services for Separated Parents and Their Children*, Gordoncare, Langdon Centre, Highett, Victoria.

Graycar, R., Rhoades, H. and Harrison, M. 2000, 'Families, Law and Family Law Reform', a paper presented to 10th World Congress, International Society of Family Law, Brisbane, July.

Gregory, B. 1996, 'Unemployment Among Men', a paper presented to the 5th Australian Family Research Conference, Brisbane.

Grief, G.L. 1995, 'Parental Abduction Justification as Ego Defense', *Family and Conciliation Courts Review*, vol. 33, no. 3, pp. 317–23.

——1998, 'Many Years After the Parental Abduction', *Family Court Review*, vol. 36, no. 1, pp. 9–31.

Grimes, A. and McIntosh, J. 2004, 'Emerging Practice Issues in Child Inclusive Divorce Mediation', *Journal of Family Studies*, vol. 10, no. 1, pp. 113–20.

Hallett, C. 1995, *Interagency Coordination in Child Protection*, Studies in Child Protection, HMSO, London.

Harries, M. and Clare, M. 2002, *Mandatory Reporting of Child Abuse: Evidence and Options—Report for the Child Protection Council, Perth*, Department of Community Development, Perth.

Hart, S.N. and Brassard, M.R. 1993, 'Psychological Maltreatment', *Violence Update*, vol. 3. no. 7, pp. 3–6.

Hay, Alison 2003, 'Child Protection and the Family Court of WA', a paper presented to the Child Sexual Abuse: Justice Response of Alternative Resolution Conference, Australian Institute of Criminology, Adelaide, May.

——2005, 'Children's Experiences When Being Assessed in Residence and Contact Disputes Where There Are Allegations of Child Abuse in the Family Court of Western Australia', PhD thesis, Department of Social Work, Monash University, Melbourne.

Hay, Alison and Brown, Thea 2004, 'The Views of Children in Residence and Contact Disputes Involving Child Abuse Allegations', a paper presented to the 15th International Conference, International Association for the Prevention of Child Abuse and Neglect, Brisbane, September.

Hester, M. and Ratford, L. 1997, *Domestic Violence and Child Contact Arrangements in England and Denmark*, Policy Press, University of Bristol, Bristol.

Hetherington, E.M. and Kelly, J. 2002, *For Better or for Worse: Divorce Reconsidered*, Norton & Co., New York.

Hiller, P. and Goddard, C. 1989, *The Physical Abuse and Neglect of Children: A Study of 102 Cases Presenting at a Paediatric Hospital*, Department of Social Work, Monash University, Melbourne.

Horner T.M. and Guyer, M.J., 1991, 'Prediction, Prevention and Clinical Expertise in Child Custody Cases in which Allegations of Child Sexual Abuse Have Been Made', 'I: Predictable Rates of Diagnostic Error in Relation to Various Clinical Strategies', *Family Law Quarterly*, vol. 25, no. 2, pp. 217–52.

—— 1992, 'Prediction, Prevention and Clinical Expertise in Child Custody Cases in which Allegations of Child Sexual Abuse Have Been Made', 'II: Prevalence Rates of Child Sexual Abuse and the Precision of "Tests" Constructed to Diagnose It', *Family Law Quarterly*, vol. 25, no. 3, pp. 381–409.

Horner, T.M., Guyer, M.J. and Kalter, N.M. 1993, 'Prediction, Prevention and Clinical Expertise in Child Custody Cases in which Allegations of Child

Sexual Abuse Have Been Made', 'III: Studies of Expert Opinion Formation', *Family Law Quarterly*, vol. 26, no. 2, pp. 141-70.

House of Representatives Standing Committee on Family and Community Affairs 2003, '*Every Picture Tells a Story*'—*Report on the Inquiry into Child Custody Arrangements in the Event of Family Separation*, Commonweath Government, Canberra.

Howitt, Dennis 1993, *Child Abuse Errors*, Rutgers University Press, London.

Hume, Marie 1997, 'Child Sexual Abuse Allegations in the Family Court of Australia', unpublished Masters thesis, Humanities and Social Sciences, University of South Australia,Adelaide.

Humphreys, C. 1995, 'Whatever Happened on the Way to Counselling: Hurdles in the Interagency Environment', *Child Abuse and Neglect*, vol. 19, pp. 801-09.

——1997, 'Child Sexual Abuse Allegations in the Context of Divorce: Issues for Mothers', *British Journal of Social Work*, vol. 27, pp. 529-44.

Hunter, Rosemary, Genovese, A., Melville, A. and Chrzanowski, A. 2000, *Legal Services in Family Law*, Law and Justice Foundation, Sydney.

——2002, *The Changing Face of Litigation: Unrepresented Litigations in the Family Court of Australia*, Law and Justice Foundation, Sydney.

Interpol n.d., website, <www.interpol.int/Public/Children/SexualAbuse/Default.asp>.

Jenny, C. 1996, 'Medical Issues in Sexual Assault',in John Briere et al. (eds), *The APSAC Handbook on Child Maltreatment*, The American Professional Society on the Abuse of Children with Sage Publications, Los Angeles.

Johnson, C. 2002, 'Familicide and Disputed Residency and Contact in Western Australia', Master of Arts thesis, School of Social and Cultural Studies, University of Western Australia,Perth.

Johnson J.R. 1995, 'Domestic Violence and Parent-Child Relationships in Families Disputing Custody', *Australian Journal of Family Law*, vol. 9, pp. 12-25.

Johnston, J. and Campbell, L. 1993, 'Parent-Child Relationships in Domestic Violence Families', *Family and Conciliation Courts Review*, vol. 31, pp. 282-312.

Johnston, J. and Girdner, L.K. 1998, 'Early Identification of Parents at Risk for Custody Violations and Prevention of Child Abduction', *Family and Conciliation Courts Review*, vol. 36, no. 3, pp. 392-409.

Jordan, P. 1996, 'Ten Years On: The Effects of Divorce and Separation on Men', a paper presented to the 5th Australian Family Research Conference, Brisbane.

Kaufman J. and Zigler, E. 1987, 'Do Abused Children Become Abusive Parents?', *American Journal of Orthopsychiatry*, vol. 57, pp. 186-92.

——1989, 'The Intergenerational Transmission of Child Abuse', in D. Cicchetti and V. Carlson (eds), *Child Maltreatment: Theory and Research on the Causes and Consequences of Child Abuse and Neglect*, Cambridge University Press, Cambridge.

Kaye, Miranda and Tolmie, Julie 1998a, 'Fathers' Rights Groups in Australia', *Australian Journal of Family Law*, vol. 12, pp. 19–67.

——1998b, 'Discoursing Dads: The Rhetorical Devices of Fathers' Rights Groups', *Melbourne University Law Review*, vol. 22, pp. 162–94.

Kaye, Miranda, Stubbs, Julie and Tolmie, Julia 2003a, *Negotiating Child Residence and Contact Arrangements Against a Background of Domestic Violence*, Research Report No. 1, Families, Law and Social Policy Research Unit, Socio-Legal Research Centre, Griffith University, Brisbane

——2003b, 'Domestic Violence and Child Contact Arrangements', *Australian Journal of Family Law*, vol. 17, pp. 93–133.

Kelly J.B. 1991, 'Children's Post Divorce Adjustment: Effects of Conflict, Parent Adjustment and Custody Arrangement', *Family Law*, vol. 21, pp. 52-6.

Kelly, L. 2000, Foreword, in P. Cox et at., *Child Sexual Assault*, Palgrave, Basingstoke.

Keough W.J. 2000, *Child Representation in Family Law*, LBC Information Services, Sydney.

Kempe, C.H., Silverman, F.M., Steele, B.F., Droegemuller, W. and Silver, H.K. 1962, 'The Battered Child Syndrome', *Journal of American Medical Association*, vol. 181, no. 1, pp. 17–24.

Kerin, P. and Murphy, P. 2003, 'Overview of an Emerging Model of an Integrated Family Court System', a paper presented to the 8th Australian Institute of Family Studies Conference, Melbourne, February.

Kids Help Line 2004, *Kids Help Line Information Sheet*, <www.kidshelp.com.au>.

Kimm, Joan 2005, 'The Family Court of Australia', a paper presented to the Higher Degree Reporting Research Seminar, Faculty of Law, Monash University, Melbourne.

Kitzinger, C. 1990, 'Why Men Hate Women', <www.newint.org/issue212/hate.htm>.

Kolko, D. 1996, 'Child Physical Abuse', in L. Berliner et al. (eds), *The APSAC Handbook on Child Maltreatment*, The American Professional Society on the Abuse of Children with Sage Publications, Los Angeles.

La Fontaine, Jean 1990, *Child Sexual Abuse*, Polity Press, Cambridge.

Lone Fathers Association (Australia) Inc., website, <www.lonefathers.com.au>.

Lyon, T.D. 2002, 'Scientific Support for Expert Testimony on Child Sexual Abuse Accommodation', in Jon R. Conte (ed.), *Critical Issues in Child Sexual Abuse*, Sage, Thousand Oaks.

Lyon, Christina and de Cruz, Peter 1993, *Child Abuse, Family Law*, 2nd edn, Jordan Publishing, Bristol.

MacDonald, Geraldine 2001, *Effective Interventions for Child Abuse and Neglect*, John Wiley and Sons, Chichester.

McCoy, Alicia 2005, 'Family Relationship Centres: Issues of Family Violence', Honours thesis, Department of Social Work, Monash University, Melbourne.

McGee, C. 2000, *Children's Experiences of Domestic Violence*, Jessica Kingsley, London.

McIntosh, J.E. 2006, *An Exploratory Study of Impacts on Parenting Capacity and Child Well-Being*, report to the Family Court, Family Transitions, Melbourne.

Malcolm, J. 1997, *In the Freud Archives*, Papermac, London.

Mayhew, C. 2000, *Preventing Violence Within Organisations: A Practical Handbook*, Research and Public Policy Series No. 29, Australian Institute of Criminology, Canberra.

Ministerial Taskforce on Child Support 2005, *In the Best Interests of Children: Reforming the Child Support Scheme—Summary Report and Recommendations of the Ministerial Taskforce on Child Support*, Commonwealth of Australia, Canberra.

Morrison, R. 2006, 'A Supervisor in a Multi-Disciplinary Team: Effecting Change and Inter-Agency Collaboration', unpublished NSW class paper, Monash University, Melbourne.

Morrison, T. 1994, *Staff Supervision in Social Care: An Action Learning Approach*, Longman, Essex.

Mudaly, N. and Goddard, C. 2006, *The Truth is Longer Than a Lie*, Jessica Kingsley, London.

Mullane G.R. 1998, 'Evidence of Social Science Research: Law, Practice, and Options in the Family Court of Australia', *Australian Law Journal*, vol. 72, pp. 434–63.

Murphy, P. and Pike, B. 2003, 'The Columbus Pilot in the Family Court of Western Australia: Some Early Findings from the Evaluation', a paper presented at the 8th Australian Institute of Family Studies Conference, Melbourne, February.

Myers, J.E.B., Diedrich, S.E., Devon, L., Fincher, K. and Stern, R. 2002, 'Prosecution of Child Abuse in the USA', in Jon R. Conte (ed.), *Critical Issues in Child Sexual Abuse*, Sage, Thousand Oaks.

Nicholson A. 1999, 'Issues Facing the Court and Future Directions', paper presented to the Queensland Family Law Practitioners Conference, Coolum.

——2003, 'Taking a Responsive Approach to the Family Law Needs of a Diversified Australia', a paper presented at the Managing Diversity Conference, Darebin Arts and Entertainment Centre, Melbourne, October.

Oates, Kim 1996, *The Spectrum of Child Abuse: Assessment, Treatment and Prevention*, Brunner Mazel, New York.

O'Hagen, K. 1993, *Emotional and Psychological Abuse of Children*, Open University Press, Buckingham.

Pagelow, M.D. 1990, 'Effects of Domestic Violence on Children and Their Consequences for Custody and Visitation Agreements', *Mediation Quarterly*, vol. 7, pp. 347–52.

Parkinson, P. 1995, 'Custody, Access and Domestic Violence', *Australian Journal of Family Law*, vol. 9, pp. 41–57.

Parton, N. 1991, *Governing the Family: Child Care, Child Protection and the State*, Macmillan, London.

Rayment-McHugh, S. and Nisbet, I. 2004, 'Intervention in Cases of Sibling Incest', a paper presented to the 15th International Conference, International Association for the Prevention of Child Abuse and Neglect, Brisbane, September.

Rhoades H. 2002, 'The "No Contact Mother": Reconstructions of Motherhood in the Era of the "New Father"', *International Journal of Law, Policy and the Family*, vol. 16, pp. 71–94.

Rhoades, H., Graycar, R. and Harrison, M. 1999, *The Family Law Reform Act 1995: Can Changing Legislation Change Legal Culture, Legal Practice and Community Expectations?*, University of Sydney, Sydney.

Rodgers, B. and Prior, J. 1998, *Divorce and Separation: The Outcomes for Children*, Joseph Rowntree Foundation, York.

Russell, D. 1984, *Sexual Exploitation, Rape, Child Sexual Abuse and Workplace Harrassment*, Sage, Beverly Hills.

Saywitz, K.J. and Goodman, G.S. 1996, 'Interviewing Children In and Out of Court: Current Research, and Practice Perspectives', in John Briere et al. (eds) *The APSAC Handbook on Child Maltreatment*, The American Professional Society on the Abuse of Children with Sage Publications, Los Angeles.

Scourfield, J.B. 2002, 'Constructing Men in Child Protection Work', *Men and Masculinities*, vol. 4, no. 1, pp. 70–80.

Schudson, C. 1992, 'Antagonistic Parents in Family Courts: False Allegations or False Assumptions of Child Sexual Abuse?', *Journal of Child Sexual Abuse*, vol. 1, pp. 111—13.

Schultz, Leroy, G. 1982, 'Child Abuse in Historical Perspective', in Jon R. Conte and David Shore (eds), *Social Work and Child Sexual Abuse*, The Haworth Press, New York.

Sheehan, G., Carson, B., Fehlberg, B., Hunter, R., Tomison, A., Ip, R. and Dewar, J. 2005, 'Children's Contact Services: Expectations and Experiences: Final Report', Attorney-General's Department, Canberra.

Sheehan, Rosemary 2001, *Magistrates' Decision-Making in Child Protection Cases*, Ashgate, Aldershot.

Smart, Carole, Neale, Bren and Wade, Amanda 2001, *The Changing Experience of Childhood, Families and Divorce*, Polity Press, Cambridge.

Smith, M., Bee, P., Heverin, A. and Nobes, G. 1995, 'Parental Control within the Family, the Nature and Extent of Parental Violence to Children', in Department of Health, *Child Protection: Messages from Research*, HMSO, London.

Southall D., Plunkett, M., Banks, M., Falkov, A. and Samuels, M. 1997, 'Covert Video Recording of Life-threatening Child Abuse: Lessons for Child Protection', *Paediatrics*, vol. 100, pp. 735–60.

Stanley, Janet 2003, 'Child Sexual Abuse in Indigenous Communities', a paper presented to the Child Sexual Abuse: Justice Response or Alternative Resolution Conference, Australian Institute of Criminology, Adelaide, May.

Stanley, Janet and Goddard, Chris 2002, *In the Firing Line: Violence and Power in Child Protection Work*, Wiley Series in Child Care and Protection, John Wiley and Sons, London.

Stanton, D., Fehlberg, B. and Sheehan, G. 2000, 'The Divorce Transition: Recent Findings', a presentation to the Family Law Pathways Advisory Group, from the Australian Institute of Family Studies, Canberra, 22 June.

Stark, E. and Flitcraft, A. 1996, *Women at Risk: Domestic Violence and Women's Health*, Sage, London.

Stevenson, Olive 1998, *Neglected Children: Issues and Dilemmas*, Blackwell, Oxford.

Strauss, M. 1994, *Beating the Devil Out of Them: Corporal Punishment in American Families*, Lexington Books, New York.

Summit, R. 1983, 'The Child Abuse Accommodation Syndrome', *Child Abuse and Neglect*, vol. 7, p. 7.

Thoeness, N. and Pearson, J. 1988, 'Summary of Findings from Sexual Abuse Allegations Project', in B. Nicholson and J. Bulkely (eds), *Sexual Abuse Allegations in Custody and Visitations Cases*, National Legal Resources Centre for Child Advocacy and Protection, Washington, pp. 1–28.

Thorpe, David 1994, *Evaluating Child Protection*, Open University Press, Buckingham.

Tomison, A. 2000, 'Exploring Family Violence: The Links Between Child Maltreatment and Domestic Violence', *Issues in Child Abuse Prevention*, no. 13, National Child Protection Clearing House Issues Paper, Australian Institute of Family Studies, Melbourne.

Toth, P. 1992, 'All Child Abuse Allegations Demand Attention', *Journal of Child Sexual Abuse*, vol. 1, pp. 117–18.

——2004, 'Child Interview Approaches in Action', a paper presented to the 15th

International Congress on Child Abuse and Neglect, International Society for the Prevention of Child Abuse and Neglect, Brisbane, September.

Trotter, Chris 2004, *Helping Abused Children and Their Families*, Allen & Unwin, Sydney.

——2006, *Working with Involuntary Clients*, Allen & Unwin, Sydney.

United Nations Convention on the Rights of the Child (adopted by the General Assembly of the United Nations on 20 November 1989; came into force on 16 January 1991).

Uviller, R.K. 1978, 'Fathers' Rights and Feminism:The Maternal Presumption Re visited', *Harvard Women's Law Journal*, vol. 1, pp. 107–30.

van Dam, C. 2001, *Identifying Child Molesters: Preventing Child Sexual Abuse by Recognising the Patterns of Offenders*, Haworth Press, New York.

Wallerstein, J.S. and Blakeslee, S. 1989, *Second Chances: Men, Women, and Children a Decade After Divorce*, Ticknor and Fields, New York.

Wallerstein, J.S. and Kelly, J.B. 1996, *Surviving the Breakup: How Children and Parents Cope with Divorce*, Basic Books, New York.

Wallerstein, J.S., Lewis, J. and Blakeslee, S. 2000, *The Unexpected Legacy of Divorce: A 25 Year Landmark Study*, Hyperion, New York.

Warshak, R.A. 1996, 'Gender Bias in Child Custody Decisions', *Family and Conciliation Courts Review*, vol. 34, no. 3, pp. 396-409.

Wiehe, Vernon R. 1997, *Sibling Abuse*, Sage, Thousand Oaks.

Wilczek, J.R. 1987, '"Conduct"—Its Rele vance in the Determination of Family Court Proceedings: The Porcupine Syndrome', *Australian Law Journal*, vol. 61, pp. 488-509.

Wilson, R. 2002a, 'Fractured Families, Fragile Children: The Sexual Vulnerability of Female Children in the Aftermath of Divorce', *Child and Family Law Quarterly*, vol. 14, no. 2, pp. 1–23.

——2002b, 'The Cradle of Abuse: Evaluating the Danger Posed by a Sexually Predatory Parent to the Victim's Siblings', *Emory Law Journal*, vol. 51, no. 1, pp. 241–347.

Wilson, C. and Powell, M. 2001, *Guide to Interviewing Children*, Allen & Unwin, Sydney.

Winfrey, Oprah n.d., website, <www.oprah.com>.

List of cases

A and A [1998] FLC 92–800

AMS v AIF; AIF v AMS [1999] FLC 92–852; (1999) 199 CLR 160

Re Andrew [1996] FLC 92–692

B and B [1993] FLC 92–357

B and B (Access) [1986] FLC 91–758

B and B: Family Law Reform Act 1995 [1997] FLC 92–755
B and B [1988] FLC 91–978
Bartholomew v Kelly (unreported) (Appeal No. NA 25 of 2000)
Blanch v Blanch and Crawford [1999] FLC 92-837
Bormann and Bormann (unreported) (Appeal Nos NA 47 and NA 54 of 2002)
Briginshaw v Briginshaw (1938) 60 CLR 336
Cartwright and Cartwright [1977] FLC 90–268
Chandler and Chandler [1981] FLC 91–008
Cooper v Cooper [1977] FLC 90–234
D and D [2005] Fam CA 356
Re David [1997] FLC 92–776
Dean and Dean [1977] FLC 90–213
Grant and Grant (unreported) (Appeal No. EA 15 of 2001)
H and W [1995] FLC 92–598
Heidt and Heidt [1976] FLC 90–077
Irvine and Irvine [1995] FLC 92–624
Jaeger and Jaeger [1994] FLC 92–492
JG and BG [1994] FLC 93–515
Re K [1994] FLC 92–461
K v B [1994] FLC 92–478
Re L (A Child) (Contact: Domestic Violence), V, M and H [2001] Fam 260
Litchfield and Litchfield [1987] FLC 91–840
Lythow and Lythow [1976] FLC 90–007
M and H [1996] FLC 92–695
M and M [1988] FLC 91–979
M and M [2000] FLC 93–006
Merryman and Merryman [1994] FLC 92–497
N and S and the Separate Representative [1996] FLC 92–655
Patsalou and Patsalou [1995] FLC 92–580
R and R: Children's Wishes [2000] FLC 93–000
Russell and Close (unreported) (Appeal No. SA 45 of 1992)
S and S [2001] FMCA fam 185
Sedgley and Sedgley [1995] FLC 92–623
T and N (2004) 31 Fam LR 257
T and S [2001] FLC 93–086
Re W (Sex abuse: standard of proof) [2004] FLC 93–192
Re W and W: Abuse Allegations; expert evidence [2001] FLC 93–085
WK and SR [1997] FLC 92–787

INDEX

A and A (1998) 36, 37–8
*A New Approach to the Family Law
System*, discussion paper 131
abandonment of a child 87, 88
abduction by a parent 6, 86, 93,
   100–1
Aboriginal families, *see* Indigenous
   families
Aboriginal Family Violence Prevention
   and Legal Service 136
ages of abused children 16, 18–19, 81,
   103
allegations of child abuse xiii, 2, 11, 12,
   14, 15–16, 61, 86–7; absence of
   specialised services for 139–41;
   alleged and actual perpetrators, *see*
   perpetrators; by Indigenous parents
   124; by someone other than a parent
   16, 21–2, *see also* perpetrators; and
   child protection services 139–40, *see
   also* child protection services; false 2,
   11, 12, 13, 14, 15, 22, 32, 46, 47,
   53–4; impact on families 17, 110–13,
   116–17, 118–19, 120–1; impact on
   partner making 118–20; myths about
   and trivialisation of 52–3, *see also*
   denial; by parents, *see* parents; reporting, *see* reporting child abuse;
   response to 139–41; substantiated
   and unsubstantiated 14–15, 81, 90,

112–15, 116–18; testing/assessing
   74–6, 133, 173–5
Andrew, Re (1996) 42
Anglicare 132
Australian Capital Territory 69, 90, 91
Australian Centre for the Study of
   Sexual Assault 136
Australian Childhood Foundation 133
Australian Domestic and Family
   Violence Clearing House 136
Australian Institute of Health and
   Social Welfare 68–9, 90

B and B (1988) 43–4
Bartholomew v Kelly (2000) 38–9
Berns, S.S. 35
'best interests of the child'
   principle/legislation 25, 26, 27,
   29–32, 40–1, 51–2, 54–5; primary
   considerations 29–30, 51–2, 140;
   child's wishes and separate legal
   representation 56–8
bias, *see* gender bias
Birrell brothers 68
Blackshirts group 136
Blanch v Blanch and Crawford (1999) 37
Bravehearts 137
Briggs, Freda 137
Briginshaw v Briginshaw (1938) 4, 45
Butler-Sloss, Justice 37, 74

Campbell, L. 2
Cartwright and Cartwright (1977) 34–5
case law under *Family Law Act* (1975)
    32–40, 43–6
case study of alleged sexual abuse
    150–62
case study of physical abuse/domestic
    violence 162–75
Cawson, P. 92
Centacare 132
Centre for Child Abuse, Melbourne
    133
Centrelink 131, 132, 137
Chandler and Chandler (1981) 33–4
changeover abuse, *see* handover
child abuse: ages of children 16, 18–19,
    81, 103; allegations of, *see* allegations;
    assessing 74–6, 133, 173–5; cases xi,
    7, Chapter 8, *see also* case law and
    by name of case; causes of 77–9,
    99–101; community attitudes and
    myths xii, 4, 47, 52–3, 66–7, 87–9, *see*
    also denial; defined in legislation 31,
    33, 41; denial of, *see* denial; distinc-
    tive features of 15, 17–19; early
    protection policy and legislation
    88–9; and family law legislation 29,
    31–2, *see also Family Law Act*; follow-
    ing parental separation and divorce,
    see parental separation and/or
    divorce; forms of 6, 13, 17–19,
    41, Chapters 4 and 5, *see also*
    contact/access abuse; emotional
    abuse; handover/changeover;
    homicide; neglect; physical abuse;
    sexual abuse; Freudian theory of
    53–4; gender breakdown 81, 96, 103,
    see also girls; and mental illness of
    parent, *see* mental illness; multiple
    forms of 92; in other cultures, *see*
    cultures, other; perpetrators of, *see*
    perpetrators; reporting, *see* reporting;
    severity of 14, 94
child protection authorities/services 14,
    66–7, 72, 74, 80, 88, 91, 92, 114, 116,
    119, 124, 134–5, 139–40, *see also*
    lobby groups; and allegations of
    child abuse 139–40; funding for 138

child protection workers: in suspected
    sexual assault case 159–62; in
    physical abuse/domestic violence
    case 166–71
Child Responsive Dispute Resolution
    Model 62
Child Support Agency (CSA) 131–2,
    137
children: impact of divorce and allega-
    tions of abuse on 110–11, 120–1;
    interviewing 74, 75–6, 121; legisla-
    tion for best interests of, *see* 'best
    interests of the child' principle;
    lobby groups for 137; numbers in
    separated families 25; rights of 27,
    28, 36, 40, 41, 55–8; services for
    133–4; wishes of children in court
    cases 55–8
Children and Young Persons Act (1989)
    (Vic) 41
Children's Cases program 62–3
Children's Courts 51, 60, 88, 135
Columbus program xii, 62, 143–4,
    147
Commonwealth Attorney-General's
    Department xv, 130, 137
Commonwealth Department of Family
    and Community Services and Indig-
    enous Affairs 137
contact/access: abuse of 18, 99;
    disputes, *see* residence and contact
    disputes; right of parent/child 27,
    28, 36, 40, 43, 44–5, 46, 54–5; in
    sexual abuse 43, 44–5, 46, 48, 83,
    158; supervised 105, 133
contact centres 98, 105, 133–4
Contact Orders pilot program *see* Parent
    Orders program
Cooper v Cooper (1977) 42
Corby, B. 87
Council for the Single Mother and Her
    Child 137
counselling 14, 48; agencies 132–3; *see*
    also family relationship centres
criminal convictions/offences,
    men/women with 19, 20, 79, 87,
    93–4, 100, 104, 112
criminal law, English 66

cultures, other xiii, 5, 19, 97; and family
law diversity 123; parenting behaviour of 123–4; professionals working
with 122–4
custody 26, 27, see also contact/access;
residence and contact arrange-
ments/disputes

D and D (2005) 38
Dads 4 Justice (UK) 136
Dads Against Discrimination 135
Dads in Distress 135
David, Re (1997) 46
Dean and Dean (1977) 34
denial of abuse: by community and
professionals 52–4, 65, 67, 68, 83–4;
by suspected perpetrator 79–80, 136;
by child victims 71–2, 76–7, 164
Department of Community Services,
New South Wales 96
Department of Human Services,
Victoria xv, 72, 95
disabilities, parents with intellectual,
see mental illness and intellectual
disability
dispute resolution 62–3, see also residence and contact arrangements/
disputes
divorce 32–3; statistics 25; see also
parental separation and/or divorce
doctor and suspected sexual assault case
155–7
domestic violence, see family violence
drugs, see substance abuse

emotional/psychological abuse 6, 13,
17, 91; causes of 100; definition of
97–8; and domestic violence 92, 100;
handover/changeover abuse as 98–9
English criminal law 66
Equality for Fathers 135
ethnic background, see cultures, other
evaluating child abuse, see allegations
of child abuse, testing/assessing
Every Picture Tells a Story report 63

Family Court of Australia xi, 24, 25, 32,
51, 129, 130, 131, 137, 140, 141, 144,

158, 162; case waiting period 47, 61,
63; Children's Cases program 62–3;
and the Magellan List 61–2, see also
Magellan program; processes and
protocols 59–60
Family Court of Western Australia
143
family law Chapter 2
Family Law Act (1975) ix, x, xii, 6, 24,
25–6; case law under 32–40, 43–6;
family violence defined 40; and
protection of children Chapter 3,
see also 'best interests of the child'
principle; child protection
services/authorities; protection of
children; and State and Territory
agencies 59–60; sections (including
former sections of the Act): s 4(1)
31, 32, 40; s 10D 59; s 60B 29, 30;
s 60B(1) 41; s 60B(1)(a) 29;
s 60B(1)(b) 30; s 60B(2) 46;
s 60B(2)(b) 28, 29, 30; s 60CA 29,
40, 51; s 60CC 29, 30, 51, 55–6;
s 60CC(2) 29–30; s 60CC(3) 30;
s 60CD(2)(a) 56; s 60CD(2)(b) 56;
s 60CD(2)(c) 56; s 60CE 56;
s 60CG 41; s 60D 25, 26, 59;
s 60D(1) 28, 31, 40, 41; s 60I 48;
s 60I(7) x; s 60I(9) 49; s 60K 46;
s 61DA 30; s 61DA(2) 30–1; s 62G
56; s 64(1) 25–6; s 64(1)(i) 26;
s 64B 29; s 65DAA 29, 30; s 65E
27, 29, 40, 51; s 67Z 60; s 67ZA 59;
s 68F(2) 27, 29, 30, 51, 56, 63;
s 68F(2)(g) 30, 63; s 68H 56; s 68K
46; s 68K(1)(b) 28, 41; s 68L 56, 57;
s 68LA 57; s 68R 41; s 69ZK 31, 60;
s 69ZK(2) 60; s 69ZV 56; s 69ZW
59, 60; s 91B 59, 60; s 92A 60;
s 100B 57; s 110A 56;
s 117AB 31, 49
Family Law Amendment (Shared Parental
Responsibility) Act (2006) 6, 24, 26,
29–32, 36, 48–9, 51, 55, 56–7, 59–60;
changes in terminology 29
Family Law Pathways Advisory Group
(FLPAG) 128–9, 145
Family Law Reform Act (1995) 26–8;

amendments 27-8, 46-7, 51; changes
in terminology 27
Family Law Rules (1994) 31, 56, 60, 62
family law socio-legal services system
Chapter 7; and absence of
specialised services for child abuse
allegations 139-41; common assessment tool 145; the core of the
system 129-31; counselling agencies
132-3; financial benefits agencies
131-2; funding for 137-8; men's and
women's lobby groups 135-7; new
specialised services 141-5, *see also*
Columbus program, Magellan
program; problems 138-41; protection services, *see* child protection
services; services for children 133-4;
strategies for managing 145-7
family relationship centres 1, 48, 131
family violence ix, 2, 14, 19-20, 26, 28,
29, 69-70, 99; between parents
33-40; case study 162-75; centres
136; and child abuse 86, 92, 98,
101-2, *see also by form of abuse*; with
children as primary victims 40-6;
defined in the *Family Law Act* (1975)
40; defined in the *Family Law Reform
Act* (1995) 28; effects upon children
34, 35, 36, 37, 38, 39-40, 101-2, 104;
following divorce 111-13; in other
cultures 123-4; and right of contact
40-1; and risks to children 37-8, 44,
78; specialist counselling services
132-3; viewed as marital misconduct
35; women's lobby groups 136-7;
women's refuges 132
Family Violence and Family Court
Research program 141, 143
fathers after separation, interests of
135-6; *see also* parents
Federal Magistrates Court 25, 32, 58,
59, 61
Federal Magistrates Service 129
feminist movement 67-8
financial benefits agencies 131-2
Finkelhor, D. 15, 70-1
Freudian theory of child abuse 53-4,
67

funding for family services system
137-8

Gardner, R.A. 2, 11-13, 22, 74
Gatehouse Centre 133, 156
gender: bias xi, 7, 12, 53; breakdown 81,
96, 103, *see also* girls; stereotypes 12,
52, 53
girls as victims of abuse 19, 42, 80, 81,
103
Goddard, C. 84, 116
Goldstein, J. 54
Goodman, G.S. 75
Grant and Grant (2001) 38-9
Gregory, B. 19

handover/changeover: abuse 6, 18,
98-9; supervised contact 133
Heidt and Heidt (1976) 34
homicide, attempted or actual 86, 93-4,
101, 119
Howitt, D. 116

illness: fictitious, *see* Munchausen
syndrome by proxy; mental, *see*
mental illness
incest 66, 71
Indigenous families, parenting behaviour
in 123-4
interviewing in investigating allegations
of sexual assault 74-6
Irvine and Irvine (1995) 42

Jaeger and Jaeger (1994) 35
Jenny, C. 74
JG and BG (1994) 36
Johnson, C. 101
Johnston, J. 2
judicial discretion 51-2, 62

K, Re (1994) 58
K v B (1994) 25
Kempe, Henry 10, 68
Kids Help Line 133, 134
Kitzinger, C. 84

L (A Child), Re (2001) 36-7
language/interpreters, issues of 122-3

legal aid commissions130, 137, 142, 144
legal representative for the child,
    separate56–8, 171–3, see also solicitor
Litchfield and Litchfield (1987) 42
lobby groups: for children 137; men's
    135–6; women's 136–7
Lone Fathers Association 135
Lyon, T.D. 71
Lythow and Lythow (1976) 26

M and M (1988) 43–4, 50
M and M (2000) 38
Magellan program xii, xiv, 15, 47, 61,
    62, 81, 91–2, 103, 111, 124, 141–3,
    144, 147, 162; List 47–8, 61–2
Magistrates Court, Federal 25, 32, 58,
    59, 61
Magistrates Courts, state and territory
    129, 130, 135, 158
marital breakdown and child abuse, see
    separation and/or divorce; research
    on 10–11
Matrimonial Causes Act (1959) 51
mediation services 130, see also coun-
    selling
medical tests/assessment74, 156
Melbourne registry, Family Court 62
men's lobby groups 135–6
Men's Rights Agency 135
mental illness and intellectual disability
    99, 101, 102, 122, 124–6
Merryman and Merryman (1994) 35
mothers: lobby groups for 136–7, see
    also parents; women
Mt Pritchard Domestic Violence Centre
    166–8
Munchausen syndrome by proxy 95–6
murder, see homicide
myths about child abuse xii, 4, 47, 52–3

National Child Protection Clearing
    House 137
neglect as abuse 4–5, 6, 13, 17–18, 86,
    87, 90; causes of 100, 102; in a
    context of parental separation and
    divorce 92, 97; definition of 96–7;
    lack of continuous schooling 97; and
    family violence 92

New South Wales 69, 87, 88, 90, 95,
    135, 142
Nicholson, Chief Justice 43, 129
Northern Territory 90
Notice of Child Abuse or Family
    Violence 31, 60
notification of abuse, see reporting child
    abuse

Oedipus complex 53

Parent Orders program 98, 134
parent responsibility shared, see Family
    Law Amendment (Shared Parental
    Responsibility Act)
parental alienation syndrome (PAS) xii,
    11–13, 22
parental separation and/or divorce, child
    abuse and xii, 1, 2–5, 6, 8, 9, Chapter
    1, 102, see also child abuse; abuse
    starting only after separation 9, 80;
    and contact/access rights, see
    contact/access; as context of abuse,
    see emotional abuse; neglect; physical
    abuse; sexual abuse; factors in 9,
    79–80; and family types 15, 19–20;
    financial benefits agencies 131–2; and
    forms of abuse, see child abuse, forms
    of; history/eras of understanding of
    10–17; impact of 109–13, 115–17,
    118–21; legislation for protection of
    the child Chapter 3, see also 'best
    interests of the child' principle; and
    post-separation services 131; risk
    factors in 79–80
parents: ascribing blame to 11, 12, 77–8,
    81; in child sexual abuse 80–1; as
    childhood victims of abuse 71; with
    criminal history, see criminal convic-
    tions/offences; impact of divorce on
    109–11; lobby groups for 135–7;
    with mental illness or intellectual
    disability see mental illness; stereo-
    typing 12, 52; with substance abuse
    problems 126–7
Partnerships Against Domestic Violence
    program 136–7
Parton, N. 84

Patsalou and Patsalou (1995) 35–6
perpetrators of child abuse ix, x, 15,
    42–3; alleged and actual 20–2; impact
    of allegations on substantiated
    112–16; impact of unsubstantiated
    allegations 116–18; parents/family
    members as 21–2, 42–3, 79, 80–1,
    103, *see also* sexual abuse; statistics
    103
physical abuse 6, 13, 17, 87, 99–100;
    case study 162–75; causes of 100,
    102; in the context of parental
    separation and divorce 91–2; and
    corporal punishment 95; defined
    94–5; and domestic violence 92,
    100, 104; Munchausen syndrome
    by proxy 95–6; recovery from
    105; state statistics 90–1
police force, federal 130, 137
police forces, state and territory 93, 130,
    135, 138
pornography, child 72
poverty/income levels 9, 79, 99–100,
    102
professionals, socio-legal 1, 3–5, 6–7, 11;
    attitude to child sexual abuse 83–4;
    client threats/violence towards 106,
    111–12, 113, 114, 115, 127; common
    framework for all 148–50; effects of
    child abuse on xiii, 3–4, 105–6;
    interviewing children 74, 75–6, 121;
    managing families after separation or
    divorce Chapter 6; and 1970s litera-
    ture on abuse 67–8; reporting inci-
    dence of abuse 31, 68–9, 88;
    strategies for dealing with families
    (in sample cases) Chapter 8; working
    with alleged but unsubstantiated
    perpetrators 117–18; working with
    alleged child victims of abuse 121;
    working with parents with mental
    illness or intellectual disability
    124–6; working with substantiated
    perpetrators of child abuse 113–15;
    working with those of other cultures
    122–4; working with those with
    substance abuse problems 126–7
prostitution 72

protection of children 6, 41; and child
    protection services, *see* child protec-
    tion authorities/services; Children's
    Cases Program 62–3; child's wishes
    and right to separate representation
    12, 55–8, 83; courts' procedure and
    protocols 59–63; and family law
    legislation/policy Chapter 3, 87–9,
    see also 'best interests of the child'
    principle; and Freudian theory of
    abuse 53–4, 67; and gender stereo-
    typing 52, 53; and judicial discretion
    51–2, 62; and the Magellan List 61–2
psychologists and psychiatrists, *see* coun-
    selling; professionals
punishment, parental 95

Queensland 69, 70, 88, 90, 91, 135

racial diversity, *see* cultures, other
Relationships Australia 132
reporting child abuse 10, 11, *see also*
    allegations; by children 71–2, 76–7; by
    professionals 31, 59–60, 68–9; cases
    substantiated and unsubstantiated
    14–15, 81, 90, 91; patterns in reported
    incidence 10–11, 68–70, 90; to the
    police 93; trends in 68–9, 89–90
research, empirical 7; first 13
residence and contact arrangements/
    disputes 11, 13, 14, 15, 16, 50, 69, 70,
    80, 81, 97, 104–5, 120, 142, 144, 158,
    see also contact/access; child sexual
    abuse in 69, 70; of other cultures 122
rights of children 27, 28, 36, 40, 41,
    55–8
risk assessment in investigating allega-
    tions of sexual abuse 74
risk to children: in contact with a parent
    43–5; in family violence 37–9
Royal Children's Hospital 133
Russell and Close (1992) 42

S and S (2001) 45
Saywitz, K.J. 75
school principal in suspected child
    abuse case 151, 153, 154–5
Sedgley and Sedgley (1995) 42

services, family law, see family law socio-
legal services system
sexual abuse, child 3, 4, 6, 13, 17, 20–1,
41, 42, Chapter 4; actual prevalence
of 70–1; after parental separation
and/or divorce 18, 19, 65, 78–80, 84,
see also parental separation;case law
43–6; case study 150–62; causes of
77–9; community attitudes to 66–7,
and contact with perpetrator 43,
44–5, 46; defined 72–3; denial of 65,
67, 68, 76–7, 79–80, 83–4, 151, 152,
see also denial; myths; discovery/
rediscovery cycle 67–8; and domestic
violence 92; evidence/investigating
allegations of 11–13, 73–6; of girls
19, 42, 80, 81; interviewing strategies
for 75–6; intra-familial 65–6, 69, 70,
71, 72–3, 74, 79, 80–1, 84–5; long-
term effects of 82; medical tests 74,
156; reported incidence of 10, 11,
68–70, see also reporting abuse; risk
assessment 74; risk factors 78–9; and
sexual grooming 73; and sexually
transmitted disease 71, 74; statistics
70, 71, 80; victims of 81–2
sexually transmitted disease 71, 74
solicitor in suspected sexual assault case
157–9, see also legal representative
South Australia 88, 90, 135, 142
Stanley, J. 84, 116
State and Territory agencies: the Family
Court 59–63; Children's Cases
Program 62–3
stereotypes, gender 12, 52
Stevenson, O. 96–7
substance abuse 126–7
Summit, R. 116
Sydney registry, Family Court 62

T and N (2004) 39
T and S (2001) 38
Tasmania 88, 90, 91
Trotter, C. 114

UK Children's Act (1989) 27
unemployment 19, 79
United Kingdom 10, 68, 87, 89
United Nations Convention on the
Rights of the Child (UNCR OC)
27, 56, 58
United States 10, 68, 69, 87, 89
US National Centre of Child Advocacy
13

Victoria 69, 70, 87–8, 91, 95
video interview xi, 74
violence, family see family violence

W, Re (2004) xi, 45–6
waiting period, case 47, 61, 63
Wallerstein, Judith 55
Western Australia 69, 88, 90–1, 97, 134,
135; family court system 129, 143
Western Australia Department of Child
Safety 135
Western Australia Department of
Community Development 94–5
Western Australia Department of
Community Services 72
Western Australian Legal Aid Commis-
sion 144
Wilczek, J.R. 33
Wilson, R. 15, 70, 80
Winfrey, Oprah 73
women, legal centres for 130, 136; lobby
groups for 136–7; refuges for 132
Women's Information and Referral
Exchange (WIRE) 136

For Product Safety Concerns and Information please contact our EU
representative GPSR@taylorandfrancis.com
Taylor & Francis Verlag GmbH, Kaufingerstraße 24, 80331 München, Germany